The Future of Schools

Student Outcomes and the Reform of Education

General Editor: Brian J. Caldwell, Professor of Education, Head, Department of Education Policy and Management, University of Melbourne, Australia

Student Outcomes and the Reform of Education is concerned with the reform of public education and its impact on outcomes for students. The reform agenda has gripped the attention of policy-makers, practitioners, researchers and scholars for much of the 1990s, with every indication of more to come with the approach of the new millennium. This series reports research and describes strategies that deal with the outcomes of reform. Without sacrificing a critical perspective the intention is to provide a guide to good practice and strong scholarship within the new arrangements that are likely to provide the framework for public education in the foreseeable future.

School Effectiveness and School-based Management:
A mechanism for development
Yin Cheong Cheng

Transforming Schools Through Collaborative Leadership
Helen Telford

The Inner Principal
David Loader

The Future of Schools: Lessons from the Reform of Public Education
Brian J. Caldwell and Donald K. Hayward

The Future of Schools:
Lessons from the Reform of Public Education

Brian J. Caldwell and
Donald K. Hayward

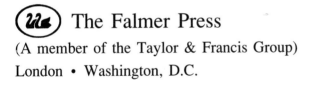 The Falmer Press
(A member of the Taylor & Francis Group)
London • Washington, D.C.

KH

UK	Falmer Press, 1 Gunpowder Square, London, EC4A 3DE
USA	Falmer Press, Taylor & Francis Inc., 1900 Frost Road, Suite 101, Bristol, PA 19007

First published in 1998

A catalogue record for this book is available from the British Library

ISBN 0 7507 07240 cased
ISBN 0 7507 07232 paper

Library of Congress Cataloging-in-Publication Data are available on request

Jacket design by Caroline Archer

Typeset in 10/12pt Times by
Graphicraft Typesetters Ltd., Hong Kong.

Printed in Great Britain by Biddles Ltd., Guildford and King's Lynn on paper which has a specified pH value on final paper manufacture of not less than 7.5 and is therefore 'acid free'.

10/25/04

Contents

Preface

Public education continues to be the subject of major reform around the world. Despite profound changes that have occurred in many places, there is a broadly held view that things are not right and that more needs to be done. This book is a reflection on what has occurred in recent years and offers a policy framework for further action intended to achieve lasting school reform in the public sector.

We believe this is the first book to be co-authored by a former Minister for Education and a currently serving Professor of Education, and only the second to be authored by a Minister of the Crown following a sweeping reform in public education in the modern era, the first being from the pen of Kenneth Baker, former Secretary of State for Education in Britain, who served immediately before and following the 1988 Education Reform Act. It is important to set down the reasons why this book was written and to explain why we came together to accomplish these purposes.

Former Ministers frequently write to 'set the record straight', describing and explaining the events of office, giving reasons why actions were taken or not taken, often revisiting matters of particular public note. As Minister for Education during the first term of the Kennett Liberal National Government in Victoria, serving from October 1992 to April 1996, Don Hayward embarked on the most dramatic transformation of public schooling in Australia, known as Schools of the Future. There is likely to be public interest in his account.

Schools of the Future was not the only major change at the time. On assuming office, the Government was faced with the task of reducing a crippling public sector debt that was placing the future of the State in jeopardy. As Minister, Don Hayward was required to manage the task in the Education Portfolio. It is only by recounting his early life experiences and his period as Shadow Minister for Education prior to assuming office that one can separate Schools of the Future from these other events, revealing it to be a coherent and thoughtful plan, some may describe it as a vision, for a future of public education in Victoria that would raise the quality of schooling and be more responsive to the interests of students and their families. It is only by appreciating this vision that one can also see that the work is unfinished.

Brian Caldwell is Professor of Education at the University of Melbourne who has had a scholarly interest for more than two decades in an approach to the management of schools that was a key component of Schools of the Future, namely, the decentralization of authority, responsibility and accountability to the school level. This started with his doctoral research on the pioneering scheme of school-based budgeting in Edmonton, Alberta in the late 1970s, and gathered momentum in the early 1980s in studies of effective schools in Tasmania and South Australia.

The latter revealed how these schools had been given or had developed a capacity to manage themselves, linking the management process to decisions about learning and teaching. A model for how this could be done was found at Rosebery District High School on the west coast of Tasmania under the leadership of Jim Spinks. Caldwell and Spinks developed a series of training programs for principals, teachers and parents that was used first on a wide scale in Victoria, in the limited self-management in the early years of the Cain Labor Government. Their books on the concept and practice of the self-managing school proved helpful in a range of settings when governments sought to restructure the public system so that more authority, responsibility and accountability were decentralized to the school level. In addition to several states in Australia, this dissemination and utilization was most widespread in Britain, Hong Kong and New Zealand.

Brian Caldwell was invited to assist in four aspects of Schools of the Future, commencing with membership of a task force to help in the design process. Then followed a continuing role in the professional development of principals, mainly through five-day residential programs in association with Max Sawatzki. He also served as Chair of the Education Committee of the School Global Budget Research Project that made recommendations to Minister Hayward and his successor on how resources should be allocated to schools in their decentralized budgets. He was also a member of a research team that monitored the processes and outcomes of Schools of the Future in the Cooperative Research Project, a joint endeavour of the Department of Education, University of Melbourne, Victorian Association of State Secondary Principals, and Victorian Primary Principals Association. This book thus provided an opportunity for him to reflect on what has been accomplished in Schools of the Future in the light of the broader international reform effort, especially in that aspect that was concerned with the concept and practice of the self-managing school.

We agreed to meet after Don Hayward left office, following his decision not to seek re-election. We discussed the merit of working together on a book and wondered whether a joint effort would add value to what could be accomplished separately. Our work had, of course, been in quite different domains, only rarely intersecting as Schools of the Future unfolded. Understandably, we had different views and values on some matters. Interestingly, what clinched our decision was a realization from the very outset that the reform was incomplete. Schools of the Future, when fully implemented, may be necessary but it is not sufficient, and much more needs to be done to achieve lasting reform and make public schools exciting places for all students to learn well in the twenty-first century. There was value, then, in a book that provided a record of what transpired in Schools of the Future, set these developments in a broader frame, and then critically and constructively explored possibilities for the further reform of public education in a much wider setting than Victoria. Such a book fitted well in the Falmer Press series on Student Outcomes and the Reform of Education, offering an unusual perspective from participants in the reform process who were prepared to be reflective and critical at the same time as give an historical account.

We proceeded in this way. Don Hayward provided the personal account of Schools of the Future in Chapter 3, setting out details of each element of the reform and of the events associated with their introduction. Successes and satisfactions, problems and pitfalls, personalities and prognoses are included. Many observers must have wondered how he managed the pressure of simultaneously taking responsibility for dealing with a budget crisis in the Education Portfolio, and designing and implementing a far-reaching reform in public education that was intended to yield important benefits in the future. Parts of Chapter 3 are a personal account of these events and a reflection on the role of the Minister in relation to colleagues and other key players in the process.

One can only understand Schools of the Future if one understands Don Hayward's early years, at home and in school, and as a parliamentary assistant before moving to General Motors and then to political office. These years shaped his views and values particularly about the importance of public education, with a period as Shadow Minister for Education before taking up office providing time for reflection and the preparation of a plan for action. This necessary background is set out in Chapter 2.

It was important to establish our agreements on the achievements and importance of public education and, following our discussions on these matters, Brian Caldwell wrote Chapter 1, which also places Schools of the Future in an international perspective on effort to achieve reform in public education. This perspective was also provided in Chapter 4, where Brian Caldwell reviewed research on Schools of the Future and similar studies of school-based management in Victoria and, especially, in other nations. Don Hayward contributed to this chapter by reflecting on his own experiences in the light of the written account by Kenneth Baker as Secretary of State for Education in Britain. It was in the course of this review of research that it became clear that the critical linkages between reform efforts, including school-based management, and what occurred in classrooms and the learning experiences of students had not yet been made to any great extent in most places. Coherent reforms such as Schools of the Future provide a starting point and a framework, but more is needed.

We thus had our separate responsibilities for the first four chapters, with the ministerial record providing the centre-piece in Chapters 2 and 3, something that is exclusively and properly Don Hayward's account, with these chapters framed by Chapter 1, which makes clear our commitment to public education and its achievements, and Chapter 4 setting events in Victoria in a broader frame, especially in the light of research.

We then devoted considerable time to the substance of Chapters 5, 6 and 7, for these look to the future. The centre-piece in this set is Chapter 6, which proposes a policy framework for lasting school reform, not as a detailed blueprint or even as a broad approach to be implemented all at the same time in a particular setting. However, we feel that the framework, taken together, lays out the territory that will be covered at different rates and in different ways if lasting change for the better is to occur. Chapter 5 explores the issues that have to be addressed in public policy-making, thus establishing the pre-conditions for a successful venture in public policy, while Chapter 7 spells out the requirements for leadership if the transformation is to occur.

These proposals for the future were developed together and were the subject of frequent review and refinement, with ideas tested with others on some occasions. It was a demanding but nevertheless exciting process carried out in many places. The early reflective work was done by Don Hayward, soon after his retirement from parliament, when he and Christina were developing their language skills in and around Venice in Italy. We met regularly over many months in quiet space at the Melbourne Business School at the University of Melbourne, and it was here that ideas for the future began to take shape. A more reflective time was needed near the final stages, and bushwalking with Christina and Marie near the Hayward retreat at Lorne was ideal for this purpose. Much of the final writing was completed while Brian Caldwell was Visiting Professor at the Chinese University of Hong Kong, and it was during this time that technology served us well, with daily e-mail exchanges of chapters, drafts and new possibilities.

We express thanks to our loved ones, for whom this became yet another mission to be accomplished, when there may have been a reasonable expectation that the task was done. We also acknowledge the countless people, many of whom are named in these pages, who helped take us this far in Schools of the Future. We pay special tribute to teachers who created the great achievements of public education down through the years, and will continue to do so if empowered in the way we envisage. May they accomplish this without the tyranny of the organization, whether it be 'the system' or 'the union'.

As we now complete these pages, we are more certain than ever that, despite much that impresses about reform in public education to date, the real effort lies ahead, and this will demand leadership by many, the alignment of key interests and, above all, the will to see it through. There is too much at stake to risk the failure of such an enterprise at this stage of our history.

Brian Caldwell
Don Hayward

1   The Crisis in Public Education

Public education has made a major contribution to the well-being of society and it continues to do so. Indeed, the public school and systems of public education would have to be rated among the great successes of the last century. Those nations that are at the forefront of economic and technological progress take pride in their public schools. Many of their leaders have come from humble origins along paths that could not have been negotiated were it not for the commitment of teachers and the contributions of communities that ensured schooling was possible for all, even in the most remote and often soul-searing settings. We both attended public schools, or state schools as we described them at the time.

The enduring nature of the public school is indicated by the fact that it remains one of the few institutions to survive through a century of social transformation. It has become almost a cliché to suggest that most organizations and institutions that were created before this century no longer exist and that most that will provide work for current students and their children have not yet been created. Yet the local school, often the same physical structure, remains at the centre of a community. A community that has no school or a community that loses its school seems to lack or lose a heart.

Despite these achievements, there is a sense of crisis in public education in much of the western world. It is a crisis that extends to virtually every aspect of schooling. That it is a crisis of the West is evident in study after study that shows that schools in the East are at the top of the heap. The release of the results of the Third International Mathematics and Science Study made this clear. In what is almost certainly the largest comparative study of student achievement ever conducted, in this case in forty-one nations, Singapore was top in Mathematics and Science, with Japan and Korea joining it in the top four, along with the Czech Republic in Science and Hong Kong in Mathematics. Despite this, places like Hong Kong still press for further improvement, as reflected in recommendations of the Education Commission on raising the quality of schooling (Education Commission, 1996).

Our book is concerned with this crisis and the future of public education, with particular attention being given to developments in three nations, Australia, Britain and the United States, although much of the commentary and analysis could be applied in other countries.

In Britain, the need for reform was recognized by former Labour Prime Minister James Callaghan in his famous Ruskin Speech in 1976, but more than a decade elapsed before the 1988 Education Reform Act of the Conservatives led by Margaret Thatcher resulted in national curriculum, national tests and the local management of schools with a capacity for 'opting out' to become grant-maintained. These reforms were triggered by allegations of politicization by the left at the local level, a faith in the mechanism of the market to stimulate parental choice and improve quality, and concern at the apparent decline in student achievement in relation to comparable nations. The outcome nearly a decade later is broad acceptance of the framework of the new arrangements, at least to the extent that the major political parties are committed to maintaining it, but with continuing and wide concern about standards and the lack of a significant or measurable impact on the achievement of students. From the perspective of the former Conservative Government, the blame lay with local education authorities, schools of education at universities, and the quality of teaching. However, schools are under-resourced in important ways, whether it be the knowledge and skills of teachers, or failure to keep pace with technology, or the decaying fabric of obsolete buildings. Teachers feel embattled in the face of apparently unrelenting criticism. The nation continues to lag in international comparisons of student achievement. The reform agenda is clearly unfinished.

The United States is a nation of more than 15,000 school districts, with constitutional power at the state level, and little leverage at the national level other than through special purpose grants and moral suasion on the part of the President. Americans speak of waves of reform but little appears to have changed in terms of broad public unease at the quality of schooling. At first sight, virtually every element in a possible reform agenda has been tried, including the adoption of national goals, state-wide testing, the creation of charter schools, private involvement in the delivery of public schooling, revenue reform to achieve a greater measure of equity across districts, and the involvement of the judiciary on a scale unknown in other places. The reform effort is fragmented, though some local or special projects have promise (as in the New American Schools projects reported by Stringfield, Ross and Smith, 1996), and there is, as in Britain, a sense there has been little impact of efforts to date.

In Australia, where constitutional arrangements are more like the United States than in Britain, though there are no districts as far as governance is concerned, reform has not engaged the public to the same extent. Efforts to secure agreement among states on a national curriculum have not succeeded, although most states have now established their own curriculum frameworks. There has been some decentralization of responsibility to the school level and increasing concern about outcomes and accountability. Resourcing is an issue but from different perspectives, being seen as inadequate by some and inefficiently deployed by others. National and international comparisons do not attract the same attention as in other countries, although there seems to be a consensus emerging about the importance of literacy and the introduction of technology. Reform has been dramatic in Victoria, where a government elected in 1992 with sweeping parliamentary majorities has introduced a series of measures that have some things in common with Britain but have a higher level of coherence. These are attracting attention in the international arena. This book examines the origins and agenda for reform in Victoria in the first instance, but is concerned in the main with the outcomes and the future of reform on a broader scale.

The program of reform in Victoria, known as Schools of the Future, was implemented at the same time that the government took measures to balance a budget and reduce state debt, both of which were seen to be out of control. It was in this climate that all public schools were chartered, a curriculum and standards framework was adopted, most of the state education budget was decentralized to schools, local selection of teachers was introduced, and a new framework of accountability was established. While there was no provision for schools to 'opt out' as in Britain, and 'league tables' of tests were ruled out, the revolution was just as dramatic as that in Britain, and in many ways was completed in shorter time. The stage is set, as it is in Britain and the United States, for further change that has its focus in the improvement of learning, that is, the agenda for reform is likely to shift from the system and school to the classroom.

However, these reforms in three nations, even if they penetrate the classroom, are likely to be insufficient to address the larger issues of the control and resourcing of public schooling, and most importantly the quality of schooling that is necessary for the individual and for society in the third millennium. While the first part of this book gives an account of recent efforts in school reform, it is primarily dedicated to the future of public education and the lessons that may be drawn from those endeavours.

The Achievements of Public Education

We return again to the opening lines of the chapter and reiterate our respect for the achievements of public education. At a strictly personal level, the authors came from families of modest means and undertook all their schooling and higher education in the public sector. Our subsequent work, where it took us into the school education field, either political or professional, has been largely concerned with public education. This book reflects a commitment to its future. It is thus appropriate to commence with acknowledgment of its achievements.

Source of National Pride and Success

Public schools have been the primary source of education for the majority of students in all nations, especially in those that have been the most successful, no matter what indicator for national success is adopted, whether it be economic strength, cultural sensitivity and tolerance, or enduring peace and civilization. Even where public education is the subject of debate or even crisis, the protagonists invariably and properly acknowledge the contribution of the public school.

Contribution to the Economy

While this achievement is often denied, the link between education and the economy has been strong over the last century, and the fact that the link is not now as strong as it was is the source of concern to many. The great systems of public education had their origins in the late nineteenth century as momentum was building for what we now call the industrial revolution. In addition to their traditional roles as sources of education and civilization, schools had the new role of preparing young people for work in the factories and the public service, both rapidly expanding as the century drew to a close.

Centre of Culture and Civilization

Public schools have helped build a sense of cohesion in the community, not only through their transmission of knowledge of history and of societal values that are enduring, but also through their success in bringing together students of many different origins and cultures. It is not uncommon in some cities for students to come from a wide range of ethnic backgrounds, with scores of languages other than the majority language spoken in the home. No other organization or institution has had to meld a community with a common purpose, but with such diversity, for such a significant part of the day for so many years.

Focus for Community

Also, from a community perspective, the school has been an important institution. For much of the last century the public school has been a source of pride in every hamlet, village, town or city. Though there were other sites for community gatherings, the school was always such, with its facilities used for a wide range of sporting, cultural, educational and social occasions. This achievement has been highlighted when a public school has been threatened with closure, even when enrolments have dwindled to a handful.

Building a Profession

The public school is associated with the rise of teaching as a profession. The school teacher has always been a person of respect in every community. Now there are millions of teachers in public schools around the world, with most in developed nations holding a university degree, including a substantial component that draws on an increasingly sophisticated body of knowledge about learning and teaching. Levels of remuneration and working conditions are high in many though not all countries. Teacher unions and professional associations have played an important role in these advances.

These achievements are, of course, not unique to public education. So far we have not referred to private schooling, which remains the choice or feasible option for a minority of parents in most nations and the majority in some. Each of the achievements can also be ascribed to private schools. We shall return to private schools in the second half of the book.

The Crisis in Public Schooling

Despite these achievements, there is a sense of crisis in public schooling in many nations. While there is no consistent view among protagonists as to the source and scope of the crisis, it is real nonetheless. Some views stem from a belief that momentum has been lost in the areas of achievement; others from the emergence of new conditions in the late twentieth century, more than one hundred years after the formation of most systems of public schooling, that suggest that a new approach may be needed.

Contribution to a Global Economy

Links between public education and the economy remained strong for most of the century. There is widespread concern in some nations that the link is now weak, and many proposals for change have been energized by the need to make it strong again, in what we now call the post-industrial age or the information revolution.

While there was some measure of disbelief as recently as the start of the 1990s, there is now almost universal acceptance that there is a global economy, and that a nation that fails to ensure its children, indeed all of its citizens, have the knowledge and skill to successfully participate in such an economy, will surely suffer a decline in standard of living and quality of life. There is such a sense in many western nations, as evidenced in projects such as the Third International Mathematics and Science Study, and the now almost continuous stream of comparisons between approaches to schooling in different countries.

Standards of Achievement

Reform has been marked in some nations by a breakdown in consensus on what ought to be taught or learned in schools, as might be reflected in a curriculum for all schools, and the abandonment of efforts to monitor the quality of schooling, either by public examination or inspection or both. One course of action, in response to these sources of concern, has been to establish a curriculum and standards framework and to monitor the level of student achievement, especially against state, national and international benchmarks.

More specifically, there is profound concern at levels of literacy in the primary or elementary school, with estimates in some countries of about 20 per cent for the number of children who complete this stage without adequate achievement. The consequences are very serious indeed, not only for the next stage of schooling, where students may experience alienation and become highly disruptive, but later in life, when no worthwhile employment can be gained. A view that the basics are not as important now, with advances in technology and reliance on calculators and computers, is quickly dispelled when one realizes that students without adequate levels of literacy are more disempowered than ever.

Cultural Cohesiveness

There is a sense that schools are losing their effectiveness in the civic or community domain. To blame social ills on the school is unfair, but some critics have a case when a loss of pride or commitment to key values is sheeted home to the absence of studies in history or the inclusion of subjects that seem to promote or tolerate or encourage a smorgasbord of values.

Keeping Pace with Technology

It seems that most schools around the world have simply failed to keep pace with the revolution in technology. Seymour Papert's graphic invitation to imagine time travellers from the 1890s visiting schools and hospitals of the 1990s and observe the great discrepancy between the two settings in terms of use of technology will immediately grasp the point (Papert 1993, p. 1). The concern here is not technology for the sake of technology. Technology empowers the learner and the teacher and other professionals in a host of ways. For the student, it means being able to access almost unlimited sources of information without spending time in limited searches in traditional sources, and in being able to manage that information in highly creative ways, including advanced problem-solving. For the teacher, it means freedom from a mountain of boring administrative chores, allowing the easy management of complex information to support their work; and freedom from standard and often out-of-date lesson plans and learning designs, allowing access to teaching and learning resources that are the world's best. These benefits are evident now in many schools; why can they not be enjoyed by all?

The Fabric of Schools

The fabric of many public schools is also a cause for serious concern. Perhaps the most critical aspect is that many schools are simply falling apart after years of neglect, especially in those communities that were established and grew rapidly with the increase of population in the baby boom following World War II. Such was the rate of construction and the cost involved that only light construction was possible in some places, and working in such structures must surely be a source of dissatisfaction for teachers and students alike. For most schools, however, the design is simply inappropriate in an age of technology. These are the schools built on factory lines, essentially a line of box-like structures through which students progress in lock-step fashion as in mass production. The range of shapes and sizes that high-tech schools require is still rare. This is not to say that some nations have not done well in the design of their public schools in recent years, or even during the boom times, especially in those communities in Canada and the United States where the majority of voters had children in schools and gave their support on ballots to secure the additional levels of property tax or bond issues to raise the funds required for state-of-the-art schools.

Levels of Resources

There seems to be agreement among all commentators that there is a crisis in the resourcing of public schools. However, this issue is, at the same time, apparently the chief cause of conflict in different views about cause and effect. Those who are concerned about the decline in standards, especially in respect to the adoption of technology, or who point to the long-neglected physical condition of many schools, suggest that lack of public resourcing is the cause. International comparisons of per capita expenditure among nations in the Organisation for Economic Cooperation and Development (OECD) are frequently employed in making the case. The value of equity is invoked when some schools can rely more on their community to provide additional resources than can others. The debate becomes bitter when public funds are also made available to private schools or when measures to encourage the foundation of private schools are taken by government, for the issue of public versus private schooling is as much about ideology as it is about parental choice. Taking all things into account in the nations with which we are chiefly concerned, many public schools are clearly under-resourced compared to their counterparts in the private sector. If the aim is to bring all schools to a standard in the areas that are important, more resources are required.

The solution, however, is not necessarily in the provision of more funds from the public purse. The reality in most places is that the community will not accept higher rates of taxation to support public education, and even where increases may be possible, they are clearly insufficient to meet the needs at hand. The need for more resourcing in education to bring all public schools to benchmark standards comes at a time when an increasing proportion of citizens are in older age brackets, and priorities in the foreseeable future are about health care and other public services. Nor can the privatization of public education be the solution if the options are limited to initiatives such as the Edison Project in the USA or the contracting out of selected services. In the overall scheme of things, these provide resources at the margin.

A related concern in the funding of schools, especially in systems of public education, is related to how resources are allocated. At issue here is the proportion of the total available funds that actually reach the school or classroom. While there is general agreement that state education departments, local education authorities or school districts should have resources to provide support services for schools or maintain a structure to provide appropriate direction and accountability, alarm bells ring for many when the central share is perceived to be excessive. Such a concern underpins the initial insistence in Britain that at least 80 per cent of the total available budget be allocated directly to schools, and why agreement was quickly reached across the political spectrum that this proportion should be higher. It also explains the consternation when it was revealed that only 43 per cent of public expenditure for New York Public Schools actually reached the classroom.

Professional Status and the Role of the Teacher Union

The professional status and levels of job satisfaction of teachers are invariably included in accounts of the crisis in public schooling although, again, there are different views about cause and effect. Certain indicators seem unassailable, including the steady decline in some nations in the ability of secondary students entering tertiary programs in teacher education, and the failure of teaching salaries and working conditions to keep pace with those for other professions. While concerns about teacher morale have been evident for many years, some contend that they are now at their highest. Interestingly, a low level of teacher morale has been claimed as a factor in the performance of students in international tests, as was the case in Australia which, while ranking in the top ten nations in the Third International Mathematics and Science Study, also had more than 50 per cent of teachers preferring to work in another field.

There is also an issue about the role of the teacher union in the late twentieth century. Having made a major contribution to the success of public education in the past, there is evidence in some places that the movement has lost its way, opposing virtually every effort at reform while maintaining a strictly industrial stance in most of its endeavours. This is not always the case, for many leaders in unions or professional associations are at the forefront of reform efforts in some nations, where members at all levels of schools and school systems are partners in the design and delivery of new reforms.

Starting the Search

Taken together, this is a formidable list of concerns that suggests that the solution does not lie in piece-meal efforts or changes at the margins in areas such as the finance of public schooling. We think they are sufficient to warrant a landmark shift in attitudes and a new framework for school education in general. We explore the options in other chapters, but signal here our view that maintaining traditional distinctions between public and private schooling will not yield a solution to the crisis. These distinctions stake out the ground for ideological debates as they have in school organization and in the classroom, where phonics versus whole language in literacy, whole class instruction versus individual work in mode of learning take on 'star wars' dimensions that leave students stranded while the battles rage. The truth is that all approaches have to be accommodated. Certainly, it is counterproductive to maintain that approaches to the organization of public education that were established in the late nineteenth century should prevail for all time.

We use as a starting point in this search for a new framework the reforms in Victoria that are known as Schools of the Future. There are many reform movements around the world that have similar features, but we turn to Victoria, not only because of our familiarity with what transpired and its outcomes, but also because the Victorian effort appears to be unusually coherent and ready to proceed beyond the initial stage of system restructuring to a new design in public schooling at every level: system, school, class and student. On this last point, some nations have in our view remain fixed in or have moved slowly through that first stage, perhaps exemplified in Britain, or have had difficulty in achieving any large scale reform across the nation or part thereof, perhaps illustrated in the USA.

In this last half of the chapter, we describe the system of public schooling in Victoria, setting recent developments in an historical context. We then offer brief international comparisons before indicating our own interest and involvement and outlining the directions we intend to take in the book.

Public and Private Schooling in Australia

The Commonwealth of Australia is a federation of six states and two territories, with the latter subject to the federal government but in most respects having the status of states. Except for being a constitutional monarchy, the parliamentary arrangements and divisions of responsibilities are not unlike the USA. The Commonwealth Parliament has a House of Representatives and a Senate, and each state has two legislatures or houses, typically referred to as a Legislative Assembly (lower house, the majority party in which forms the government) and the Legislative Council (upper house, or house of review). In this nation of about 18 million people, constitutional powers to make laws related to education lie with the states, but the Commonwealth has considerable power because it has the exclusive authority to levy income tax, the major source of public revenue in Australia, and its capacity to make grants to the states to which conditions may be attached. To a large extent, the Commonwealth has taken responsibility for the higher education sector, mostly consisting of universities and colleges of technical and further education. The states exercise their powers for school education and raise the major part of the funds for the resourcing of public schools, the remainder coming from special purpose grants from the Commonwealth and from local fund-raising efforts.

Across the nation, approximately 70 per cent of school students attend government or public schools, administered for the government by departments of education. The remaining 30 per cent attend non-government, independent or private schools, with most of these in systems of Catholic schools and an increasing number of smaller systems of denominational schools. A small but significant number of non-government schools are independent, many with deep historical traditions along the lines of the English public (private) school and most have some affiliation with a main-stream church. Various categories of non-government schools have been established, and all receive at least some public funding on a scale, dependent on their capital resources and capacity to raise funds through fees and other means. Systems of Catholic schools receive most of their funds from government, because their capacity to raise money from fees and private effort is relatively low compared to the traditional and well-endowed private school. Most government funding for non-government or private schools comes from the Commonwealth.

In the sense conveyed in the previous paragraph, it is perhaps inappropriate to distinguish between public and private schools in Australia since all receive some

9

funding from government. Similarly in the Australian distinction between government and non-government schools. Such distinctions were sensible until about the late 1960s, for until this time there was no government funding for private schools. Now that all schools receive some funding from the public purse, Australia is rapidly approaching the point that it is appropriate to refer to all schools as public schools, with contribution from government according to the capacity of the school to generate funds by private or community effort. The issues that underpin these distinctions are deep-seated and historical, but we advocate a more realistic approach to the matter, as will become clear as we develop the major themes in this book.

The Transformation of Public Schools in Victoria

Victoria is one of six states in Australia, being a former crown colony of Britain that joined with others to form the Commonwealth of Australia in 1901. It has a population of more than 4 million, the majority of whom live in metropolitan Melbourne, a bustling cosmopolitan city of more than 3 million, described in an international survey in the early 1990s as 'the world's most livable city'. It is relatively compact by Australian standards, but with wide sweeps of farmland as well as remote communities in mountainous parts of the state.

Its population after colonization was mostly European, mainly British with a significant Irish minority, a balance that prevailed until the second half of the twentieth century. In the nineteenth century, there was a series of gold booms which, combined with a thriving agricultural sector, mostly wool, meant that 'marvellous Melbourne' became one of the wealthiest cities in the world by the 1890s, and much of the gracious architecture of the period remains intact. The boom turned to bust with the depression of the 1890s.

Along with other Australian states, and other parts of the world, systems of public education made their appearance toward the end of the nineteenth century as the needs of a growing industrial revolution and increasing urbanization made their impact. From 1872, Victoria has had a public education system that is 'free, compulsory and secular', administered by an Education Department under a Minister of the Crown. Like other states, a highly centralized system of public or state schools was established, ensuring a relatively uniform system of primary and later secondary schooling. As we noted earlier, this was a signal achievement given the dispersion of the population and the remoteness of many communities. Existing side-by-side was a relatively large private sector, the largest in Australia, explained to a degree by the wealth of the population in the nineteenth century, leading to the establishment of the large mostly Protestant independent schools in the great 'public school' tradition of Britain. At the same time, a relatively poor but nonetheless robust Catholic community, energized by a mostly Irish immigration, ensured the emergence of a system of Catholic education.

The system of government schools grew steadily throughout the twentieth century, with a small number of secondary schools making their appearance in

Melbourne and the main provincial towns and cities. It was a stable and well-regarded system that generally met the needs of the state. A small minority, less than 10 per cent in most instances, completed secondary education in high schools and proceeded to what was then the state's only university, the University of Melbourne. Curriculum at the secondary level was dominated by the needs of university entrance, or matriculation, and the primary curriculum was determined by the Education Department, with implementation monitored and consistency ensured by a system of district inspectors. Technical schools to the tenth year led most students to apprenticeship or, for a few, to institutes of technology. Unemployment levels were low, almost non-existent by current standards, with most employed in agriculture, industry and a small but growing service sector. These were times when links between education, especially school education, and economic need were tight and expected, perhaps because the economy was mostly community-based or local. Apart from the export of wool and mostly unprocessed minerals from mines, there was no sense of an economy beyond the state or nation and, for manufactured goods, high tariffs ensured that this would remain.

This sense of stability and well-being was disturbed in the third quarter of the century by several significant developments that affected the nation.

Rapid Increase in Population

The first development was the rapid increase in population. The massive post-war immigration, mostly from Britain, the Mediterranean and Eastern Europe in the early stages, but enriched from Asia in more recent times, led to the population of Australia doubling, and a transformation of society. The impact on schools was profound, not least as far as rapid growth was concerned, for this movement was accompanied by the baby boom of the 1950s and 1960s. Schools were constructed by the hundred in a very short time, most unfortunately of light timber construction with limited life expectancy and closer together than in comparable cities in the case of metropolitan Melbourne, a decision that would lead to some profoundly difficult times when the population of school-age children in many communities dwindled in the 1980s and 1990s.

Grants to Private Schools

The second force was the outcome of some epic 'state aid' debates in the 1960s that led to government funding of private or independent schools for the first time, allowing the construction of facilities not possible in the past, especially for the less wealthy schools. As a consequence, the proportion of students in non-government, independent or private schools grew rapidly to exceed 30 per cent in Victoria by the 1990s, the largest proportion in any state in Australia. This public support for non-public schools came later than in other nations, especially Britain and New Zealand, where what are regarded as non-public schools in Australia are readily accommodated in a public system (with very few truly private schools) and in Canada, with its system of separate school districts that allow full public funding of minority Catholic or Protestant schools at the same level as the public school districts.

Changing Attitudes to Authority

The third force was associated with the great social movements of the late 1960s and 1970s that led to such outcomes as a weakening of or challenge to authority in a range of social settings, whether it be Vatican 11 in the Catholic Church, or the protest movement and the Vietnam War, or the rise of feminism, or a more acute sensitivity to the needs and aspirations of the disempowered or minorities. In schools in Australia, especially in Victoria, this meant a challenge to the authority implied in a centralized curriculum, resentment at a tight system of external examinations, rejection of boards of inspectors, the formation of the Australian Schools Commission that dispersed Commonwealth funds to the states to meet particular purposes and redress disadvantage, the creation of school councils or other community-based participation structures that restored a measure of community involvement not evident in the public system for many decades, and a weakening of the authority of principals. The ranks of teacher unions were greatly expanded with the rapid growth of the teaching force, and members from the baby boom generation providing a great source of energy and militant action. Teachers colleges, formerly operated by the education department, became state colleges and ultimately a system of relatively autonomous tertiary institutions.

Much of this development occurred from the mid 1950s to the early 1980s under a right of centre Liberal Government. The election of a Labor Government with Premier John Cain in the early 1980s continued the process, with a stronger emphasis on school-based decision-making, including curriculum, on the one hand, but also more centralization or re-centralization on the other, especially in the continued growth of regional and head offices and the establishment of the Victorian Certificate of Education for senior levels in secondary schools. Teacher unions had unprecedented levels of influence in determining policies and priorities, at the system level and at the school level, where principals were required to consult with Local Administrative Committees before any action of significance. Recommendations to significantly shift further responsibility, authority and accountability to the school level in 1986, especially in respect to decisions on resources, were opposed by teacher unions and parent organisations and, ultimately, by the government (see Government of Victoria, 1986 for an account of the outcomes).

Transition to a Global Economy

During the 1980s and early 1990s, Labor Governments at the national level under Prime Ministers Bob Hawke and Paul Keating took action to help Australia in the transition to a global economy, the fourth of the major forces to impact school education in the last half of the century. De-regulation in a number of sectors and lowering of tariffs led to the decline of many industries, a process made more severe by the effects of the recession in the early 1990s, a combination of effects that hit Victoria hard. While state revenue declined sharply, and unemployment rose and several financial institutions collapsed, the state maintained high levels of expenditure in the public sector, especially in education. Reductions in the latter, such as occurred in neighbouring New South Wales, were resisted. Several national commissions pointed to the growing gap between knowledge and skills required in the modern economy and those that were addressed in schools. State debt and budget deficits were high, and school education was in turbulent times as an increasing number of interests expressed concern at directions in curriculum and a capacity to meet the needs of a restructured economy. School education and the needs of the economy that converged for more than a century of public education now diverged sharply.

Impact on Schools

The outcomes of these forces were a greatly expanded school system with a more diverse make-up of students, the targeting of funds to meet the needs of particular groups of students, more school-based curriculum development than ever, increased involvement of parents and teachers in decision-making, and higher levels of retention of students to the end of secondary school. In structural terms, education departments across the nation expanded greatly to become among the largest bureaucracies to be found in the public service in any setting. New head offices had to be found. In Victoria, for example, what was mostly housed in a single building at 2 Treasury Place behind Parliament House was shifted and dispersed, ultimately to occupy much of one tower of Melbourne's tallest building, The Rialto. The organization chart became complex as small units were established to manage funds for the scores of discrete special purpose grants. Despite this high level of centralization, there was some decentralization. Administratively, this came in the form of regional arrangements, with an array of district support centres by the early 1990s. Each school had a council with powers to set policy, within guidelines provided by the Minister, and to approve the school budget. Principals were selected locally.

Schools of the Future

Don Hayward tells the story of the design and implementation of Schools of the Future in Chapters 2 and 3, respectively. The major features of this reform in the first term of the Kennett Government are briefly described here in Chapter 1, and then placed in international perspective, so that the reader may locate these events in the overall scheme of things, as efforts are made around the world to sustain systems of public education.

Figure 1.1: The four dimensions of Schools of the Future

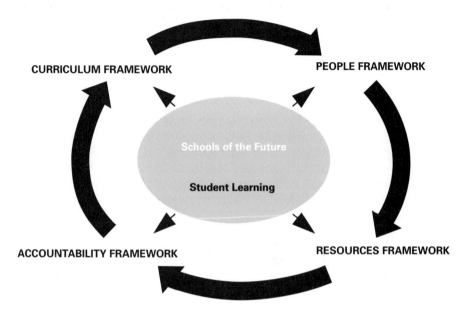

The Labor Government in Victoria was defeated in elections in late 1992 and a Liberal National Coalition Government led by Jeffrey Kennett was elected with sweeping majorities in both houses of parliament. Don Hayward was appointed Minister for Education. The Government of Victoria moved quickly in a series of measures to restore the financial condition of the state. It had clear evidence from the Commonwealth Grants Commission over many years and its own Commission of Audit to show that Victoria was spending more than its counterparts in the delivery of public education, especially in the light of the more geographically compact nature of the state, with no discernible advantage in terms of outcomes for students. The physical condition of schools was very poor, and many schools had enrolments too small to sustain a program suited to the needs of society in the late twentieth century, especially in some communities where other schools were available. Consistent with this analysis, incentives were provided for teachers to retire, effectively reducing the number of teachers by more than 6500, and decisions were made to close or amalgamate more than 300 schools, reducing the number to about 1700.

While these measures were taken to address issues of efficiency in the public education system and manage a crisis in the state's finances, a package of reforms to restructure the system was designed in late 1992 and early 1993, and released under the banner of Schools of the Future. In broad terms, this package had four dimensions as illustrated in Figure 1.1. A Curriculum and Standards Framework was established for all years from Preparatory to Year 12, designed by the recently-established Board of Studies. About 90 per cent of the state's school education budget was decentralized so that each school had a 'school global budget' to manage for virtually all areas of recurrent expenditure, including teaching and non-teaching staff, the only exceptions of note being capital expenditure and certain categories of expense for system and school support. Regional and central offices were severely down-sized, with the number of employees at these levels being reduced from more than 2300 to less than 600. Local selection of teachers was introduced, though permanent teachers continued to be employed by the Education Department. A capacity to select teachers at the school level and develop a school workforce plan was curtailed in the early years by the fact that the overall number of teachers in the system was still considered in excess of requirements, so many schools carried a number of 'over entitlement' teachers. A Professional Recognition Program was introduced to provide a new career structure for teachers, with provision for appraisal of staff. The accountability system provided for annual reports to the Education Department and school community and a process of triennial review was trialed for implementation in the second term of the Kennett Government following its re-election in early 1996. A Learning Assessment Project was implemented at the primary level with all students being tested in literacy, mathematics and science at years 3 and 5. Results were used for school-level planning and report to parents; 'league tables' of results were not introduced in contrast to practice in Britain. These features were all implemented within a framework of a school charter, a short document that sets out the priorities, programs and special characteristics of each school, being an agreement between the school, its community and the Education Department that will shape its operations for a period of three years.

These developments were part of a more comprehensive program of the Kennett Government that was broadly endorsed by the community at the elections of early 1996. All were characterized by an absence of union influence that, in the previous Labor Government, was frequently a determiner or constraint on action. This comprehensive program included an effort to transform the industrial relations scene.

A particular characteristic of Schools of the Future was the manner in which it moved relatively quickly through structural reform to address matters related to learning and teaching. Notable was an initiative in early literacy in 1995 known as Keys to Life that made available more than A$50 million to help ensure that all children could learn to read well in primary school. Also prominent was the manner in which the government responded to advances in technology and the consequent changes in the workplace for students and teachers. The revolution in technology may be considered the fifth of the major forces that have re-shaped or will re-shape public schooling, the others identified earlier in this account of developments in Australia in the last half century being large-scale post-war immigration that diversified the social make-up and transformed society in Australia, the 'state aid' debate and the funding from the public purse of non-public (non-government, private and independent) schools, the challenge to traditional authority and concern to empower and redress disadvantage, and the emergence of a global economy and the critical scrutiny placed on knowledge and skills that are addressed in schools.

These developments notwithstanding, the sense of crisis in public schooling remains in the manner described at the outset. The agenda for further reform is the primary purpose of this book after a more detailed account is offered of the processes and outcomes of Schools of the Future.

Schools of the Future in International Perspective

Observers of the international scene will readily identify counterparts, not only of forces shaping the reform of school education, but also the policy responses. Most systems or nations now have the equivalent of a curriculum and standards framework, with the British national curriculum having many similarities to what has unfolded in Victoria. Victoria provides for all schools to have a charter, as does New Zealand, but this concept is different to that used in the charter movement in the United States, that usually connotes a school being freed from the constraints of a school district and many of the regulations that bind all schools. There is no charter for schools in Britain, although all locally managed schools are expected to have a school development plan.

There are also similarities in policies that decentralize responsibility for staffing and budget to the school level. In Britain, this is known as the local management of schools, but a capacity in that country for schools to 'opt out' and become 'grant-maintained', with public funds coming to the school directly from the Funding Agency for Schools, has no counterpart in Victoria. New Zealand also has decentralized the budget but the reform was not completed, with extensive opposition to the so-called 'bulk funding' of schools.

There are few counterparts in the USA. While most states have established something similar to a curriculum and standards framework, few of approximately 15,000 school districts have moved significantly and comprehensively to school-based or local management of schools. Decentralization has different connotations. In New York, for example, it meant decentralization to subdistricts or regions within the city system, with little authority and responsibility shifting to the school level. In early 1997, these subdistrict arrangements were abandoned amidst calls for a higher proportion of district resources to be allocated to schools. Chicago has empowered communities through representation on school councils, but little appears to have changed at the school level.

There are similarities in the charter school movement in the USA that is now gathering momentum. These schools are freed from control by the school district but receive public funds, so in this respect they are like grant-maintained schools in Britain, hence may be considered to have gone further than Schools of the Future on this dimension. Charter schools are now described as 'the hottest trend in American education reform' with President Bill Clinton declaring himself 'a great champion' of the movement (Jouzaitis, 1997, p. 1). Indeed, Clinton proposed an increase in federal support for charter schools from US$51 million to US$100 million in 1997 (Harris, 1997, p. 12) at a time of budget constraint, with bi-partisan support of Democrats and Republicans now apparent.

The Learning Assessment Project in some ways echoes the testing programs in Britain and the United States, but there are no 'league tables' of raw results that show how schools perform against one another. Britain maintains a sophisticated approach to the inspection of schools, a practice abandoned in Victoria in the 1970s. There are no counterparts in the United States. On the other hand, there is provision in some states in the USA to close down non-performing systems, as there is in Britain for the closing down of schools, but these powers have rarely been exercised. No schools in Victoria have been closed for non-performance; the criterion for school closure has been student enrolment.

Victoria has moved through the structural reforms relatively quickly to respond to the need to restructure learning, teaching and school organization in the search for improved performance and the adoption of new technologies. One senses from reading the headlines that Britain and the United States are setting the same priorities, with public debate probably more robust than in Australia. Whereas Britain has also progressed through the structural reforms, although somewhat slower than Victoria, that started later, it is clear that structural constraints may impair the effort in the USA for some time. By this we refer to the fact that there are more than 15,000 school districts in that nation and that each state has a virtual mountain of regulations to be addressed in the implementation of reform. The USA has perhaps the most impressive collection of approaches to the re-design of schools and school systems that are intended to penetrate the classroom, including the nine designs that make up the New American Schools (NAS) program (Stringfield, Ross and Smith, 1996) and the several initiatives funded by the Annenberg Foundation, the Pew Charitable Trust, and the Edison Project. NAS incorporates many initiatives that may be better known by their discrete titles, such as the National Coalition of Essential Schools founded by Ted Sizer and the programs developed by Robert Slavin, Success for All, and Roots and Wings.

Teacher unions in the USA have maintained an important strategic role in the design and implementation of reform, in contrast to what has occurred in Victoria, where they have been sidelined in most respects. The relatively more powerful role in the USA is understandable, given the manner in which union leaders have seen the need for reform and have repositioned their organizations from reaction to leadership. After a late start, it is apparent that teacher unions in Britain now embrace the major elements of the reform agenda and are keen to move on to change that will have a real impact on learning and the re-building of the teaching profession.

There are important differences in these nations as far as private schooling is concerned. There are few truly private schools in the USA, where there are constitutional restrictions on the use of public funds in support of this sector. In Britain and New Zealand, what might be considered private schools in Victoria and elsewhere in Australia, are aided schools with public funding, and these are generally considered in the same broad category of public schools.

This international overview has been restricted to developments in Australia, Britain, Canada, New Zealand and the United States but there are parallels in some areas in other nations. We are hard-pressed to name any nation where there has not been a trend to decentralize some authority and responsibility to the school level. Similarly in concern for performance and measures against international benchmarks, such as those provided in the Third International Mathematics and Science Study. All are challenged by advances in technology.

In general, the Victorian reforms emerge as remarkably coherent in an international perspective, warranting closer attention as far as design, implementation and outcomes are concerned. They provide a useful starting point for considering the long-term future for public schooling, in Australia and elsewhere around the world where there is a sense of crisis despite impressive achievement over more than a century.

The Authors' Perspective

It is important to make clear the authors' perspective at the outset. Don Hayward was Minister for Education during the first term of the Kennett Government. He was educated in public schools in New South Wales and graduated from the University of Melbourne after working as a parliamentary assistant for a short period. His substantive career before entering parliament was in the corporate sector, serving as a senior executive in General Motors. He was Shadow Minister for Education in the Opposition Liberal Party for several years before the election of the Kennett Government in late 1992. He was Minister for Education throughout the first term of this government and had oversight of the design and implementation of Schools of the Future. He did not seek re-election to parliament in 1996.

Brian Caldwell is a Professor of Education at the University of Melbourne. He was educated in public schools in Victoria, graduated from the University of Melbourne, and was a teacher of mathematics and science in government schools in Victoria and in a public school in Edmonton, Alberta, before completing postgraduate study at the University of Alberta. His interest in restructuring was sparked through doctoral research on school-based budgeting in Canada, notably the Edmonton Public School District, in the late 1970s. He has served as consultant to several governments on matters related to school reform, especially on the allocation of resources to schools. He provided advice in the design of Schools of the Future, contributed to leadership development programs for principals in Victoria, helped research the processes and outcomes, and served as Chair of the Education Committee for the School Global Budget, providing recommendations on the funding mechanism for schools to Minister Hayward and his successor, Phillip Gude.

Outline of the Book

In this first chapter, we set out the accomplishments of the public school but made clear the sense of crisis that is evident in several countries after more than a century of public schooling. We then described the context in Victoria, Australia, where an unusually coherent program of reform known as Schools of the Future commenced in early 1993. We use this as the starting point to consider the future of public schools.

In Chapter 2, Don Hayward provides a personal account of the origins of Schools of the Future, revealing a sense of planning and sensitivity to concerns about public schools. This account belies the views of critics of the reform on both counts.

Don Hayward continues the account in Chapter 3, documenting the implementation of Schools of the Future, providing details of how each dimension of the framework illustrated in Figure 1.1 was designed and implemented. He reflects on what it was like to be Minister leading the most extensive reform in public education ever undertaken in Australia.

In Chapter 4 we provide a commentary on Don Hayward's experience, matching it with the account of Kenneth Baker, Secretary of State for Education in Britain at the time of implementation of reforms in that country that flowed from the 1988 Education Reform Act. We then report research on the processes and outcomes of Schools of the Future. Our starting point is to account for its success as a large-scale policy change in education. We draw on the policy model of James Guthrie and Julia Koppich (Guthrie and Koppich, 1993) to show how all of the elements for success were present, as illustrated in the accounts in Chapters 2 and 3. Findings from the five-year Cooperative Research Project are cited, especially those that have suggested links between the major features of Schools of the Future and improved learning outcomes for students. Reference is also made to independent evidence in the studies of Allan Odden, University of Wisconsin at Madison, whose four-year study of the Victorian reform was part of a multi-nation international study funded by the Office of Educational Research and Improvement in the USA (Odden and Odden, 1996). Findings from studies of comparable reforms in other countries are presented. Other local studies that are critical of the reform are also described and appraised.

We turn our attention in Chapter 5 to the issues faced by public schools at the dawn of the third millennium. These lie in the areas of teachers and teaching, learners and learning, the relationship between education and the economy, the resourcing of schools, and the role of government. We describe six pre-conditions to achieve lasting school reform. We acknowledge that reforms such as Schools of the Future are a necessary but not sufficient pre-condition.

We begin Chapter 6 with a vision for schools of the third millennium which reflects a commitment to public education and a recognition that schools will change in profound ways, with technology a major driver of the transformation of learning. We then develop a policy framework to achieve lasting school reform. This framework is built around four key concepts: 'public', 'entitlement', 'contribution' and 'design', the outcome of which is a framework with fifteen elements. Taken together, these constitute our preferred scenario among three that we put to the test. The framework in its entirety is intended for Australia, but most elements apply to all countries that are pursuing a reform agenda in public education.

What we propose is arguably the most sweeping transformation in public education, at least in Australia. Making this change will call for high levels of leadership, and the alignment of all with an interest and stake in achieving lasting school reform that yields benefits for all students. We consider in Chapter 7 the implications for four groups of leaders, being those in government; bureaucracies; teacher unions, being organizations we propose be reconstituted as professional associations; and principals and other leaders at the school level. We conclude that the crisis in public education is fundamentally a crisis in learning. The book is titled *The Future of Schools* but at its heart lies the future of learning.

2   Foundations of Reform

In this chapter, Don Hayward provides a personal account of how the foundation was laid for Schools of the Future in Victoria. After setting the scene when the Liberal National Government came to power in 1992, a deeply personal account is given of his early upbringing and work experience that shaped his attitudes to schooling and the role of government. This experience lay in politics, as a parliamentary adviser, but most notably at senior levels in the corporate sector. He outlines how a program of reform was developed during the years in Opposition, ensuring mobilization on assumption of power.

The Education System I Inherited

Victoria is the second most populous state in Australia. At one time it had been Australia's wealthiest state, mainly due to gold finds, long since exhausted. For many years it had been the financial hub of Australia. It had also been the centre of much of Australia's manufacturing industry. In 1982, a Labor Government won power in Victoria. Through financial mismanagement, this government incurred deficits in recurrent expenditure and significantly increased the state's debt. These disastrous policies led to the downfall of the State Bank, the Victorian Economic Development Corporation and other institutions. Just as importantly, it also undermined investor confidence in the state. As a result, new investment dried up, and many business firms began to leave. Victoria was frequently referred to as 'a rust bucket' and, at meetings in other states, Victorian business people found themselves the butt of jokes.

Education, which is so vital to social and economic development, also suffered a decline in public confidence in Victoria during Labor's decade of mismanagement. I was acutely aware of this because of my own work as a Member of Parliament in my electorate of Prahran. From talking with parents it became abundantly clear that their preference was for their children to attend private schools. I knew many parents who could not really afford to do this, but who would work at two jobs each to pay for their child to go to a private school. This occurred very frequently in migrant families who knew the value of a high quality education to the future prospects of their child. Across the state, more than 30 per cent of all students attended private schools.

The rhetoric of the Labor Government was that their education system would help the most disadvantaged children. However, from my observations of such children in my own electorate, I came to the conclusion that the system was actually working to their disadvantage. This was confirmed by my experience when, for a time, I was Shadow Minister for Community Services. The irony was that the Labor Party's attempts to make everyone equal tended to perpetuate social disadvantage for many children. The Labor Party's approach was essentially ideologically driven, with slogans such 'equality of outcomes' and 'parity of esteem'. It sought to use the education system for 'social engineering' purposes.

When I tried to analyse the reasons for this, it seemed to me that the effect of the Labor Party's slogan-driven education policies was to set the lowest common denominator as the benchmark and to encourage mediocrity. However, I knew from my own childhood experiences that, to escape the poverty trap, one must be encouraged to excel and achieve one's full potential. It was only my good fortune in participating in a stimulating learning environment, with inspiring teachers, that I was given a chance for the future.

From my talks with teachers and Education Department bureaucrats I reached the conclusion that the system had lost its sense of purpose. Many of these people had begun to think that the system was there for their own comfort and convenience and to provide them with employment. Further, the system had been captured and was controlled by teacher union officials and other special interest groups who were pushing an ideological agenda at the expense of a high quality and demanding education for our young people. In *Yes, Prime Minister* chief bureaucrat Sir Humphrey Appleby considered the purpose of the English comprehensive education system to be 'to improve the living standards of teachers, not the educational standards of children . . .' I believed this description could be equally applied to the education system in the State of Victoria.

These problems of attitude were compounded by the centralized nature of the Victorian education system. This facilitated control by teacher union officials. In fact, the Labor Government had entered into centralized agreements with these teacher union officials that regulated virtually everything that happened in schools. School principals had become the captives of teacher union officials, who could veto their decisions.

These observations of the way in which the Victorian education system was operating against the interests of many of the children in my electorate, on top of my own childhood experience where education had lifted me out of poverty, had a significant emotional effect on me. I became personally committed to reforming the system so that it would actually give children from disadvantaged circumstances a chance for the future, as it had done for me, for the twenty-first century will be immensely more complex and challenging for our young people than the twentieth century was for us. We must help our young people to develop the resourcefulness and flexibility which will enable them to grasp the new and ever changing opportunities.

Formation of My Views on Educational Reform

Early Years

I was born in Broken Hill, a mining town in the far outback of New South Wales. Because my father worked in a number of nomadic jobs, and then joined the Royal

Australian Air Force, our family moved a great deal. My brother and I once calculated that we had attended fourteen different primary schools in various States. In one especially itinerant year we attended four different primary schools in three states, two of which were Catholic parish schools. As my mother's maternal grandparents were Irish Catholic, or 'bog Irish', to use the vernacular, she often favoured a local Catholic school.

At the end of World War II, we finally settled in Sydney. My father applied for and secured the tenancy of house in a New South Wales Government Housing Commission estate in Sutherland Road, Auburn, an industrial suburb in the western suburbs of Sydney. The main industries in this area were slaughter houses and meat processing works.

I have vivid memories of this house. The area itself still had a raw feeling about it, with open fields and unmade roads. The house, which was on an unfenced block of barren land, was of basic fibro construction and lacked most amenities, such as sewerage. However, we were amazed to have a house to live in after so many years in rented furnished rooms. Also, it seemed extraordinary for us to be settled in one place, rather than always on the move.

My father tried to make the most of the house and built a fence around portion of the yard to grow vegetables and to keep chickens for meat and eggs. As a result, we became, to some degree, self-sufficient in food. Also, my brother and I got after-school jobs delivering meat and groceries for local shops, which added a bit to the family income. Each week there was precise planning of the family budget to cover expenses. I can well remember the discussions between my parents as to what sort of food we could afford that week and whether there was enough money for the boys to go to the pictures.

Of course we soon got to know the other kids in the neighbourhood. At first they tried to bash us up. However, I was strongly built, and packed a good punch. Also, what my brother lacked in size, he made up in agility. Together we were a good defence team and were able to repulse this aggression. After a while, we earned the grudging respect of the local mob.

For these neighbourhood kids, school was a time to be endured, and they 'wagged' it as often as possible. They planned to leave school as soon as legally possible and get a job. This usually meant a job in the large meat works in the area where most of their fathers worked. There is no doubt in my mind that I would have ended up working in the meat works as well, except for a minor miracle.

That miracle was the opportunity to attend Homebush Boys' High School. This school was located some miles away from our home. At that time it was a selective school, in that prospective students had to sit for an exam and were selected on their results. Somehow or other it was arranged that I should sit for this exam and, as a result, I was selected to attend the school.

I clearly remember setting out from home for my first day at Homebush Boys' High School. I rode my bike to Auburn Railway Station, where I locked it in the bike rack. Then I took the train to Flemington Railway Station. From Flemington Railway Station I walked to the school. During that walk I could see on the hill in the distance the large, imposing, dark red brick school building . It looked daunting, and I remember feeling very anxious. However, I also remember feeling a new sense of excitement. I think I knew that this was an important turning point in my life. Instinctively, I realized that day was the beginning of a new phase in my life that would lead to an escape from poverty and from a life at the meat works. When I walked in the school gate, I felt a miracle had occurred.

At Homebush Boys' High School I discovered a totally new and exciting world, peopled by gifted, inspiring teachers and boys with quick, alert minds. It was a world of ideas and knowledge which intrigued and stimulated our young minds. It was a place where knowledge was sought and valued for its own sake. For most of us, school became the most important part of our lives. We did not come to school because we had to. We came because we wanted to, even though, in my case, coming to school involved two hours of travelling every day. Life became synonymous with learning.

At Homebush Boys' High School we learnt the joy and beauty of the English language and English literature. We revelled in the spoken word, both through drama and debating. We learnt the strange and appealing logic of mathematics. We learnt the excitement of science and the adventure of history. In fact, our life itself became an adventure.

We were lucky in our teachers at Homebush Boys' High School. I can remember two in particular. John Tierney was our English Master. His was a family tradition of school teaching and writing. His father, John Tierney senior, had taught Henry Lawson at Eurunderee School, a small bush school in New South Wales. As well as being an inspiring teacher, John Tierney was an author in his own right. He had written a number of novels and short stories under the pen name of Brian James. The best known of his novels was *The Advancement of Spencer Button*, a story about a school teacher (James, 1950).

Norman Lindsay said the following in an introduction to a volume of John Tierney's short stories: 'It is a remarkable coincidence that the two best short-story writers Australia has produced spent their childhood in the same small country town . . . (Eurunderee).' He was referring to John Tierney and Henry Lawson. John Tierney made literature, especially Australian literature, come alive for me, and gave me a love of writing that has made my whole life richer.

Andrew Watson was our Headmaster and taught us science. He had trained as a geologist. He had been to the Antarctic on one of Sir Douglas Mawson's expeditions. Mawson named Watson Bluff, at the east end of David Island, after him. Watson had then gone into teaching. He fired our imagination and taught us that science is a never-ending voyage of discovery through the natural world. He made us realize mathematics was a glorious game with a logic and beauty of its own.

The school taught us the value of self-learning. Often we learnt as much from each other as from the teachers. I clearly remember a group of us going repeatedly to the Mitchell Library in Sydney to research the early days of the settlement of Sydney. We looked forward immensely to these visits, which became like an adventure into the past. I also remember expeditions by the same group to the Royal National Park south of Sydney to look at the plants the first settlers saw when they landed in 1788.

On another occasion, I organized a group of boys from the school to make the long journey to Broken Hill to learn about mining in the outback. We all stayed in Broken Hill with my extraordinary relatives. My aunts made such an impression on my friends that, nearly fifty years later, they still talk about them. One friend describes them as though they were characters in a Patrick White novel.

The atmosphere of excitement for learning and the general ethos in the school was such that we all did well when it came to our final matriculation examinations. What amazed me about my own results was my success in mathematics and science. I considered that I had no natural aptitude in those subjects and I was sure that my results were due to the inspiring teaching of Andrew Watson. Based on my matriculation results, I was awarded a scholarship that took me to the Law School of the University of Sydney.

University and a First Appointment in Politics

Through debating at school we had become very aware of the issues of the day, and had developed a degree of political awareness. It was therefore not surprising that a number of us from Homebush Boys' High School gravitated to the political clubs at the university. In my case, it was the Liberal Club. I became very active in the Liberal Club and after a while, was elected President.

I am still somewhat puzzled why I was attracted to the Liberal Club at that early stage, especially in view of a strong tradition of trade unionism in my family. My mother's maternal grandfather had allegedly led the striking miners in their march down Argent Street in Broken Hill. In retrospect, I think the reason was that my life so far had taught me the value of enterprise. The Liberal Club said it stood for individual enterprise, whereas the Labor Club seemed to be all about collectivist action.

During an election campaign, the Liberal Club decided to ask the Prime Minister, Robert Menzies, to speak at a lunch time meeting at the university, which he accepted. The attendance at the meeting, which I chaired, was enormous, with the Wallace Lecture Theatre filled to overflowing. A lot of students had come to the meeting to heckle Menzies. However, he turned this heckling to his advantage in such a clever and good humoured way that he carried the crowd with him. As a result, the meeting was a great success, and Menzies left it in great good humour, and apparently quite well disposed towards me.

Subsequently, when one of his Ministers, Bill Spooner, Minister for National Development, happened to mention to Menzies that he was looking for someone with a political background for his private office, Menzies suggested me. In no time at all I found myself on the staff of a Federal Minister, and doing my Law course part-time.

Bill Spooner was a very unusual man. He had been the partner in a prominent firm of Sydney accountants, but had also been involved in the Liberal Party and its predecessor all his adult life. He had been the New South Wales State President of the Liberal Party before being elected a Senator for New South Wales. When the Liberal Party, led by Menzies, won government in 1949 he was immediately appointed a Cabinet Minister. On the surface he seemed a brusque, rather cold man, but underneath he was warm and genuine.

Spooner was also a very hard worker. As Minister for National Development he was responsible for the huge Snowy Mountains Hydro-Electric Project. A major task was negotiating the agreement between the Federal Government and the State Governments for the use of the electricity and irrigation water resulting from the project. These negotiations proved very troublesome indeed. What nearly drove me mad was his habit of working on these on Sunday mornings. As a young man, Saturday night was always 'the big night', and one would always welcome a little more sleep on Sunday morning. However, the telephone would often ring at about 8.00 am on a Sunday morning. There was no 'Good morning'. The only words spoken in Spooner's gruff voice were 'Get over here'. Somehow I would get myself dressed, would gulp a quick cup of ghastly instant coffee and be on my way to Spooner's home at Balgowlah. We always got a lot done at these sessions, and it taught me that Ministers have to start working early in the morning, even on Sundays.

I thought Spooner was very bright, but not everyone shared that view. The Secretary of the Department of National Development, Sir Harold Raggatt, had his doubts, probably because Spooner gave him such a hard time. After a particularly exasperating session with Spooner, he said to me: 'When I come to see the Minister at Parliament House, he invariably turns his chair in the middle of our discussion and looks at the Senate rose garden. At first, I used to think that he was thinking'. With this in mind, almost in memory of Spooner, when I eventually became Minister for Education I would often turn in my chair during discussions with bureaucrats and look at the view from my office on the twenty-fourth floor of the Rialto Building in Melbourne. I didn't care whether they thought I was thinking or not.

As well as the need for hard work, my time with Spooner taught me a number of things that were helpful to me when I became a Minister in due course. I instinctively realized that what I was seeing and hearing was worth recording and I kept notes in an exercise book with a blue cover. The following are some of the things he said to me, often when we were sitting next to each other on an aeroplane.

> If you want to be a really successful Minister, you have to believe in what you are doing. You have to have a personal commitment to it, and to be emotional about it. Then it doesn't matter what your opponents say about you. You can shrug them off. Don't be afraid of emotion. Harness it to help you. You will find you can use it as a driving force.

> If you want real change, you have first to work out in your own mind exactly what you want to achieve and then go after it. You can't leave it to the bureaucrats, they find the status quo far too comfortable.

> You have to lead these bureaucrats. In fact, you have to drive them. Then you have to follow them up and make sure the buggers have actually done

it. You can't leave it to them. They will always find reasons for not doing it the way you want.

One should not be too matey with bureaucrats. You will have to give them hell most of the time. You need a good working relationship with them and be able to talk properly with them, but they should always fear you a bit, and think you a bit of a bastard.

It was very difficult to concentrate on my Law studies and still work at the pace and pressure that Spooner demanded. We would often be at Parliament House in Canberra until late into the night, and I would try to study then. Spooner had a habit of pushing a buzzer when he wanted something. Annoyed at being disturbed when I was studying I got into the habit of saying 'Damn!' every time the buzzer sounded, not realizing that Spooner could hear me. Eventually Spooner could bear it no longer and, with a pleading tone in his voice, said 'I know I am diverting you from your studies, but would you please refrain from saying "damn" every time I buzz you because it is giving me a guilty conscience'.

After two years with Spooner, I was offered the job as Private Secretary to the President of the Senate, Sir Alister McMullin. In the mistaken belief that I would have more time for my studies, I took it. However, I found McMullin just as demanding as Spooner, but in a different way. Whereas Spooner was preoccupied with the development of policy and running a Department of the executive government, McMullin was intent on expanding the role and relevance of the Senate. In fact, McMullin laid the groundwork for the remarkable increase in the influence of the Australian Senate in recent years by embracing the concept of the investigatory committees which are a feature of the US Senate.

It was always my firm intention to enter the legal profession and I had already made arrangements to become an articled clerk with a firm of solicitors. There then appeared on the Canberra scene Earl Daum, Managing Director of General Motors-Holden's (GMH). Daum became a special mate of McMullin, and when Daum visited Canberra, McMullin would entertain him at luncheon or for a drink in the President's suite. Often McMullin would be called away to Chair the Senate or for some meeting, and I would end up hosting Daum. Also, when Daum had VIP visitors from General Motors Corporation, I would be given the job of guiding them around Parliament House and providing them with refreshments. Consequently, Daum and I became quite friendly.

The General Motors Years

Late one night over a whisky, during one of his visits to Canberra, Daum said to me, 'I have wanted to talk to you for some time but Alister has stopped me. I want to offer you a job in GMH. I have to tell you that Alister is opposed to this. He thinks you should go into politics'.

This was totally unexpected. I had no desire to enter the automotive industry. I had every intention of becoming a lawyer. I said that I was very grateful for the compliment he had paid me by offering me a job, but I was not interested.

Over the coming months Daum made the offer two more times. The last time he said to me, 'We do not make promises in General Motors, but it is my prediction that, if you join us, you will be a member of the Board of Directors of GMH within ten years'.

As Sir Alister McMullin had already stated his views against me taking the GMH job, I went to Spooner and asked him. His response was that, 'You have to take it. If you don't you will be wondering for the rest of your life what you might have missed. If it doesn't work out, or if you don't like it, you can always leave after a while and take up the Law'. On the basis of that advice, I took the job, and thus began a second, unplanned, career.

I made rapid progress in GMH, and, as predicted by Earl Daum, I was appointed to the Board of Directors at the age of 33. I was later transferred to General Motors Overseas Corporation, and, in 1972, became Managing Director of General Motors Philippines. I learnt one of my most important lessons in General Motors from Alfred P. Sloan. Sloan had been President and the Chairman of General Motors for much of its life. Sloan developed and then implemented the concept of decentralized operating autonomy, combined with centrally coordinated policy, that had served General Motors so well for many years. He wrote a book entitled *My Years in General Motors*, which I believe should be prescribed reading in any business school (Sloan, 1964).

As a young man being fast-tracked, I was sent by GMH to the USA to learn more about General Motors Corporation. This induction included some time at the General Motors Building in New York. One day a Vice-President took me as his guest to lunch in the Executive Dining Room in the General Motors Building.

By this time Sloan was an old man, and was no longer involved directly in the operations of General Motors. He had in fact become a living legend in General Motors and in the American business community. In recognition of his enormous contribution to the development of the corporation, when Sloan retired as Chairman of the Board of General Motors, the Board made him its Honorary Chairman. He still enjoyed coming into 'The Building' for lunch from time to time, and was there the day the Vice-President took me up to lunch.

My host, obviously in awe of the great man, took me over to be introduced and to pay homage. I can still see Sloan clearly in my mind's eye. With the extraordinary courtesy and good manners for which he was renowned, he rose shakily from his seat to greet us. I can remember him as having a gaunt figure, a thin, lined face and piercing eyes.

When it was explained to him that I was a young up-and-coming executive from Australia, he obviously felt obliged to give me some words of wisdom to take back 'down under'. 'There have been two secrets for the success of General Motors', Sloan said. 'The first is always putting the customer first. The second is the balance between decentralized operating and coordinated policy. When General Motors loses that balance it will decline'.

He was right. In the years to come the bureaucrats in the General Motors Building in Detroit began to impose centralized control on the operations of the various production and sales units. As a result, General Motors lost touch with the needs of the customers and lost the flexibility to respond to those needs, and the fortunes of the company declined, as Sloan had predicted. It is only in recent years that General Motors has rediscovered Sloan's wisdom, and has become profitable again. However, much of the damage is irreparable. My years in General Motors taught me that bureaucracies flourish in both the private and public sectors, and they develop a life of their own that has only limited relevance to the mission of the organization.

Those years also taught me how to manage a large organization. Much of what I learnt was through observing the mistakes that General Motors made. I learnt financial management, and the critical need to control expense. I also learnt how to manage large projects, including the need to precisely identify the objectives of the project, for careful planning, including planning effective and practical strategies to implement the objectives, and the need for constant monitoring to ensure the project is meeting the objectives. All these skills were vital to me in my work as Minister for Education.

Above all else, my years in General Motors taught me the importance of building the team to undertake a project or mission, the need for leadership for the team, and the need to develop and nurture every member of the team. However, they also taught me the need to be stern and unrelenting when people are not performing. Even more importantly, they taught me to recognize and reward contributions and achievements by team members in both material and non-material ways. The achievements in Education in no small measure resulted from building and managing effective teams to implement our reform program.

The years I spent with General Motors in Asia were of special value in another respect. I learnt at first hand the dynamic nature of the growth of Asian countries, especially south-east Asian countries. I learnt of the drive and energy of the young people and how they saw education as a priceless resource that would give them a future. I saw the refocusing of effort of many of those countries on the intellects and creativity of their people. These countries began to place a high value on the intellects of their people, rather than seeing the people as just low cost labour. I realized that if Australia was to keep pace with rapid development in this region we must use the minds of our people more effectively. We would need to complement the growth of south-east Asia, rather than try to compete with it. We would need to concentrate on knowledge-intensive industries. In all of this, improving the education of our children would be of crucial importance.

There is no question that my years in General Motors gave me an immensely valuable experience and the knowledge and skills to run a $3 billion operation as Minister for Education. They also helped me to achieve the massive reforms in education in Victoria. That experience was unique in the Victorian Government, because noone else in the Government had ever run a large organization. It may be that I mainly learnt from the mistakes of General Motors, but the taxpayers of Victoria were the beneficiaries of those mistakes.

My four years as Managing Director of General Motors Philippines in Manila left a profound impression on me in still other ways that greatly influenced my future work as Minister for Education. It was my job to establish two new manufacturing operations in Manila, and also a distribution network throughout the country. One of these plants was to produce automotive transmissions and involved sophisticated manufacturing operations that required well-trained people. We planned to provide extensive technical training for the new employees for this plant, but were concerned that these new employees would lack an adequate level of education on which to base this technical training. However, we soon found that these people had excellent skills and made rapid progress in the technical training. Some were so good that, after a few months, we were able to send groups of them to GMH in Australia for advanced training.

I was so impressed by the ability of our workers and their technical skills that I sought information about their education. I found that the education they were receiving both in the villages and in the city had a sound basis in language and in mathematics. Also, it had an emphasis on technical skills and vocational education. This stemmed from the years when the United States administered the Philippines and had put a priority on establishing a network of schools throughout the islands. However, I also discovered that these schools were woefully under-resourced. Despite this lack of resources, the students learnt well. I was told that this was mainly because of the dedication of the teachers and the attitudes of the students, who saw education as the way to escape what appeared to be intractable poverty.

As I travelled around the Philippines, I often took the opportunity to call in to the local schools. As Managing Director of General Motors Philippines, and a potential source of jobs, one was warmly welcomed. In fact one's visit turned into a type of celebration. The thing that I noticed in these schools was the strong emphasis on technical skills and vocational education. I learnt that these schools were teaching practical skills to children from a very early age, and were proud of it.

Even during the period of misrule by President Ferdinand Marcos, these village schools continued to operate effectively. I was told that this was mainly because the local barrio (or village) looked upon the school as its own, and, despite desperate poverty, would support it.

Because these people had a good basic education, combined with practical skills, they were able to adapt to new technology in industries such as the automotive industry. This enabled them to escape from the dreadful poverty so evident in the Philippines, and to live better lives. This drove home to me again that the most effective way to overcome disadvantage and give people a better chance for the future was through education.

Election to Parliament

After twenty years with General Motors, it was suggested to me that I should seek preselection for the Liberal Party for a seat in the Parliament of the State of

Victoria. My first reaction was to scoff at the suggestion because the prospect of being a Member of the Victorian Parliament had no special appeal to me. In any case, I thought my chances of gaining pre-selection were virtually nil.

My wife, Christina, and I discussed this over a number of days. I had been with General Motors for most of my working life. Having been appointed to a senior position in General Motors at an early age I had already experienced most things that many executives of my age were still seeking to achieve. Also, as a family, we had no desire for a further overseas posting with General Motors. Talking all this through, we came up with the surprising conclusion that I might as well give the pre-selection a try. This decision was reached in the sure expectation that I would not win the pre-selection anyway, but we thought it would be an interesting experience. So I joined the field of candidates for pre-selection for Monash Province in the Legislative Council. To my surprise, and, I suspect, that of everyone else, I was pre-selected. I went on to win the seat in the next elections and thus became a Member of the Victorian Parliament. Thus began my third unplanned career.

After six years in the Legislative Council (Upper House), I moved to the Legislative Assembly (Lower House) following my election as the Member for Prahran.

The Liberal Party was in Opposition in the Victorian Parliament for a number of years. I had various 'Shadow' portfolios over those years and at one stage I had been appointed Shadow Minister for Community Services. I was pursuing the Labor Government over a series of scandals, the most dramatic of which was its appointment, without proper checks, of a paedophile with overseas criminal convictions to care for children at risk. I was personally outraged by the Labor Government's mismanagement of community services. I saw my main mission in life as hounding them and exposing their ineptitude.

The Liberal Parliamentary Party had a love–hate relationship with its parliamentary Leader, Jeff Kennett. Through the Machiavellian activities of a small group of personally ambitious Members, a 'spill' motion was passed at a regular Party Meeting which declared all positions vacant. In the subsequent elections the Deputy Leader, Alan Brown, replaced Jeff Kennett as Leader of the Opposition.

Following his election, Brown scheduled appointments with a number of us to tell us our fate. Were we to continue as Shadow Ministers, and, if so, in what portfolio? I had a long standing arrangement to meet with some community organizations in Geelong that day, so my appointment was delayed until late that afternoon. I went into Brown's office expecting to be reconfirmed as Shadow Minister for Community Services, because I had developed a strong personal commitment in that area.

Brown said, 'Sit down Don, and hold on to your chair'. I did not like the sound of this, and I thought he was going to tell me that I did not have a job on the frontbench. 'I want you to take on Education. It is an area where the Labor Party's performance is disgraceful, and I want you to go after them'. I was astonished, but I told him that I would love to get my teeth into it. I departed from his office wondering what I was to do next, because Brown did not have any instructions or suggestions.

Shadowing Education in Opposition

Being in Opposition is terrible. You have virtually no resources, nor access to information. You are expected to attack, which I found was at odds with my nature. At the same time you are expected to develop exciting policy initiatives that appeal to the voters, and thus help get your Party into Government.

When Jeff Kennett was deposed as Leader of the Opposition, at his request, he became Convenor of the Liberal Party Education Bill Committee. These parliamentary party committees are essentially 'Bill' committees in that their main function is to consider proposed legislation in the form of Bills and make recommendations to the Parliamentary Party as to whether it should support, seek to amend or oppose the Bill. Usually Convenors limited themselves to just convening meetings. However, Kennett, with his unbounded energy and creative mind, decided that he wanted to play a part in the policy development process as well.

Kennett and I had long talks about our objectives for Education in Victoria. We both believed that the most important responsibility of our generation was to give the next generation the opportunity of a high quality education. It soon became apparent that we would not be content with just running the education system. We were determined to make fundamental reforms of the system so as to give each child the best chance for the future. In fact we both believed our most vital task in Government was to make those reforms. We saw as an important part of those reforms increased accountability of schools for student learning and also the introduction of objective, statewide assessment.

I realized that I needed assistance both in attacking the government and in preparing our policies and I began to search for a research assistant. A contact at the University of Melbourne suggested a young student called John Roskam. I asked Roskam to come and see me and one day in my Prahran office I looked up from the computer terminal and saw a thin, sandy haired young man in his early twenties coming through the door. Thus entered John Roskam, whom my wife and I later came to regard as a fourth son.

Roskam was completing both Law and Commerce degrees at the University of Melbourne, and was also deeply involved in conservative politics and debating there. It struck me immediately that there was a remarkable parallel between his situation and my own when I went to work for Bill Spooner. However, he seemed more affluent than I was at the time. Also, whereas I had come from an Anglo-Irish background and was fifth generation Australian, his father was born in Holland and his mother was born in Poland. As I looked at him when he walked through the door, he did not look very robust, but he later proved to have considerable stamina, both physical and intellectual.

It was very clear from our first discussion that Roskam was very intelligent, that he had highly honed political instincts, that he was articulate and persuasive with people, and that he understood how to present issues publicly. I immediately appointed him my research assistant and thus began a partnership that was pivotal to the reform of education in Victoria. He went on to become my Senior Adviser in Government.

I then began the process of developing my own philosophy of educational reform. My starting point was my fundamental belief that if you wanted to give a child the best chance in life you had to give them access to an educational opportunity that would help to bring out the best in them, and enable them to achieve their potential. My own personal experience had taught me that. Also, I had seen it time and time again in my own electorate where poor families especially poor migrant families worked night and day to earn enough to send their children to high quality private schools, and that this had opened up a new world of opportunity for the children.

Also, I believe the key was the individual learning of each child. One had to excite the child's interest to learn, so that learning became an adventure. The good teachers at Homebush Boys' High School, as well as imparting knowledge, had excited our desire to learn and had guided us in our discovery of knowledge. Further, I was convinced that not only would information technology change the world, but it would also change the nature of learning and greatly improve access to knowledge.

I had the view that, in the past, education had not been driven by the needs of the student, but rather, by the needs of, and for the benefit of, those individuals and organizations that were part of the 'education club'. I was convinced that if we wanted to focus on the individual child's needs and bring out that child's full creativity, the emphasis had to be on the individual school, rather than on a centrally controlled 'system'.

We already had models of highly successful schools in the non-government, or independent schools, which were attended by more than 30 per cent of Victoria's school students. What we needed to do was to make all our schools 'independent'. We needed to dismantle 'the system'.

Finally, we needed to put the power where it belonged, in the hands of families. Students needed to access a diverse range of innovative providers of educational services that would meet the individual needs of each student so as to bring out the student's full creativity and potential. This meant that the support that the government gave to education should be provided direct to families as 'education credits'. The student could then take his or her education credit to the approved provider of education services that best met his or her individual needs. Whether that provider was in the government or private sector was irrelevant. In fact the compartmentalization of schools into government and non-government was artificial and had been devised and maintained by those with a vested interest in the status quo. With this new approach must come strict auditing of the standard of education services being provided by the providers, which would include standardized assessment across the state.

It seemed extraordinary to me that, except for the two senior years, there was no curriculum in Victoria. If a child went to another school, the curriculum in the new school could be so different from that in the old school, that it could seem as though the child had travelled to another country. I was determined that we would develop a proper curriculum and standards framework for schools throughout Victoria.

My research had convinced me that 'the system' had failed those it was supposed to help, the socially disadvantaged. For young people to break out of the poverty trap, they needed a high quality education that would prepare them for the new work opportunities of the twenty-first century. They would not get this in a centrally controlled system. They would best get it in a school which was part of its local community and which was responsive to the individual needs of its students.

If one wished to dismantle 'the system', and give families and students the ability to access the education services that best met their individual needs, one first had to enable schools in the government system to become autonomous, independent providers which could offer their services to families and students. This was very revolutionary stuff, and would be strongly opposed by those who had a vested interest in the status quo. I realized that I first had to sell the ideas, because, in history, ideas have ultimately prevailed over vested interests.

I realized that I must try to focus attention on the future. Although, in my view, schools in future would not necessarily play the same pivotal role in a child's education as in the past, I realized that we first had to reform schools. Therefore, I came up with the name Schools of the Future for my reform program.

I then began an intense series of discussions with academics, school principals, teachers, parents, business people and others to canvass as wide a range of views as possible on these issues. On the whole I was very encouraged by these discussions, which seemed to support the thrust of my policies. School principals seemed very supportive of the concept of operating autonomy for schools. However in discussions with some school principals, they urged that all schools should move towards autonomy at a slow, gradual, uniform pace.

I saw many objections to this. First, it meant that all schools would proceed at the rate of the least ready schools and the advanced schools would be held back. Also, if you are going to make fundamental cultural change, you have to move quickly, before those who have an interest in the status quo can organize their opposition. All my experience told me that the most effective way to achieve change is to have some who move at the forefront of change, and act as exemplars for the rest. Further, I had the view the Schools of the Future program would only work if schools wanted to be part of it. In other words, a school's involvement would be voluntary, and the school would have to apply to become a School of the Future. This meant that we would have to persuade schools of the advantages for them, and this could best be done through the examples of the schools already in the program.

I then began to develop my strategic objectives and plans to implement them. For government schools, my strategic objectives were to make them autonomous (ultimately independent) centres of learning where children would be encouraged and excited by the adventure of learning and guided and facilitated in pursuing that adventure. For curriculum, my strategic objectives were to develop a rigorous curriculum that would help our children to become culturally literate, that would give them core knowledge and would equip them for the newly emerging opportunities of the twenty-first century. For assessment, my strategic objectives were to develop an effective process of standardized assessment, together with proper reporting to parents, that would give parents the confidence that their child was making proper progress at school. If not, the diagnostic aspect of the assessment would help the teacher and the parent to develop an individual learning plan for the child to ensure that the child made proper progress.

A specific objective was to reform the curriculum and assessment system that was then in place for the final two years of secondary school (Years 11 and 12). This system was called the Victorian Certificate of Education (or the VCE). The Labor Government had developed the VCE as part of its plan to use education for social engineering purposes. As a result, it had little credibility with parents. It was also plagued by glitches which were gleefully highlighted in the media. The public perception of the VCE was so poor that I gave serious consideration to abolishing it altogether. I drew up a plan to reinstate the previous Higher School Certificate (HSC), but to realign it closely with the HSC in New South Wales. Because New South Wales and Victoria between them make up about 60 per cent of Australia's population, this would then have meant that about 60 per cent of Australia's senior students would follow a nearly identical curriculum and undergo assessment of a similar standard. If this were the case, it was possible that the other states might follow suit also, and we would then have a national curriculum for all Australia.

Another option that I seriously researched and studied was making the International Baccalaureate widely available in Victorian secondary schools. Students would then have the opportunity to choose the International Baccalaureate as an alternative to the VCE or HSC. After much soul searching on this issue, I decided that to move completely away from the VCE would be disruptive to those students who were then already caught up in the VCE. I therefore decided to retain the VCE, but, in Government, to significantly reform it. I decided to establish a new Board of Studies to undertake this reform, as well as develop a curriculum and standards framework for Years Prep to 12 and a process of standardized assessment for student achievement.

One aspect of planning was to find a chief executive officer who had the strength to drive these changes through the bureaucracy. Naturally, because of my business background, I thought first of someone from outside education. However, experience in other states had shown that this rarely worked. The bureaucrats in both government and the vested interest organizations always seemed to be able to bamboozle an outsider. We really needed someone who could understand their jargon and who could fight them at their own game. I searched Victoria, and then Australia, for the right person.

At this stage another interesting character entered the scene. This was Shane Stone, then Minister for Education in the Northern Territory, and subsequently Chief Minister. Shane Stone was originally a Victorian, where he had practised Law. He had been bitten by the political bug early. He had tried on various occasions to get pre-selection for the Liberal Party for a parliamentary seat in Victoria. However, in their infinite foolishness, the Liberal Party had rejected him. Stone had heard that there were good opportunities in both the Law and politics in the Northern Territory, so, for Stone, it was 'go North young man'. In Darwin, Stone succeeded in both.

I first met Stone at one of the meetings of Liberal Ministers and Shadow Ministers for Education that were regularly convened by the then Federal Liberal Shadow Minister for Education, David Kemp, who went on to become Federal

Minister for Schools in the Howard Government. Sadly, we were then mainly 'Shadows', the only places where we were in Government being the Northern Territory, Tasmania and New South Wales.

After one of these fairly unproductive meetings Stone said to me, 'I want you Victorians to get in next time, and what you need is help. Some of my senior people and me are coming to Melbourne in about three weeks for an inter-government meeting. It's on a Friday. We'll stay over to the Sunday, and we'll spend the whole of Saturday briefing you on the big education issues'.

Stone was true to his word, and early one Saturday morning we went to work in the sitting room of his suite at the Windsor Hotel in Melbourne. Stone had brought four people with him, but the person doing most of the briefing was Geoff Spring, Secretary of the Department of Education and Training in the Northern Territory. Spring was a large, well-built man who seemed strong in every sense of the word. He had a reputation for being tough, and the teacher union officials in the Northern Territory had nicknamed him 'the Crocodile'. By the end of the day, I was convinced that he had the strength to make the Victorian bureaucracy implement our reform.

That night we all had dinner in the main dining room of the Windsor Hotel. As the evening progressed, I raised with Stone whether, if we won the election in Victoria, he would 'lend' me Geoff Spring for a year 'to get us started'. Shane said he would, but we would have to 'talk Geoff into it'. The process of 'talking Geoff into it' went on for some weeks, mainly over the telephone. As was his way, he played hard to get. Finally, I gave up on him, and started to draft up an advertisement which we would put in the newspapers immediately after the elections. When he heard I was doing this, and that I was prepared to forego the opportunity of his services, he agreed to come to Victoria for a year to help us get the reform process under way.

After Spring had been in the job for a few months, I decided that I wanted him to continue as CEO, rather than return to the Northern Territory at the end of a year. It therefore became necessary to enter into a contract with him, which was the standard contract for senior bureaucrats. He was reluctant to do this because he believed the superannuation and the termination provisions in the contract made his situation in Victoria less secure than in the Northern Territory. In fact, he decided to leave Victoria and return to the Northern Territory. He then visited Darwin, the capital of the Northern Territory, to make arrangements to take up a position there, as, by then, someone had been appointed to his previous position. When he arrived back in Melbourne from Darwin, further protracted discussions occurred, following which he reversed his decision and decided to remain in Victoria. Nothing in my term as Minister caused me more anxiety and distress than this episode.

The Scene Is Set

When the election was called, we had developed both our strategic objectives and the action plans to implement our revolution in education in Victoria. We had also chosen our Chief Executive Officer.

It is history that we won the election with a record majority in both Houses of the Victorian Parliament. In Education, we were then able to move into Government and hit the ground running from day one. It is unlikely that any other new Government had ever been so well prepared in the education area on assuming office.

A revolution is never easy. There has to be the one big, powerful idea in which people could believe passionately. There also had to be the political will, and the political power to make the idea work. There also has to be a climate in which the public will accept the revolutionary ideals.

All of these existed in Victoria in 1992. We had the powerful idea. It was to help each child achieve his or her potential so as to give them the best chance for the future in the rapidly changing world of the twenty-first century. We had the political will. Kennett and I were strong characters who would not be dissuaded once we had decided that what we are doing is right. After the election, we had the political power and authority, because the record majority in both Houses of Parliament constituted a very powerful mandate.

The climate was ripe for reform.

3   Schools of the Future

In this chapter, Don Hayward continues his personal account of the reforms in public education during the first term of the Liberal National Government in Victoria, during which time he served as Minister for Education. Chapter 2 contained personal reflections on early life and career experiences that shaped his views on schooling and on the management of change in large organizations. It concluded with his description of the process of preparing for office, an opportunity that came to fruition with election to Government on October 2, 1992. In Chapter 3, different facets of reform are presented, including taking up the office of Minister for Education, the legislative experience, implementation of Schools of the Future, the role of the bureaucracy, and reflections on the experience.

The Revolution Begins

The revolution began on the morning of Wednesday, October 6, 1992. I had been sworn in as Minister for Education the previous day. At a little after 7.00 am that morning Geoff Spring, who was to serve as Director of School Education; Isabel Keeling, my personal secretary; Keith Cameron, my driver; and I arrived in my newly acquired ministerial car at the basement car park of the Rialto Building in Collins Street, Melbourne. The Rialto was a fifty-five storey skyscraper and the Department of Education had twenty-four floors in the main tower.

Our first problem was to get into our office. After talking persuasively to various security guards, we eventually gained access to the twenty-fourth floor, where the Minister's office was located. There we were confronted by a locked door with an electronic entry number code. Of course, we did not have the code. After we banged on the door for about ten minutes, two bureaucrats eventually appeared and opened the door.

When I reached the Minister's office I was struck by the spectacular view over most of the city and Port Phillip Bay beyond. In fact, I could see most of my electorate of Prahran. It proved a perfect view to turn my chair and look at when I got fed up with listening to bureaucrats. The next thing that struck me was the starkness of the office. Virtually everything moveable had been removed, especially the computer equipment. Even some of the furniture had gone, purloined by bureaucrats who had put the twenty-four hours vacuum between the two administrations to good advantage. The remaining furniture was shabby and in need of a good clean.

I spent the first morning meeting people and reading the Department's briefing books. From even a cursory glance at these it became abundantly clear that the

Labor Party had grossly mismanaged the Department and had left it with a horrend-ous and immediate budget crisis. I therefore demanded that the senior bureaucrats provide me with a budget review that afternoon.

The scene that confronted me after lunch will forever be in my memory. Lined up on one side of a long table in my room were the senior officers of the Depart-ment. On the other side were Roskam and me. It was reminiscent of scenes from *Yes Minister*.

One officer opened the batting with the cheery statement, 'Minister, we are sorry to have to inform you that the previous government made commitments for the recurrent budget far in excess of the funds available. In fact, it can be said that there is a black hole in the budget of at least $40 million, which is likely to get bigger'.

'And then there is the time bomb', chirped up another. 'Time bomb!' I repeated, in a state of alarm. 'Yes', he said. 'We have about 8000 teachers out on unpaid long term leave, mainly maternity leave. When a teacher went off on leave the previous government appointed a new permanent teacher in his or her place. We have like a phantom army of teachers out there. They have the right to come back anytime they choose, and we have to give them a job. As far as the budget is concerned it is like a time bomb ticking away, and can add tens of million dollars expenditure at any time.'

'And we must not forget the backlog', declared a third, almost joyfully. By this time I was feeling somewhat irritated. 'What the hell is the backlog?' I demanded. 'Well Minister, for ten years your predecessors have starved the capital and maintenance side of the budget and used the funds to pay for the extra cost of the work practices set out in the agreements with the teacher unions. We estimate there is a backlog in school maintenance of more than $600 million. It is believed that the physical condition of about half the schools is such that they do not meet the standards set under the occupational health and safety legislation.'

I instructed the bureaucrats to go away and prepare a series of options to deal with the immediate budget crisis, and I closed the meeting with a feeling of exas-peration at being handed this problem on my first day in the job.

Dealing with the Budget Crisis

In addition to dealing with 'the black hole', 'the time bomb' and 'the backlog', we also had to make our contribution to eliminating the overall deficit in the total pub-lic sector budget of more than $1 billion left by the Labor Government.

The previous government had borrowed to pay recurrent operating expenses. Even worse, they borrowed to pay the interest on the borrowings. The effect of this was that nearly a third of the state's income was being used to pay the interest costs on the borrowings, and this was compounding each year. As a result, the percentage of income available to pay for government services, such as schools and hospitals, was rapidly declining.

The Cabinet decided that it had no option but to eliminate the recurrent deficit in the shortest possible time. The Cabinet was opposed to increasing taxes on an ongoing basis and decided that the deficit should be eliminated by reducing the operating expenses of the departments. As the Education Department made up about a quarter of the Government's operating costs, we had to carry our share, as did the other large departments, such as health.

The first things we looked at were the out-of-school costs, which were mainly the salaries of bureaucrats. We reviewed every item and applied the test 'does this add value to a student's learning?' In many instances the answer was 'no', because we found that many of the administrative activities were due to bureaucrats making work for themselves, students being forgotten in the process. Sometimes when speaking to bureaucrats, I had the feeling that they thought students only existed for their convenience, in other words, to give them a job. I had to remind them time and time again that the only justification for their existence was to serve students.

As a result of this rigorous review, we were able to reduce the out-of-school bureaucracy by more than 60 per cent. The central bureaucracy was a special target, and this came down from more than 2300 to less than 600.

Another area of high cost was school cleaning. School cleaning was done by direct employees of the Department, and there was a lot of evidence to show that it could be more efficiently and effectively done by independent contractors. We quickly contracted out school cleaning, and were thus able to reduce the direct employment in the Department by more than 4000 by this move alone.

The main expense item in the Department's budget was the salaries of the 45,000 teachers. The agreements made by the previous Labor Government with the teacher unions had introduced costly changes in the work practices of teachers. In particular, the staffing formulae in Victoria, in terms of teacher/student ratios, were more generous than the Australian average, and of most other states. Clearly, if we were to place the education budget on a secure and stable basis, we had to address this issue. We therefore adjusted the staffing formula to bring it more in line with the Australian average.

The Maintenance Backlog and School Organization

I ordered an immediate review of the physical condition of our schools. This showed that we had inherited a maintenance backlog of more than $670 million. Many of our schools were in a shocking condition, and we did not have enough money to fix them all.

Over its ten-year reign, the Labor Government failed to address the issue of demographic shifts in population, and the effect of these on school enrolments. As a consequence, in some of the older established areas there was an excessive number of unused places in schools. For example, in one inner city area alone there were more than 2000 unused secondary school places. At the same time, the Labor Government had failed to keep up with the demand in the rapidly growing outer suburbs for new schools, and for increased capacity in existing schools.

There was an urgent need to make schools decent and secure places in which to learn and teach. Also, with the rapid growth in information technology, there was the need to significantly reinvest in schools to re-engineer them for twenty-first century learning technologies. This included installation of Local Area Networks (LANs) to link computers and software throughout the school.

Clearly, we had to transfer under-utilized resources to areas of greater need. Also, in the face of the chronic shortage of funds left to us by the Labor Government, and the urgent need to upgrade schools, it was essential to reassess the long term viability of schools with declining enrolments. In making this reassessment we had to consider the following questions:

1 Was there a long term declining trend in the school's enrolment?
2 Was there an excess of student places in that area?
3 Was there convenient access to an alternative school?
4 Would students have access to a broader curriculum choice if a merger took place?

If the answers to these questions were in the affirmative, consideration should be given to the school merging with another school in the district, and to the closure of that school site.

Under the previous government, a group of bureaucrats had been working away on 'school reorganization' for some years. We reviewed their work and it was abundantly clear that about fifty-five schools should be closed immediately. In fact, the previous government had planned to close these schools, but had lacked the political courage to implement the plans.

As it was approaching the end of the school year and people would need to make their plans for the next year, it was essential that the matters be resolved immediately. I took the decision to close fifty-five schools. I did not seek Cabinet approval for this, but, to inform them, I made a white board presentation to the Cabinet in which I outlined the rationale behind the decision, and the specific reason for each closure.

The Coalition Parties were scheduled to meet later that morning, so I arranged for the same white board to be taken from the Cabinet Room to the Party Room at Parliament House and made the same presentation to all the Members of the Coalition Parties. Following this, in the early afternoon, I used the same white board to make the same presentation to the media.

For the media this was a major story. 'Fifty-five schools to close!' was a great headline for them. The treatment of the story by television, radio and the print media was sensational and emotional. The irony was that the media portrayed the decisions as driven by 'budget cuts'. It was true that the closures would bring some savings in the recurrent budget. However, these were marginal, because most of the costs in the system were salary related, and the staff from the closed schools would have to be deployed elsewhere.

In fact, the decisions were about three things:

1 Improving the educational opportunities of the students through giving them access to a broader curriculum;

2   Redirecting resources to where they were most needed; and
3   Not investing scarce capital to upgrade school which did not have a long-term future.

Every later decision to merge or close a school was for the same three reasons.

In most cases the closure of the schools occurred without incident. However, in two cases there was long drawn-out drama. The first of these was the case of Richmond Secondary College, where the teacher unions and groups of left-wing agitators decided they would cause the Government as much pain as possible. They occupied the building, and brought a case against the Government in the Equal Opportunity Board. Their case did not succeed, but they refused to vacate the premises. Our plans were to use the premises to establish a new girls' secondary school, Melbourne Girls College, from the beginning of 1994. As 1993 was coming to a close, it was necessary to start preparation for this new school, and, after repeated passive efforts, the police moved to evict the occupiers. The occupiers wanted to create the maximum publicity and resisted, hurling abuse at the police.

Provoked beyond their tolerance, the police decided to charge against the occupiers. This was a decision by the police, and was not at the request of the Government. As a result, the television that night featured footage of the occupiers being dragged from the building, together with allegations of police brutality. This of course was just what the occupiers had been hoping for. Some of these scenes were replayed on CNN and other international news services. Unfortunately the police, in attempting to solve the situation, played into the hands of the occupiers, and gave them the publicity they were seeking.

In fact, the occupiers were not genuinely interested in the local students, but were extremists who were attempting to exploit the situation, as they did in other 'protest' situations. Fortunately the general public recognized this and the occupiers gained very little community support. It was also recognized by senior people in the trade union movement, as distinct from teacher union officials. In fact, one senior trade union leader unofficially helped to broker a settlement that helped us to get the new Melbourne Girls College up and running in time for the new school year.

Melbourne Girls College was established and has proved to be an outstanding success, with girls from all over Melbourne seeking enrolment. It is already being recognized as one of the top girls' schools in Australia and an example of what I was trying to achieve with Schools of the Future. It is an autonomous, independent school whose future is in the hands of its own school community. Its aspirations for its students are high. Its aim is for each girl to achieve her full potential at the school and to develop her talents to the utmost so as to give her the best chance for the future. From among its students will come women who will lead our community in all aspects of life including artistic, scientific, social and business endeavours.

Melbourne Girls College knows exactly where it is heading. It is catering for a specific market, which is high quality girls education. It is deliberately aiming for, and is achieving, high academic standards and high discipline standards. It is also a good example of how a government school can compete with non-government schools. Parents now see Melbourne Girls College as providing an equal or super-ior education for their daughter as a private girls school. Clearly, there is no reason why other government schools can't learn the lesson from the success of Melbourne Girls College and do the same.

The second school to take the Government to the Equal Opportunity Board was Northland Secondary College. This school had a limited number of aboriginal students and had some special programs for them. However, the quality of education in the school was inadequate. Also, it was not the type of learning environment that would best equip aboriginal students for the competitive world they would inevitably face after school. In addition, it was located in an area where there was a massive oversupply of secondary places. Further, the physical condition of the school was very poor, and it would require major capital expenditure to put it in order. This was because the previous Labor Government, realizing that the school did not have a viable long term future, had spent virtually no money on repairs and improvements during the previous ten years.

The recommendation of the Department was that the school should close because of the oversupply of places in the area, the declining enrolments at the school, the poor quality of education being provided and the physical condition of the school. The Department assured me that the programs for aboriginal students at the school could be easily transferred to another school in the area. Based on this recommendation, I decided the school should close.

The hearings before the Equal Opportunity Board and consequent appeals were protracted and costly. Finally, the Equal Opportunity Board ordered the Government to reopen the school. In my view, this decision was wrong, and is working against the interests of aboriginal students, because the quality of education available to them at the school is inadequate for their needs.

Northland is in sharp contrast to the high quality education available to aboriginal students in the excellent Koorie Open Door Education (KODE) schools. The KODE schools involve a high level of self-determination and involvement by the aboriginal community, and the progress of aboriginal students in the KODE schools is outstanding.

In retrospect, although the decision to close Northland Secondary College was correct, perhaps there were other approaches to closing the school. Because the school had been captured by activists who were determined to exploit both the media and the Equal Opportunity legislation, we should have looked at it in isolation and developed a strategy that may have neutralized the opposition in the school. However, the Department's recommendation was that the school should be treated in the same way as the other schools involved in the reorganization process, and it was one occasion when I allowed the Department's view to override my instinct.

If we had looked upon Northland Secondary College as a special case, perhaps we could have brokered a merger with one of the other schools in the area and a transfer to the site of the other school. However, the people in the school were so obstinate in their demands that the school stay in its existing location that I doubt if such a compromise would have worked. Also, when so many other schools were closing, it seemed a breach of faith with those other schools if we gave special treatment to Northland just because they were able to exploit the media and invoke the Equal Opportunity legislation.

Leaving aside the fifty-five closed schools, and given that our mission was to help students fulfil their potential, the question had to be asked as to whether the existing configuration of some of our schools was such as to best do that. In particular, we had the responsibility to consider whether the merger of schools would result in students being offered access to a curriculum of greater breadth and depth.

Also, with a larger cohort of students, a merged school had the opportunity to build a team of teachers with a range of different skills and backgrounds. This would broaden the educational experience for students and help the school to meet the different and individual needs of each student. It would also enable a synergy to develop and grow between a group of teachers with different talents, which together could make the school a much more vibrant, creative and exciting place.

As one of the essential tenets of my philosophies was to give schools back to their local community, I decided that it was important to encourage local communities themselves to face these questions. In effect, I wanted local communities to review the way schools were organized in their area. The objective of this review was to identify possible improved configurations of schools that would give students a better chance for the future. What we were seeking to do was to improve the quality of the educational services provided to students in their local area, so I called this process Quality Provision.

For the community review and decision making, I established Quality Provision Task Forces across the state. These task forces consisted mainly of representatives of school communities, and they were resourced by bureaucrats from the respective regional offices of the Department. The work of the task forces was quite arduous, and they had to face some very tough questions. In particular, they had to clear their minds of their previous preconceptions and their own emotional attachment to a particular school. Also, they had to put the best interests of the students as a whole before their own personal convenience, because, in some cases, the school in question might be in a more convenient location to them personally, as compared to a new proposal which might bring benefits to the students overall.

In the vast majority of the cases, the task forces did their work very well and came up with properly researched, logical, common sense, and, in some cases, very creative and forward looking proposals. The proof of this was that I was able to accept and approve the recommendations of 85 per cent of the task forces.

The work of the task forces resulted in the creation of new configurations of schools that gave students the best access to a quality curriculum and which also established schools with a viable long term future. This then allowed us with confidence to invest funds from the sale of surplus education properties to improve the physical facilities of the schools and equip them with the latest learning technologies. The outcome was a large number of mergers of two or more previous schools on the site of one of the previous schools. As a consequence, we were able to close more than 250 previous school sites.

One experience drove home to me the value of the work of the task forces. There was a woman who was a member of the school council of a small primary school in western Victoria and strenuously opposed the task force recommendation that her school merge with a nearby school. She vigorously fought the proposal publicly at local meetings, and in the local media. She came to Melbourne and met with me, and gave me a very hard time, using strong and colourful language. However, the local community saw the benefit of the merger in terms of a richer educational experience for the children, and voted in favour of it.

Some months later I was visiting the area with the local Member of Parliament and he took me to visit the new, merged school. The lady who had opposed the merger came up to me and said, 'I know I got stuck into you about the merger, but I can see how this school can now offer my kids more, so I am getting behind it and giving it all I've got'.

I was able to gain the agreement of the Cabinet to reinvest every dollar from the proceeds of the sale of the surplus real estate back into school improvement. This was to be in addition to our regular capital works and maintenance budget. Over a three year period we raised nearly $200 million from asset sales. With this, and money from our regular budget, we were able to reduce the Labor Party's legacy of a $670 million maintenance backlog by about half.

Reforming the Bureaucracy

When I became Minister, I realized that a primary task was to reform the bureaucracy. There were some good people in the education bureaucracy, but, as a group, they had lost their way. They had forgotten the purpose of their existence. Many had come to believe that the purpose of the education system was to provide them with a job. It was there for their personal convenience, comfort and advancement. With these preoccupations, the bureaucrats had lost sight of the fact that the only justification for their existence in the public service was the improvement in the learning of children. As Sir Humphrey Appleby says in *Yes, Prime Minister*, 'Nobody at the DES (Department of Education and Science), however, ever mentions children'.

I saw my foremost task as changing the culture of the bureaucracy to that of service, as distinct from the prevailing culture of control. We had to identify the services the bureaucracy should provide, and develop a structure for the effective and efficient provision of those services. All other unnecessary bureaucratic activities and structures would then be abolished. Of course there would also be the continuing need for officers to advise on policy development, administer the accountability mechanisms and manage the distribution of resources to schools.

The 'customers' of education are the students and their parents. It was the responsibility of the school to meet the needs of these customers. Clearly we had to assess which services the bureaucracy could and should provide to schools. Research was needed in this, and also, of course, we had to seek the views of school principals and teachers. Obviously, the bureaucracy itself should not do this research, because their functions would be under scrutiny. Therefore, we sought assistance of an outside group of consultants.

These consultants spent weeks visiting schools and talking with school principals and teachers. From this came a clear picture of the essential services that should be provided by the bureaucracy, and recommendations as to the best way in which these services could be provided. As a result of this research, the bureaucracy was radically restructured and reduced. In this restructuring, we constantly asked the question whether the function or activity under review added value to a child's learning.

After the Schools of the Future program had been in operation for some months, we reviewed the bureaucratic organization again in the light of our experience, and undertook a further significant restructure and reduction. In the case of both reorganizations, the money that was saved from the reductions in the bureaucracy was redirected to schools through their global budgets.

I took a keen personal interest in all these restructures because I am extremely aware that they are often used as devices by bureaucrats to achieve their own agenda, and to place their cronies in key positions, with the ultimate objective of frustrating the Minister. I ensured that the reorganization was such as to better serve students and parents, and effectively implement the reform program.

I was determined that in these reorganizations we should value and use people who had a contribution to make to the reform program, no matter what their background or past affiliations. There were a number of people who were perceived as being close to the previous Labor Government. Various Liberal Party politicians tried to persuade me to immediately dispense with these people for that reason alone. I resisted this. I decided that each person should be judged on their quality, their ability, their willingness to contribute to the reform program, and their commitment to it. On the other hand, we sent on their way people who had little to contribute and showed no enthusiasm for or commitment to the program.

This approach of recognizing quality, merit and contribution, and dispensing with the non-performers sent a clear message to the whole organization and had a very healthy and beneficial effect. This was reinforced by the fact that I continued to support and encourage people who, although being perceived as closely aligned to the previous Government, had proved themselves to be high performers and contributors.

Although the restructures improved the bureaucracy, they did not make it ideal for implementing a radical reform program. Bureaucracies of their very nature have inherent inertia. Bureaucrats have a significant self-interest in preserving the status quo. They view the status quo as less threatening than the unknown of a new organizational structure and radical new policies. Also, of course, if the purpose of the restructure is to take power and authority from bureaucrats and hand it over to schools, the natural and instinctive reaction of bureaucrats is to be reactionary.

The very nature and behaviour of large organizational structures makes it difficult to focus on a specific mission, to build a team dedicated to that mission and to apply attention, energy and resources to its pursuit. To my mind the sensible thing was to identify specific strategic objectives, and assign them to teams established with the clear and express purpose of achieving them. If the people in the team are given the responsibility for achieving the objectives, together with the necessary authority and resources to do so, and are told that they will be held personally accountable for such achievement or otherwise, it concentrates their minds and energies remarkably, and produces effective effort and results.

This approach was successfully adopted for a number of key tasks and functions. These included various aspects of the design and implementation of the Schools of the Future program, the organization of schools through the Quality Provision Task Forces, improvements in literacy, the introduction of new information technology based learning methods and a range of other planning and implementation activities.

Schools of the Future

When we were planning the reform program in Opposition I had decided that it should come under the general banner of Schools of the Future. It was a valuable phrase from a marketing point of view. However, from my point of view it had its limitations because the revolution went further than schools. In fact, I believed that, in the future, schools would not play the same pivotal role in the delivery of educational services as they had played in the past.

My short-term objectives were to make schools autonomous and largely independent of the system. My medium-term objectives were to put power into the hands of families, as distinct from it being wielded by those who ran the system. However, I realized that my medium-term objectives would take a number of years to achieve. Indeed, I was realistic enough to realize that they would take longer to achieve than I was prepared to stay as Minister. I was very aware that the confrontationist nature of politics was at odds with my nature, and there was a limit to how much of it I would tolerate.

My personal strategy, as distinct from any official strategy, was to try to drive the reform process as far as possible in the first term of government. It was my hope that I would create sufficient momentum with the reforms as to make the reform process irreversible. I was in no way certain that the person who followed me as Minister would have the same commitment to the reforms as I had.

I saw the high priority items in the reform process as being:

1   Operating autonomy for government schools;
2   Accountability for government schools, especially in terms of the learning standards of their students; and
3   The establishment of curriculum and standards that would prevail across all schools.

I saw the vital elements in giving government schools operating autonomy as being:

- a school charter;
- responsibility and accountability for spending their own budget; and
- responsibility over their own staffing.

The School Charter

I established a special team to plan the introduction of school charters. The main work of this team was to develop guidelines to help schools prepare their own charter. They also developed the system for the review and endorsement of the charter by the Department. Then they set up a system of training for school people in charter preparation.

The school charter is the document in which the school seeks to set out its educational philosophy, its aspirations for its students in terms of learning improvement, and its vision for the future of the school. The school charter must set out specific objectives for students, strategies to achieve those objectives and timelines for achievement. The school charter becomes an understanding and a contract between the school council and the Minister for Education as to how the school will operate, and it is the means by which the Minister transfers operating responsibility and accountability to the school.

The charter must describe the school's plans for improving student learning in the future. It also describes the school's plans for curriculum development and whether the school will place special emphasis on particular areas in the curriculum. In its charter the school also sets out its philosophy about its staff, the personnel practices it will follow and its plans for enhancing the professional development and professional standing of each member of its staff. It outlines the school's plans for the physical facilities of the school, including its buildings, its equipment, its information technology resources and infrastructure. The charter also outlines any special approaches for student learning, such as new concepts of 'guided discovery learning', and changed configurations in the classroom and the school generally.

Schools usually set up a special group from within the school community to develop their charter. It was a difficult task and usually required many long hours of discussion. To demonstrate the importance I placed on the charters, I had the Department organize ceremonies at which I formally presented the school charters. These were happy occasions, and were a celebration and culmination of an extraordinary amount of dedicated effort by a committed group of people at the school. Over a cup of tea, often with a musical group from one of the schools playing in the background, I was told time and time again by school representatives of the enormous amount of work they had done in preparing the school charter.

I was so taken with the remarks of one school council president that I wrote them down straight after the meeting. He said, 'It took us weeks. Because we are all so busy, we would often meet at the school at 7.00 am for an hour; the school would provide us with coffee and little rolls, brioches I think you call them'.

'When we were doing all this, we often cursed you, although we had never met you, because we saw you as the one who was pushing us. But, do you know what? We really enjoyed the feeling of working hard at it as a group, and a real team spirit grew amongst us, and it brought the whole community together and gave us a focus for the future. And now we are fiercely proud of this charter, and we think it will make us a better school, and will give our kids a better chance for the future.'

I had similar conversations with many others at these ceremonies.

Budget

Funding for education in Australia is in a state of disarray. Funding eventually trickles down to schools from both Federal and State sources through various administrative structures. Large amounts are syphoned off on the way to pay the salaries of the bureaucrats who administer these structures. On the whole, these bureaucrats and administrative structures add nothing to the quality of learning of the student, whom it is all supposed to be about.

I believed there is a much more direct and effective way of funding education. I believe that the funding from both the Federal and State Governments should be attached to the student (and thus the family). In that way, the student is able to access the education service that best suits his or her individual needs. There can be a range of education services, including schools. If schools are able to transform themselves into centres of excellence in learning, the school is likely to be the provider of choice for parents and students, in most cases.

I planned to do this in Victoria. In preparation for this, I established a major research project to develop what we called the Student Resource Index (SRI). The purpose of the SRI was to develop a formula for allocating funds to each student. This is an extremely complex thing to do, and has never been done successfully anywhere else. In essence, the formula should address the learning needs of the particular student, taking into account learning difficulties arising from the personal characteristics or situation of the student. The following are examples of these:

- the student has a disability or impairment;
- the student comes from a non-English speaking background;
- he or she is a 'student at risk'; or
- the student lives in an isolated situation in the country.

This research project, because of its pioneering aspects, attracted some lateral thinkers with creative minds, and substantial progress was made quite quickly. A practical solution was emerging which excited the intellect of those working on the project. People began to talk, and rumours began to fly around about the likely impact on schools. The less confident principals from the less effective schools became very anxious because the Minister was raising the dreaded concept of parental and student choice, which they found quite threatening. This was despite the fact that, because zoning had been abolished, parents and students were already free to choose any appropriate school. These principals also started to mutter the word 'competition', which was anathema to them.

Because of all this agitation, I met with a number of school principals to talk through the issue. No one persuaded me against the basic concept that the funds should attach to the child. However, some of the wiser principals convinced me that to implement this effectively, we needed to wait until the schools were fully autonomous. Further, those schools must develop the skills and experience to operate on their own, as distinct from needing the state to prop them up. In other words, Schools of the Future need to be fully established and operating effectively before we could introduce education credits for students.

I therefore decided that it was premature to attach funds to the student at this stage, and that we should put in place an intermediate step. We called this the school global budget. I set the same team to work to develop it. Much of the work that had been done in developing the SRI could immediately be picked up for the development of the global budget, especially work on the formula for allocating funds in accordance with students' learning needs.

The main differences are that the school is allocated a base grant that is simply calculated on a per capita basis, depending upon the school's enrolment. Then the school is allocated additional funds depending upon the student profile of the school, and the characteristics of the students in that profile.

To guide the development of the school global budget, we engaged the assistance of an independent Education Committee under the Chairmanship of Professor Brian Caldwell, a recognized world expert in this area and co-author of this book. Professor Caldwell's committee provided us with a series of educational principles that underpin the development of the global budget. The basis of these are the pre-eminence of educational considerations and student learning. The Committee continually emphasized that the funding formula for the school global budget should be both fair and transparent.

Developing the school global budget involved a two year research and modelling exercise, which was guided by the Education Committee. The school global budget became a reality, but further research was undertaken by the Education Committee to monitor its operation and recommend refinements and adjustments.

The school global budget gives the school principal and school council complete control over the school's resources. They are now able to decide the allocation of their budget so as to best meet the individual learning needs of each of their students. The school global budget is designed to ensure that the school can be held fully accountable for its expenditure at all times.

In accordance with the recommendations of the Education Committee, each school's global budget consists of a core allocation plus additional special allocations that correspond to the individual learning needs of each of its students. The core allocation comprises about 80 per cent of the school's overall global budget and is directly related to the overall enrolment in the school. The special allocations are in a number of categories. These include students with disabilities and impairments, students at educational risk and students from non-English speaking backgrounds. There is also a special allocation for rurality and isolation where the school's location makes this appropriate.

School Staffing

I believe that Victorian schools are blessed with some high quality, dedicated teachers. I never missed an opportunity to praise the teachers in our schools. I often asserted that, in my view, Victoria had the best teachers in Australia. I believed that one of the most vital aspects of a School of the Future is to have control over its own staffing.

The successful School of the Future would need a team of dedicated, highly professional, well-trained teachers to inspire, excite and guide the learning of the students. Given that student improvement is highly dependent upon the quality of the teacher, and the ability of the teacher to spark the interest of the student to learn, I considered that one of our highest priorities must be to improve the professionalism of teachers. Placing the responsibility to select teachers for the school with the school principal, as distinct from the old arrangements where teachers were allocated through a centralized staffing system, was an important first step.

In my view each teacher should be considered as an individual, not part of a great amorphous mass. I was determined that provision be made for the proper recognition of the teacher's professional achievements, with rewards flowing from this recognition.

There is a crisis in the teaching profession in Australia. There has been a downgrading of teaching from a professional culture to an 'industrial relations' culture. The esteem of the public for teachers was declining and the salary levels of teachers were falling badly behind other professions.

I was determined that this downward trend in the status of teaching should be reversed. I believed that much of the solution was at the school level. I considered that, of all the responsibilities of the school principal, the most important was advancing the personal and professional development of each teacher. This would better equip them to add value to the time that each student spent at school so as to help each student attain his or her potential.

I believed that the teacher, in conjunction with the principal, should be encouraged to develop his or her personal objectives for improvement for students. The teacher and the principal should then identify those areas of the teacher's personal performance and skills that need development so that the teacher would be in the best position and be best equipped to achieve his or her objectives for student improvement. The teacher and principal should then, together, develop a personal professional development plan for the teacher that should include both school-based and external activities. At the end of each year, the principal and the teacher should then review the teacher's performance in terms of the previously agreed objectives. Following the review, improved performance should be recognized in various ways, including increased remuneration.

To test these concepts, I organized informal meetings with groups of principals across the state. I made a white board presentation to the principals at these meetings and explained each aspect of the proposals. I then had a vigorous discussion with the principals present. The range of feedback I got was quite wide. To some of the principals, this approach was a revelation. Others said it was only common sense, and that they were already conducting annual reviews of teachers. All were impressed by the fact that it was a coordinated and cohesive approach in which there were benefits for all, including the teacher, the student and the school.

Without exception, these principals gave this plan their enthusiastic support, but said there were two impediments to its implementation. The first was that there was no system in place that enabled them to provide the mutually agreed personal professional development program for each teacher. The second was that they were sure the teacher unions would vigorously oppose the concept of the annual review of each teacher's performance and rewards flowing from it.

With this positive and constructive feedback, I was determined to push ahead with the plan. To implement it, we established two special programs. The first dealt with the key issue of teacher professional development. When I initially discussed teacher professional development with the Department, it proposed a 'top–down' approach. By this it meant that it would devise a series of programs that it thought best for teachers, consisting mainly of lectures to groups of teachers. It even proposed the bussing of groups of teachers into central locations to attend these sessions.

I was completely opposed to this approach. In my view, the professional development should be planned to meet the specific needs of the individual teacher and thus help her or him achieve their personal objectives in terms of improving students' learning. Also, of course, the teacher should play the key role in planning this individual program. Without this, the teacher would not feel a commitment to the program, and would not get full value from it.

We therefore developed the Personal Professional Development Program. Essentially this program provided the resources to enable the teacher and the principal to jointly develop and implement an individual personal and professional development plan for each teacher that reflects the school's priorities and addresses the teacher's needs. To achieve this, we more than doubled the amount of professional development funds already allocated to schools in their global budget.

The second program was the Professional Recognition Program. This makes provision for the annual review of the teacher's performance by the principal in terms of the previously agreed objectives. In that sense, it could nearly amount to self-assessment by the teacher, with the principal auditing the assessment. Following such assessment, improved performance would be recognized and rewarded through promotion and increased remuneration. It also provides a career structure for teachers, with four professional levels within the school and promotion based on merit.

My objectives in the Professional Recognition Program were to give teachers recognition for their improved performance. Also, I considered our teachers were underpaid. This program helped us to give our teachers a pay rise, but, at the same time, to achieve improvements in the quality of teaching. An important feature of the program was that it allowed highly skilled teachers to receive substantial recognition for their skills and contributions to student learning but still remain in the classroom. This is because the salaries at the top levels overlap the salaries for the Principal Class. In the past, to gain higher salaries, teachers had to forsake teaching for management positions in the school. Positions at the top levels of the program are tenured for up to five years and are renewable. As a further encouragement for professionalism, teachers have the opportunity through the program to take one year's leave in five on 80 per cent of salary.

It was my plan that participation in the Professional Recognition Program would be voluntary for teachers, and they should have to apply to join. Joining brought with it salary increases as of right, in addition to the potential to gain performance-related increases. Over a few months, nearly half of the teachers opted to join the program. The teacher union officials were very opposed to the program, because it tended to undermine their own power base, and they mounted a vigorous campaign against it. They were also opposed to it because it incorporated the concept of payment for performance. These union officials were losing ground as more and more teachers joined the program, so they resorted to the Australian Industrial Relations Commission, hoping to have the Commission outlaw it. Instead, the Commission supported the program, and incorporated it in an award, which meant that 100 per cent of teachers became part of the program. The union officials' strategy of resorting to the Commission to destroy the program had exactly the opposite effect.

In summary, a basic tenet of Schools of the Future is that each teacher in each school is an individual professional. The ultimate aim of Schools of the Future is for each teacher, as an individual professional, to have a contract of service with his or her school. That contract would meet both the needs of the school and of the teacher. For example, the teacher may wish to negotiate flexibility in the days or hours during which she or he will be at the school to enable the pursuit of a personal interest, project or course of study.

It is the principal's responsibility to build a strong team in the school, and to ensure that each teacher is an effective, contributing member of it. This includes selecting high quality, dedicated teachers in the first instance and contributing to the personal and professional development of each teacher.

Leadership in Schools of the Future

Clearly, to be successful in this massive cultural change, there had to be well-trained leaders in the Schools of the Future. We entered into a service contract with a school council organization to provide training for school council presidents and other members of school councils.

The role of the school principal was especially vital to the success of the School of the Future. Ideally, the principal of a School of the Future should have vision, commitment, the capacity to think laterally and creatively, and the ability, through effective communication and leadership, to persuade his or her team at the school to share that vision and commitment. In the early stages, we were particularly eager to identify schools and their principals that would be exemplars that others would follow.

A small group that included Professor Brian Caldwell provided invaluable advice and assistance in leadership development programs for school principals and other key people in the school community. Those who participated in training sessions provided by this group were enthused by them and we received excellent feedback.

I also sought the advice of a group of outstanding principals concerning ways to enhance the leadership skills of principals. We invited them to a hotel at the seaside resort of Queenscliff for a couple of days for 'think tank' type discussion sessions, in some of which I was able to participate. These sessions were really exciting and productive, and I was delighted to see and hear these principals working so effectively and productively together. We ended with a list of the qualities and behavioural characteristics of team leaders in Schools of the Future, and we left Queenscliff very enthused, excited and energized.

One of the things that really encouraged me during these discussions was the way in which a number of principals who had previously been close to the Labor Party became convinced of the potential of the Schools of the Future program to help them and their teachers give students a better chance. Not only were they converted to the program, they also became some of the most successful in implementing it and advocating it amongst other principals.

I then sought the best international advice on team leadership development. I travelled to France and sought advice from top academics at INSEAD, a prestigious business training institute near Paris. In the UK, I sought advice from leading authorities in this field at the London Business School and at Cambridge University. In the US I sought advice from people in a number of business schools. As a result, we were able to put in place an outstanding program which is helping our principals to become some of the best in the world. It is also providing remarkable personal development opportunities for aspiring principals.

Another development that I supported with enthusiasm was the establishment of the Australian Principals Centre at the University of Melbourne. This is very much the project of the professional associations of the primary and secondary principals and aims at providing principals from Victoria, and from other parts of Australia and overseas, with outstanding leadership training. The Australian Principals Centre will provide accreditation and high quality professional development for aspiring principals as well as ongoing professional development for existing principals, which will give them the opportunity for personal renewal.

One of the most important things I did in leadership development was to establish a committee to encourage and assist women to take a greater leadership role in schools. This committee was chaired by a remarkable woman leader herself, Mrs Lorraine Elliott, Member for Mooroolbark in the Victorian Parliament. This committee not only guided leadership training for aspiring women principals, it also gave them practical help and advice on how to be actually selected for a principal's position. The result was a dramatic increase in the number of women principals and assistant principals to the stage where women now occupy about half of all these positions in Victorian schools.

One possible tension in a School of the Future is in the respective leadership roles of principal and the Chair of the school council. It is a delicate balance of responsibilities, but in the vast majority of cases, it works well. This is because we always made it clear that the school council is the overall governing body of the school and is responsible for setting policy and approving the annual budget. However the school principal is the chief operating officer of the school and is responsible for the day-to-day operations. The analogy is between the roles of the chair and managing director of a public company. In nearly 1700 Schools of the Future there have only been one or two instances where a dispute has occurred between the principal and the school council that has required the intervention of the Minister.

In my view, the status and remuneration of principals would improve significantly if they could have an individual, five year contract, linked to an annual performance review and remuneration system. We set up a team to work on this, including principals, and sought the best advice so that we could develop an approach that was in accordance with world best practice. In the result, the principals' Performance Management System was introduced. This system has two key elements, accreditation and assessment. Principal Accreditation Centres were established which are probably unique in the world. The annual assessment process is on the basis of performance against previously agreed objectives. Bonus payments are linked to the annual assessment. All principals are now part of this system, with five-year performance based contracts.

In summary, the school principal is the chief operating officer of the School of the Future and is responsible for the day-to-day administration of the school. It is not expected nor intended that the school council president nor school council members will become involved in the day-to-day operations of the school. The most important responsibility of the school principal is to build, develop, enthuse and inspire the teaching and administrative team at the school. The school principal has the responsibility for selecting members of the staff. However, the school principal's responsibility concerning his or her team extends well beyond this.

Under the Professional Development Program the principal has the responsibility to identify with each staff member that staff member's personal objectives for the year in terms of student improvement. The principal and the staff member must then, jointly, prepare a professional development plan to help the staff member achieve those objectives. If required, the principal provides resources to implement this plan from specially allocated funds. The school principal has the responsibility for monitoring and reviewing with the staff member his or her performance in terms of the achievement of the staff member's personal objectives. The principal must then provide recognition for that performance and achievement. That recognition can take a range of forms, both material and non-material. The material recognition can include a bonus payment or a promotion with salary increase.

Where the school is of sufficient size, the principal is assisted in the day-to-day administration of the school by a business manager or bursar and appropriate administrative staff. Also, highly successful and comprehensive computer software systems have been installed in schools to assist with administration and other functions. These systems are called Computerised Administrative Systems Environment in Schools, or CASES. The systems cover virtually every aspect of the school's operations, including financial, personnel, student records, timetabling and many more. They have proved to be extremely valuable to schools in local decision making and in the allocation and control of resources. The systems are also electronically linked to the information technology systems of the Department of Education.

Accountability Framework for Schools of the Future

With the autonomy given to Schools of the Future I was determined that they be fully accountable to their local community, and to the wider community, for student improvement and for their performance in terms of their own objectives as set out in their school charter. To ensure this happened, I directed that an accountability framework be developed for Schools of the Future.

In my view, this should have two main elements, an annual report by the school to its local community, and an objective triennial review. The main purpose of the annual report would be for the school to report to its local community on its progress in terms of its charter objectives. For the triennial review, a review team would be set up, including school-based and external people, to review the school's progress in achieving its charter goals and priorities. This triennial review will also indicate areas where the existing school charter could be updated. In addition to these, the school will be subject to a professional financial audit each year. In summary, strict accountability to its parents, its local community and to the taxpayers is an imperative for each School of the Future.

In the accountability framework, the most important element is the Annual Report. Not only must the school report on its operations during the year, especially in terms of student improvement, but also on progress in achieving the objectives and timelines set out in the school charter. Each school's annual report is carefully reviewed by the Office of Review, and any matter requiring attention is brought to the notice of the school council and the Minister for Education. When the school council presents its annual report to the community meeting during the first term of the following year, members of the local community have the opportunity to question the school council on any aspect of the school's operations.

The other important element is the in-depth review of the school's performance every three years, especially in terms of the school's charter objectives and timelines. Each School of the Future is also subject to a stringent audit each year of its financial management and performance. These are contracted out to independent professional auditors.

Learning for the Twenty-first Century

When I became Minister for Education, there was no common curriculum for Victorian schools for students in years Prep through 10. In effect, schools taught what they liked. Sometimes, when a student went from one primary school in

Victoria to another, it was like going from one country to another in terms of what was taught. Nor was there any statewide assessment linked to common statewide standards. For Years 11 and 12, there was the Victorian Certificate of Education (VCE), which had a prescribed curriculum and a statewide system of assessment. However, the VCE was the subject of intense public controversy, and public respect for it was low.

I was determined that we would develop and implement a world class curriculum that would help prepare students for the new opportunities of the twenty-first century. I thought it essential this be done outside the Department, and with very extensive input from teachers. I therefore established a new Board of Studies with members who were respected experts in a range of fields, not limited to education.

I directed the Board to engage in the most extensive process of consultation with teachers that had ever occurred in Victoria. Following this, I directed them to develop a curriculum that was at the forefront of world knowledge and would take students into the twenty-first century. Over a period of some months, the Board of Studies conducted a massive consultation process involving more than 10,000 teachers. Consultation of this nature and magnitude had never been attempted before.

Following this process, teacher-led teams developed a draft document entitled the Curriculum and Standards Framework (CSF), which reflected the views and advice of teachers in the consultations. Essentially this document consisted of new curriculum content and student performance standards for eight key learning areas and for each of the learning stages. The standards described what students should know and be able to do at each stage from the Preparatory Year through to Year 10. The schools were able to decide themselves how the curriculum was to be provided. For example, the CSF can be used for 'horizontal' age-related classes, or for multi-age, 'vertically integrated' classes.

This draft document itself was then subject to further consultation with teachers, and then refined. The result is a rigorous curriculum that challenges students, but also one which teachers feel they own and with which they can work. The cooperation and support of teachers in this curriculum development process is in sharp contrast to other parts of the world where a curriculum was imposed on teachers without any proper input from them, with the result that they never gave it their full support.

I considered one of our fundamental responsibilities was to report effectively to parents on their child's progress at school, which would help build the confidence of parents in their child's learning. We now had the CSF, with standards against which to report. I therefore decided to establish a system of statewide assessment for students at various stages of learning. Such a system could provide both the parents and teacher with additional, high quality information about the student's progress in relation to statewide standards. Such a system would also have important diagnostic value. It would identify areas of strength where a student could move ahead at a faster rate. It would also identify areas where a student needed further strengthening and more individual assistance and support.

I therefore gave directions to the Board of Studies to develop a statewide system of assessment, based on the CSF, which would be used initially for students in Years 3 and 5. Again, the Board of Studies entered into an extensive process of consultation, and developed a new statewide system of assessment that we eventually called the Learning Assessment Project (LAP).

Choosing the name was quite an interesting process. In the early days of planning, the Board proposed that it be called the Primary Assessment Program, or PAP. I did not like this, firstly because it was always my intention that the assessment process be extended, in 1997, to secondary schools, and secondly, because the initials PAP seemed inappropriate. My wife and I were walking in the Royal Botanic Gardens one evening and I began to discuss this with her. She said it was all about learning and that the word 'project' was better than program, and she suggested Learning Assessment Project, or LAP.

The LAP combines both assessment by the teacher and the use of objective statewide assessment instruments over a two week period. By these means, the school is able to assess the student's actual level of learning in comparison with the learning levels laid down in the CSF. This is a diagnostic process for each student in that it clearly identifies for the parent and the teacher areas in which the student may need additional assistance, and those areas in which they excel. This enables the school to provide even higher quality reporting to parents on their child's progress. It also enables the teacher and the parents to develop strategies to help the child progress more strongly at school. This concept eventually developed into the concept of the Individual Learning Improvement Plan for every student, not just those who had participated in the LAP.

The LAP clearly showed that some children were still having major problems with literacy. Literacy is fundamental to a child's progress at school and to their life thereafter. It is also vital to a child's personal development. If a child cannot read or write at the level of their peers, their self-confidence is undermined, and they fall even further behind in all their studies. For a long time there had been anecdotal information from employers, the armed services and others that a significant proportion of young people presenting themselves for employment, enlistment etc. could not properly read or write. Some secondary school principals had reported up to 20 per cent of students coming from primary schools could not read or write properly. The LAP was the first time a scientifically designed assessment system had identified and quantified the extent of the problem.

This was obviously a matter of crucial importance, not only to the children involved, but also to the nation, and urgent action was required. I instructed the Department to immediately develop a response. The result was a comprehensive range of initiatives which were collectively called the Keys to Life program. Basic to the Keys to Life program was the professional development of teachers, in other words teaching the teachers how to teach literacy. Then there were made available a series of programs which had proved to be highly successful in helping children to improve their literacy. Finally there were remedial programs for students who were not keeping pace with their peers in literacy. Foremost amongst these remedial programs was Reading Recovery which provided one-to-one expert assistance for children. This is recognized worldwide as a highly effective way of dealing with the problem. Another important element was increased parental involvement in their child's learning because there was extensive evidence that showed this to be extremely valuable in helping to improve the child's literacy skills.

There was no question that literacy was the foremost priority for schools, and must take precedence over all other activities. To assist schools in dealing with it, a total of $52 million was allocated over a number of years. These funds came from internal reallocations of priorities from the Department, not from 'productivity savings owed to the Treasury', as was subsequently stated. When the Department of Education embarked on another series of school mergers in 1996, there was an attempt to blame these on alleged budget problems because of expenditure on Keys to Life program. Nothing could be further from the truth. The Keys to Life program was a fundamental and integral part of the long-term planning of the Department and its cost had been factored into the forward budget estimates and forecasts.

I believe that the combination of the LAP and the Keys to Life program will effectively deal with the problem of a child going right through primary school and into secondary school with inadequate levels of literacy.

The LAP received enormous support from parents, as it met a long-felt need for additional information about the progress of their child at school. However, the reactionary teacher union officials opposed it, and tried to put a ban on it in schools. This ban was unsuccessful as the vast majority of teachers realized that the LAP would provide them with additional valuable information which would help them in their task of adding value to each of their students. By its second year, every primary school in Victoria was offering the LAP, despite the union ban.

The curriculum and assessment for the senior years of schooling needed immediate attention when we came to Government. On 13 October 1992, about a week after I became Minister, I met with the then Victorian Curriculum and Assessment Board (VCAB), the predecessor of the Board of Studies, which then had responsibility for the VCE. The VCAB members were somewhat wary of this meeting because they were extremely aware that I had been one of the harshest critics of the VCE. We made small talk for a while over coffee so that I could put them at their ease. Then I gave it to them straight.

I told them that I was gravely concerned about the VCE and I directed them to make immediate improvements to it. In particular, I told them they had to improve the quality of the study designs, to reduce the work load for students and teachers, to increase the amount of external assessment for subjects to at least 50 per cent and to establish an independent inquiry into the fairness and effectiveness of the assessment process, especially the discredited 'verification' process. I told them that these improvements were essential to rebuild public confidence in the VCE. VCAB acted quickly and carried out my directions.

To deal with the curriculum aspects of the VCE, committees with a strong university presence were established, and these reviewed, strengthened and re-accredited all the courses. As there had been particular problems with the quality and lack of rigour in some courses, including English, Physics and History, even the revised courses in those areas were given only provisional accreditation, so they could be more fundamentally revised over time.

The social engineers in the Labor Party had seen the VCE as a way to achieve 'equality of outcomes' and 'parity of esteem' through shifting the balance in the final years away from the learning of knowledge to 'process'. The practical effect of this was to reduce assessment by external examinations, so that these became less than 50 per cent of the total assessment process, and place a great reliance on school assessed projects, called Common Assessment Tasks (CATS).

The irony was that, like much of social engineering, this had exactly the opposite effect to what was intended. This was because the parents of students who lived in the more affluent suburbs, and many of who were university graduates themselves, were able to provide or buy assistance for their daughter or son in their preparation of the CAT, even though this was against the rules.

Also, with this great reliance on school-based assessment, there were horrendous problems in trying to ensure that this assessment was comparable between schools across the state. Otherwise, students in schools where the teachers marked easier would have an advantage over those in schools where the teachers marked harder. To try to deal with this, the previous Labor Government had set up a complicated, cumbersome, costly and ineffective 'verification' process, the effect of which was to create terrible inequities between students from different schools. This had a devastating effect on the future higher education and prospects for life of some students.

Following my direction, the level of external assessment was raised to at least 50 per cent in most VCE subjects. Also, the 'verification' process was abolished, and replaced with the General Achievement Test (GAT). This established learning levels within schools against which the schools marking of the school assessed CATS could be compared. Also the amount of project work for students was reduced, and schools were given more flexibility in the organization and timing of this work. This reduced the workload and pressure on students and teachers.

The quality of the marking of the externally assessed work was also improved by clearer and more effective procedures. At my urging, there was an increase in the remuneration of those teachers and academics who undertook the arduous and time consuming task of marking the examination papers.

Because of these reforms, the curriculum for Year 11 and 12 students became more rigorous and would help to better prepare students for the world of the twenty-first century. Also, the VCE assessment system became more valid, more credible, more effective and fairer. As a result, there was a significant improvement in public confidence in the VCE. Before the reforms began, research had shown that this was at a low of less than 30 per cent. When most of the reforms were in place, research showed that this had grown to more than 85 per cent.

Learning for Work

In earlier times, Victoria had a dual system of secondary education. High schools catered for the more academically inclined who had aspirations to attend a university or other institution of higher education. Technical schools catered for those who were seeking a more vocationally oriented secondary education, and who would probably leave school to seek a job after Year 10.

The Labor Party thought this dual system 'elitist' (the high school students being the 'elite'). It proceeded to abolish the technical schools, and create a 'comprehensive' system of secondary education. The VCE was an integral part of this 'comprehensive' approach. However, rather than helping the less academically inclined students, it put them at a disadvantage. In particular, it failed to meet the expectation of these students that their secondary education would help to prepare them for work. For many of these students, school became increasingly irrelevant; they resented the time they spent there, and this was reflected in their behaviour at school.

I was extremely conscious that the secondary schools were failing to give many students a real chance for the future. I also believe that, in the world of the twenty-first century, those who had the skills, the ability and the flexibility to grab the new opportunities emerging from change, especially that being driven by new technology, would prosper. The rest would probably be condemned to a life of unemployment, or underemployment in mind-stifling jobs. I discussed this issue extensively with business firms, secondary teachers and with groups of students. I was convinced the VCE needed to be further modified to enable schools to provide high quality, relevant 'learning for work' opportunities, and I directed the Board of Studies to do this.

This became part of the Dual Recognition Program. Under this program, students in the senior years of secondary school could concurrently study for sub-jects that would earn them credits towards their VCE, and also subjects provided by a technical and further education (TAFE) college that would earn them credits towards the relevant TAFE certificate. Very importantly, part of this program incorporated practical 'at work' training in a business or industry for a number of hours each week.

This can best be illustrated by a specific example. Elwood Secondary College decided to establish a dual recognition program in the hospitality industry. It made arrangements with the Swinburne College of TAFE to provide the TAFE course components. It then persuaded the Novotel Bayside Hotel in St. Kilda to allow the students to take their practical work training there. Novotel initially did not see much benefit in this program for them, and agreed to it more as a community service. The plan was that the students would come to Novotel on certain days and carry out normal work in various sections of the hotel. For example, the students studying food and beverages took over the operations of the main dining room on a Tuesday, usually a quiet day. They planned the menu, cooked the food and served it, as well as the drinks. After a while, the news got around that the kids were doing a great job in the dining room on Tuesdays, and that the food was terrific. The result was that, rather than this being just a public service, the hotel found that the dining room became very busy on Tuesdays, and the training program was adding to their business. Hotels and restaurants heard that these young people were both creative and professional, and they had no difficulty in getting jobs.

Elwood Secondary College's experience in the hospitality industry was repeated by other schools in a range of other areas, including business services, electronics, information technology, horticulture, and many others. Students have discovered that these dual recognition courses make their time at school more relevant to the future and give them a better chance in the job market, and enrolments in them are increasing rapidly.

There is no question that Victoria is now a leader in vocational education, and that this approach to education will expand rapidly in the future. An important aspect of the Victorian approach is that it allows students to simultaneously undertake general and vocational education without creating two streams of different status.

In many ways the reforms in vocational education were some of our most important in terms of the immediate benefits they brought for students. They made school more relevant, and brought about dramatic improvements in the attitudes and behaviour of many students in secondary schools. At a time of high youth unemployment, they provided practical training and assistance for students which significantly increased their work prospects after school. In the best vocational education programs in secondary schools, especially where local industry and business play a role in the development and delivery of the programs, nearly 100 per cent of participating students obtain jobs at the end of their schooling. A further development now is the ability of students to undertake apprenticeships while at secondary school.

New Methods of Learning

I felt very strongly that we were at a watershed in learning. There was an explosion of knowledge and it was estimated that the volume of new knowledge would double every three to five years. Also, there now existed the remarkable potential of information technology and telecommunications to improve access to knowledge, to help students to learn and to overcome disadvantage. I decided that, if we were to give students the best chance for the future, we had to embrace with vigour the new learning methods emerging from information technology and telecommunications, especially multimedia.

The first thing we did was to establish an interactive satellite learning network, with all schools connected through a satellite dish installed at the school. This was named SOFNet, which stands for Schools of the Future Net. SOFNet transmits learning programs live from studios to classrooms in all Victorian schools. While watching the programs, students have opportunities to communicate with the presenters in the studio, using telephones and facsimile machines.

One of the early applications of SOFNet was the learning of languages other than English. Over 100,000 Victorian primary students are participating in the SOFNet language programs. The languages available include Indonesian, Japanese, Mandarin Chinese, French, Italian and Modern Greek. Australia prides itself on being a multicultural society. In such a society, the learning of languages is of special importance.

Another important application of SOFNet learning is in science, with more than 1200 schools in Victoria participating. Students are showing great enthusiasm for these science related programs, which have a strong emphasis on practical experiments. These programs are especially important in the light of the shortage of high quality science teachers, particularly in our primary schools.

SOFNet has also proved extremely valuable for the professional development of teachers and for information, training and support for teachers in curriculum development. Also, where there is a gifted teacher in a particular subject area, it is valuable to share that teacher beyond a single traditional classroom situation. This is especially the case in a country like Australia where some schools are in relatively isolated situations. From this emerged the concept of the extended classroom, which is called Telematics. Telematics involves joining classrooms in more than one location through various telecommunications links, including telephone, fax and computers linked by modems for computer conferencing.

Of course the advent of the Internet has greatly advanced the use of computer conferencing. This has brought big benefits in terms of collaborative learning involving students from more than one school. The next logical step is video conferencing, and this is occurring as the upgraded telecommunications links become available.

Time and time again we were demonstrating the extraordinary learning benefits for students through the use of new information technology and telecommunications. I believed that it was important for us to move ahead as quickly as possible so that the current generation of students could get maximum benefit from these. I also wanted to put Victoria to the forefront of the world in these developments, and for Victoria to be seen as a world leader. To better focus attention, energy and resources on these aims, I established the Classrooms of the Future project, with the mission of ensuring that the learning of each young Victorian is enhanced through the appropriate use of information technology and telecommunications.

Although it is not yet fully appreciated, I am sure these new technologies will create a revolution in learning and will profoundly change the way students learn and the organization of the school and the classroom. They will challenge the very nature and configuration of the classroom.

As in all dramatic change, it is best to proceed by showing people successful examples so that they can see the benefits for them in the changes to encourage them to enthusiastically embrace those changes. We therefore adopted the concept of the Navigator School to model the most advanced techniques, using these new technologies, and established fourteen of them. These Navigator Schools are not only required to demonstrate the most effective use of new learning technologies and to provide professional development for teachers in them, but also to continually ensure that they are at the leading edge of world developments in these technologies. These schools are provided with the most advanced equipment, and are supported by the Education Department with additional staff and training. In turn, they are expected to make these facilities fully available to students and teachers in other schools, for demonstration and experience purposes.

Schools across Victoria are already demonstrating the remarkable benefits of the Internet for students to access information and for students to engage in collaborative learning. We supported this through a program called Global Classroom, which provided advice and assistance to schools and professional development for teachers. It also facilitated the participation by schools in I*EARN (International Education and Resources Network), which is an international network for collaborative student projects and learning, using the Internet. To further assist schools, we established our own site on the Internet, which we called SOFWeb, which stands for Schools of the Future Web.

SOFWeb provided students and teachers with low cost 'point and click' access to relevant and up-to-date Internet-based information. It also enables students to work collaboratively between schools in project-based learning, and to link to global student projects. Through SOFWeb, students are able to publish their work on the Internet for worldwide readership. At the same time, we provided assistance for all schools to be connected to the Internet.

Of course the roles of the teacher as guide and facilitator are always paramount, and a massive program of professional development for teachers is under way. Already thousands of Victorian teachers are very advanced in their knowledge of these new technologies and their practical application for learning, and over the next few years 6000 teachers a year will have access to further training in their use.

For me, the most dramatic example of how these new technologies can advance student learning and overcome disadvantage is the Koorie Open Door Education Campus at Kurnai College in Morwell, Victoria. In my view, the approach of the previous Labor Government to Koorie (Aboriginal) education had been disgraceful. There was little self-determination by the Koories themselves; rather they had to put up with what others thought best for them.

I was determined that we should put the Koorie child first, and that the Koorie community should decide the type of education they wanted for their children, and should have a significant involvement in providing it. At the same time I was determined that this education should give the Koorie students an understanding of the remarkable history of the Koorie people in Victoria and of their rich cultural heritage, including their languages, which were all but lost. In other words, I wanted to provide each Koorie child with a high quality education, while still maintaining a focus on Koorie culture and identity.

To achieve this I started discussions with the leaders of the Victorian Aboriginal Education Association Incorporated (VAEAI). I remember our first discussion at Parliament House in Melbourne, and, in particular, their incoming President, Mary Atkinson, a great leader and a very warm and genuine person. It soon became clear that we all shared a strong personal commitment to the cause of Koorie children, and we pledged ourselves to making real progress for them. We were all so moved by the meeting, and by our mission, that we were all nearly in tears when we parted.

The result was the Koorie Open Door Education (KODE) project, and the establishment of two campuses, one at Morwell and one at Glenroy, a suburb of Melbourne. As Lionel Bamblett, General Manager of VAEI said to me, 'The KODE campuses are a dream that has been realized. Their success in their first year has been greater than our most optimistic hopes'.

Both campuses are doing well, but of all the exciting things that are happening in them, the use of learning technologies by students at the Morwell, or Woolum

Bellum, KODE Campus is the most remarkable. The teachers and parents at the Woolum Bellum Campus decided that it needed a breakthrough to overcome the learning disadvantage from which most of the Koorie students suffered, and to change their attitudes towards learning. They decided that the best approach was to integrate the learning technologies 'seamlessly' across the whole curriculum and spread the computer resources across each of the teaching areas.

A local area network (LAN) was established in the school to link the computers and software across the campus and the access of each classroom to global communications through the Internet. This enables students to access the knowledge of the world, and to engage in collaborative projects with students in other countries and to participate in worldwide student projects. The most exciting thing they are doing is communicating with other First Nation schools around the world, jointly studying issues of interest to indigenous people, and publishing their work in this area to the world through the World Wide Web.

It began this way. The Woolum Bellum students sent an e-mail message to the office of the Vice-President of the United States, asking to be put in touch with a First Nation school in the US. Within two days the Woolum Bellum students were in touch through the Internet with the Zuni Reservation school (A:Shiwi) in the north-west corner of New Mexico.

From getting to know Charley Bullock and his students at A:Shiwi they progressed to developing a worldwide indigenous schools network via I*EARN. The 'First Peoples Conference', as this network is known, now provides an active forum for indigenous communities around the world to contribute to issues relating to their culture, and publish their work globally. Students at Woolum Bellum are contributing actively to this. What is more, this provided the incentive for Woolum Bellum students to start to rediscover the local Koorie languages.

The students at Woolum Bellum have wholeheartedly adopted the new learning technologies, and have shown an extraordinary adaptability and enthusiasm for them. The teachers say that it has helped them to lift their learning levels in a remarkable way and at a much faster rate than is the norm in mainstream schools across Victoria. It has also been a delight to have watched how their attitudes to learning have changed since their involvement with the new learning technologies. They have shown an increased motivation towards all aspects of school life, including attendance, behaviour, application to task and good concentration and participation in all areas of the curriculum. To quote Andrew Mowat, one of their gifted teachers,

> I have seen eyes literally light up when students are told that their work is to be published globally . . . It has also been exciting to watch the development of literary skills in the students that began the year with so few skills. As their confidence in their ability rose so too did the educational risks they were prepared to take . . . It has been both inspiring and thrilling . . . we know now that our Koorie students have a wonderful educational future.

What will really drive the revolution in the new learning from now on will be the influence of multimedia. This has proved to be very attractive and powerful for students in the field of entertainment and it is only commonsense that we should harness it for education. Popular culture and the entertainment media are powerful forces in the lives of young people. Students who make little progress at school often absorb prodigious amounts of information from the entertainment media in out-of-school settings.

To study this, I set up a special project called Digital Chalk. I was fortunate to get the agreement of three outstanding people to be the steering committee for this. They were Professor Peter Hill, Deputy Dean of the Faculty of Education at the University of Melbourne, and a world authority on student learning; Professor Dale Mann of Teachers College at Columbia University, perhaps the leading thinker in the world on the use of multimedia in student learning; and Steve Vizard, a leader in the Australian multimedia industry.

The task I gave them was to study the way in which multimedia can improve student learning and the development of new methods of learning, incorporating multimedia. Also I asked them to consider how to encourage the multimedia industry to produce high quality, relevant multimedia content for use in this learning. Although it was expected that this new learning would bring benefits for all students, the special focus of the project would be on young people aged between 10 years and 16 years who often become disengaged, or even alienated from schooling.

Another project for which I had a strong personal commitment was the establishment of science and technology centres for schools. An objective was to form an interconnected network to promote excellence in science and technology education and the application of information technology across the curriculum. After a great deal of consultation and planning, and after checking latest developments in the UK, Europe and the US, we decided to establish six science and technology centres and to strategically locate them across the state.

These centres provide resources and are a focal point for schools in science and technology. A key role for the centres is the provision of professional development to support the adoption of improved teaching and learning approaches in science and technology. They also have advanced facilities and equipment which is available for use by adjacent schools and, out of school hours, by local industry. Local industry plays a key role in these centres, which is very valuable to students in helping to prepare them for future work opportunities in those industries.

Managing the Reform Process

The Role of the Minister

I came to the early conclusion that I must personally drive the reform process. Even the best bureaucrats need leading. They may be committed to the government's reform process but, by nature, they are reactionary. They have a vested interest in the status quo. It is safer, more comfortable and requires less physical and emotional effort. Also, any change tends to threaten their power base. This was especially so with the changes I was implementing. In effect, I was dismantling their system. I was also substantially downsizing their numbers and transferring most of their power to schools and parents. I could understand it if they were less than enthusiastic about my reforms.

I found that a vital first step was to develop a clear, simple mission statement that everyone could understand instantly. Then I had to keep pushing it until it penetrated everyone's subconscious and became part of the conventional wisdom. I knew I was succeeding in this when the bureaucrats started quoting the mission statement back to me as if it were their own. That mission statement was, 'To help each child to achieve his or her potential so as to have the best chance for the future'. I also developed a simple test for all proposals and expenditure. This was: 'Does it add value to a child's learning?' If the proposed or existing expenditure did not meet that test, I said 'Scrap it'.

I found that I had to take a direct part in planning the reforms. I set up special action groups for the strategic planning of the reform process. These groups usually comprised a cross-section of bureaucrats, including some from the middle ranks who were good lateral thinkers. In these discussions, a white board was an important aid. I would often find myself standing up in front of the white board trying to capture the new ideas as they began to flow. The white board helped to make the discussions dynamic because one could quickly change the statement of ideas on it as the ideas themselves developed. These were not unstructured 'think tank' sessions. I clearly spelt out, on the white board, the goals I wanted to achieve, and I challenged those present to come up with the best way to achieve them.

In these discussions, we did not limit ourselves to policies and strategies, but got into their implementation as well. Many years of experience in business had taught me that the implementation was often more important than the policy formulation. The best policy in the world is useless if it is not implemented properly. Good implementation can often fix a poor policy, but poor implementation is disastrous for even the best policy. Being involved in the implementation earned me the reputation amongst some bureaucrats that I was too 'hands on'. They probably considered this a criticism. I took it as a compliment.

I also involved myself in developing the right team to implement the strategies and achieve our goals. I have already described the recruitment of Geoff Spring from the Northern Territory as Chief Executive Officer. The commitment he showed to the reform process confirmed the soundness of this appointment. However, we recruited others from other states with mixed results. In some cases the people were highly successful. One example was Merrill Hausler whom we recruited from New South Wales and who proved to be an excellent Regional Manager in the Melbourne metropolitan area. However, we were greatly disappointed with some other appointments. I found it encouraging that some of the most creative people in the team were from within the existing organization. They had never had the chance to blossom under the previous Labor Party regime, which favoured Labor Party loyalists over other more talented, non-political people.

The other key people in implementing the reforms were my personal staff in my private office. These were the people who deal with the mass of administrative matters. More importantly, they advised me on policy formation, and helped me to manage key political and media issues. They also helped me to deal with the Government's parliamentary backbench, as well as outside groups and organizations.

One's personal staff is also a vital resource in handling the business of Parliament. This included helping me to prepare for Question Time and the Adjournment Debate and ensuring that my legislative program was properly managed. During my time as Minister I had a group of talented and hard working people assisting me in my personal staff. It would not be appropriate to mention each by name but to each I owe a great debt of gratitude.

Dealing with Cabinet

It is important to remember that the Westminster system is a system of Ministerial government, as distinct from Cabinet government, although the principle of collective responsibility always applies. The Minister is expected to administer his or her department within the broad policy parameters of the government. The Minister only brings to Cabinet issues of fundamental policy that affect the government as a whole, proposals for legislation or appointments that need to be made by the Governor-in-Council. Even budget matters are not dealt with by the Cabinet as a whole, but in direct negotiations with the Treasurer and at the Budget and Economic Review Committee of Cabinet.

That is the way we operated in the first Kennett Government in Victoria, and it worked very well. That is not to say one does not go to great lengths to inform one's Cabinet colleagues of major issues in one's Department. A well-informed colleague is in a better position to support you when the going is tough. However, one tends to do this informally, often at the lunch that follows the Cabinet meeting.

Question Time

Question Time is potentially a highly dangerous time for a Minister. More Ministers have been mortally wounded in Question Time than in any other way. Unlike some Parliaments, questions in Question Time in Australian Parliaments are 'without notice'.

As a young man, I once heard 'Black Jack' McEwen give advice about how to deal with Question Time to my then Minister, Bill Spooner: 'Treat every question as though it is a genuine request for information, although, of course, it is not. Get to your feet, say the bare minimum to answer the question and then sit down again'. McEwen went on to become Prime Minister for a short while, after Harold Holt disappeared in the surf. Ironically, McEwen did not always follow his own advice.

There are two types of questions in Question Time. There are the questions from the Opposition, the primary aim of which is to catch a Minister out. Then there are questions from Government Members ('Dorothy Dixers') which are usually stimulated by the Minister to whom the question is addressed. The purpose of these questions from Government Members is to give the Minister the opportunity in Question Time to announce some good news that will benefit the Government. Sometimes they also provide an opportunity to reveal something bad about the Government in an attempt to neutralize it before the Opposition gets onto it.

Usually you do not actually answer the Opposition question, but one similar to it that suits you better. As long as your answer is relevant to the Opposition's question, the Minister is in order as far as the Standing Orders are concerned. As McEwen said, it is best to make your answer to an Opposition question as short and succinct as possible. For 'Dorothy Dixers' from the Government side, the Minister can be more expansive in the answer. However, even for these questions, the Minister should still prepare the answer in advance and stick pretty much to the 'script', because Ministers have got into trouble answering these questions as well.

In the Victorian Parliament Question Time occurs each sitting day at 2.00 pm. At 12 noon each sitting day I would meet with key members of my personal staff to prepare for Question Time. We would discuss the issues running in the news media, and anything that we had heard 'on the grape vine'. We would try to predict the questions that the Opposition spokesman on Education might try to throw at me. We would then prepare what we thought to be appropriate responses to these, have them typed up, and place them in the Question Time Folder. In practice, I rarely referred to this folder. However, the mere fact that we had done this preparation work gave one more confidence when one got to one's feet to answer the questions.

I was once blessed with the experience of the Opposition asking me every question during each Question Time for a whole parliamentary week. This was on the issue of the appointment of District Liaison Principals, who were people appointed to assist clusters of schools in the change management process during our reform period. The Opposition alleged that political pressure had been brought by my Parliamentary Secretary, Mr Stephen Elder, to have appointed people who were sympathetic to the Government. This was not true, and the Opposition were merely mouthing the claims of a few disgruntled, unsuccessful applicants who had not been appointed because they were not good enough. The Opposition had talked themselves into thinking they had me 'on the run', and day after day asked me questions based on stories told to them by these unsuccessful applicants.

As the District Liaison Principals had in fact been appointed on merit, I decided to say just that in response to each question, rather than try to dispute each of the unfounded allegations that were the basis of these multiple questions. I would thus be following the McEwen rule. This simple statement in response to each question infuriated and frustrated the Opposition. They eventually gave up their attack without scoring any points and having used a whole week of Question Time to no effect whatsoever. The phrase 'on merit', went into the parliamentary lexicon, and the Opposition would yell it at me whenever I rose to answer a question, no matter the topic, which suited me fine.

Communications

A vital element in any reform program is communications. For me, the most important people with whom to communicate were those in schools, being the school principals, the teachers, the members of school councils and parents.

My first public act as Minister for Education was to write to each school principal and advise them concerning the Schools of the Future program. We followed this up with frequent communications from the Department to school principals concerning developments and progress with Schools of the Future. The purposes of these communications were not only to keep school principals informed about developments, but to seek their advice and recommendations as well. Also, the Schools of the Future Task Force held extensive consultations with principals to gain their input on specific aspects of the program. Over the following months and years I held many meetings with groups of principals across the State to hear their views first hand. Also, during my countless visits to schools, I took the opportunity of discussing the program with the principal on an individual basis.

Because of this massive communications effort I felt confident that I knew and understood the views of principals about the Schools of the Future program. It was abundantly clear that the principals overwhelmingly supported the principles under-lying it, although they did not always agree with specific aspects.

The support of school principals for the Schools of the Future program stemmed from a long held yearning amongst them to be free of the operating constraints of the system and the dominance of trade union officials over the day to day opera-tions of schools. That had been clear to me from the very first days of my appoint-ment as Shadow Minister for Education when the Liberal Party was still in Opposition. From my first discussions with principals, I was convinced that schools would embrace the freedom of the Schools of the Future program with enthusiasm. My Department and my advisers did not always share that view. With hindsight, it is now clear that the willingness of schools to join the Schools of the Future program was underestimated by everybody except me.

A massive effort was also made to communicate effectively and directly with teachers. In the past, teachers had mainly obtained information through teacher union publications and bulletins. This made them very dependent on the union and undermined their status as an independent professional. I was determined to change this. I wrote individually to teachers on at least two occasions. Very importantly, I established a weekly newspaper that provided them with news and information. The key to the success of this newspaper was for it to gain credibility with teachers, and for them to see it as a reliable and balanced source of information. I therefore gave instructions to the Department to ensure that the newspaper was produced with high ethical and professional standards. However, this did not stop the union officials from claiming that it was a propaganda medium for the Department and the Government.

Also, a great deal of work was done to communicate directly with school council members and parents. I was determined that these communications should be clear, succinct and interesting. This was not always easy, because education bureaucrats like to use obtuse and jargon-ridden prose. I would often have fights with the bureaucrats about these communications, which they would draft in a form that was 'educationally valid', but would be meaningless to parents.

I had learnt very early in my term as Minister that when a decision was made that was controversial, effective communication of accurate information was vital. If there were to be criticism of a decision, we owed it to ourselves to at least ensure that criticism was based on accurate information, rather than the distortions and misinformation that was provided by the unions and other vested interest groups. In this regard, we did not hesitate to use paid advertisements in the media to communicate directly with parents. For example, we placed advertisements in newspapers across the state to ensure parents received accurate information about the reorganization of schools, following the work of the Quality Provision Task Forces.

Of course, we went to great lengths to effectively communicate with the news media. In this, I was greatly helped by an outstanding young man named Ian Smith who occupied the position of my Press Secretary for a while. In my experience working in Government and during my years with General Motors I have worked with many press officers, but none as good as Smith. Smith was extremely alert to the media danger or potential benefit in any issue and could rapidly develop a strategy to manage it. He was invaluable when we were dealing with the reorganization of schools as part of the Quality Provision process. He developed a program for early and full information about all the proposed changes, the rationale behind them and the benefits for students that would result in terms of better facilities, better access to curriculum and provision of new learning technologies. What could have been a media nightmare turned out to be positive news for the Government.

My experience with the media presents an interesting case study. Politicians and the media have long held varying degrees of suspicion about one another. The more emotive the issues, the more difficult it is to factually portray them, and education, along with health, is undoubtably a government's most emotive portfolio. I made the assessment early on that with the action I would have to take to place the Education budget on a stable and secure basis, and with the controversial nature of the reforms that I planned to introduce, it would be very difficult to get favourable media coverage. Rather than seeking to be a slick media performer, for which I lacked the personal attributes anyway, I was determined to always deal with the media with candour and seek to communicate accurate information about my decisions and the reasons and rationale behind them. Above all else, I wished to build up credibility with the media and to break down the attitude of suspicion that they had towards Government Ministers, and the Government generally.

I was also determined to watch the details of items that appeared in the media, including relatively small stories that might be positioned well back in the newspaper. My reason for this was my belief that public perceptions are often built up by a cumulative combination of many small things. The way I would plan a media release or comment was to ask my staff what headline we would like to see above the report of the release, and plan an approach to an individual journalist or newspaper to try to achieve such a headline, or something like it. It was amazing the number of times we succeeded in doing this.

In most cases when trying to decide upon the best approach to a media issue, I would rely on my instinctive judgment. After all, I had over thirty years' experience of dealing with the news media in the private and public sectors. That instinct usually proved right, but not always. My tendency was always to be cautious, whereas my staff often tended to be more adventurous. They would try to talk me into a particular course of action, which I would resist. After lengthy discussion, and their persistent urging, I would sometimes reluctantly agree, against my best judgment. In most of these situations, my staff were right, and their plan paid off.

The media is made up of a range of different people. There is a tendency of some politicians to consider them all a pack of hounds baying for blood. That, however, is not true or fair. There are some who genuinely want to understand the issue, and the background to it, and to report it in an intelligent and balanced way. There are others who do not want to go to that intellectual effort, and who simply want to publish a story in the most sensational, superficial manner. There are some who respect candour, and the desire of a Minister to describe an issue accurately, and without trying to score political points. There are others who view this as weakness, because you are not going for the political jugular.

We are fortunate in Victoria to have a number of respected journalists in the first group and they come from varying sections of the media: press, television and radio. This undermines the argument of some who believe complex issues cannot be accurately reflected in a 90 second radio or television report or 15 centimetre newspaper article. These respected journalists included Brendan Donohue, the State political reporter of the Channel 7 television news service; Steve Harris, the then Editor-in-Chief of the *Herald Sun* newspaper group; Alan Kohler, the then Editor of *The Age*, and Chris Richards, Education Editor of *The Age*, to name just a few. These people took the trouble to understand the nature of the fundamental reforms I was implementing in Education. Their treatment of the reporting of these reforms was not always favourable, but it was thoughtful, accurate, balanced and professional.

There were others who were primarily interested in the political dogfights, and who tended to see me coming off second best in these. I do not mention them by name as some would see it as an honour to be highlighted and that is something I would not want to bestow on them! They saw me as a poor political infighter who did not score enough political points. They did not know that I had little interest in scoring political points. My interest was to give the present and future generation of children in Victoria a better chance for the future.

The results speak for themselves. The Government did achieve my revolution in education in Victoria. This was against predictions from long-time observers of education reform who said I did not have a hope, and that I would be destroyed in the process. Also, when the 1996 elections came around in Victoria, the polling undertaken by the Liberal Party showed that, far from being a negative, education was a positive for the Government in the voters' minds. I believe those are far more important achievements than scoring political points in political dogfights.

Dealing with Teacher Union Officials

For a decade under Labor Party rule, Education in Victoria was run by teacher union officials. Under the centralized agreements, these officials virtually told the Education Department what it could or could not do. The agreements stipulated how schools should be run in an extraordinary degree of detail, and local union dominated committees could veto any decision by a school principal. A former Labor Premier, John Cain, recognized this in his account (Cain, 1995) of his own government, when he indicated that the power wielded by the teacher union officials created major problems for his government.

The control of Education by teacher union officials was never better illustrated for me than in a discussion I had with one of them shortly after I became Minister for Education. He told me about a special arrangement he had with a Minister for Education in the previous Labor Government. Under this arrangement, if a decision was made with which he did not agree, he had a special telephone number to contact a ministerial adviser who sat just outside the Minister's office. The union official told me that, using this arrangement, he could guarantee to have an unfavourable decision reversed within twenty minutes.

I was determined that I would free Education from the domination of teacher union officials. For a start, I found ways of freeing ourselves from the constraints of the agreements, and I restored full authority to school principals. This was no mean feat because, of all the reforms of the Kennett Government, those in Industrial Relations proved the most difficult. In fact, I believe that it was only in Education that we succeeded in freeing ourselves from the power of the trade union officials.

I clearly understood that the unions could only exercise as much influence as we allowed them to have. I was firmly of the belief that each teacher should be treated as an individual professional. Teaching is a profession, not an 'industry'. It was my hope that every teacher would, one day, have his or her own individual contract, drawn up in a way that suited their own particular requirements. Trade unions are at odds with the concept of professionalism, and the 'industrial action' by trade unions over the years had done much to downgrade the professional status and respect for teachers in the eyes of the public. Unions are inconsistent with professionalism and are therefore irrelevant in the teaching profession, and I decided to treat them as such and to ignore them.

Teacher union officials attempted industrial action on a number of occasions, but as a diminishing number of teachers came out on strike, they resorted to legal action before the Industrial Relations Commission. On the whole their actions before the Industrial Relations Commission were unproductive from their point of view, and decision after decision reconfirmed the validity of the Schools of the Future reforms. However, in one important and costly respect they were successful. From time to time, because of changes in enrolments, some schools need more teachers and some need less. An action by the teacher unions before the Industrial Relations Commission resulted in a decision which effectively prevented the Department of Education from transferring a teacher from a school in which they were not required to one where they were unless that teacher agreed to the transfer. This resulted in a considerable number of schools with over entitlement teachers, the cost of which the Department of Education had to bear. This resulted in budget problems for the Department of Education which later, incorrectly, were attributed to the costs of the Keys to Life literacy program. (The costs of the Keys to Life program had, in fact, been fully budgeted.)

I was determined that my push to recognize the professional standing of teachers and have the Department deal directly with each teacher as an individual professional was not biased by any personal animosity towards unions. After all, my great-grandfather had been a mining union leader in Broken Hill, and I had once received a plaque from a motor industry union praising my support for their workers. Therefore, at the beginning of my term as Minister, I arranged for Geoff Spring and I to have lunch with the leaders of the main teacher unions at Slattery's Restaurant in Melbourne. Everything was very cordial, the union leaders probably thinking this was a continuation of the previous system under which the Minister danced to their tune.

I am sure their tactic was to soften me up early in the meal, and, over coffee, to put the hard word on me in regard to their outrageous demands. Sadly from their point of view, the opportunity to do this disappeared when I received a call on a mobile telephone. This was about an urgent news media issue that had arisen, and it became clear to me that I must return to the office to deal with it by way of a radio interview. This I did, leaving Geoff Spring to continue to enjoy the company of the union leaders. The hilarious thing was that the myth later developed in teacher union circles that this lunch had been cut short by a telephone call from the Premier, who had heard that I was getting 'matey' with union officials and did not like it. The reality was that the Premier never even knew that I was lunching with them, and could not have cared less, even if he had known.

The unions were opposed to the concept of Schools of the Future because they considered, correctly, that it would undermine their control of schools. However, I did receive an unofficial approach from one union leader. He said that if I would agree to a series of proposals from them that were designed to reinforce union control over school operations, the unions would desist in their opposition to Schools of the Future. I did not respond to this offer.

Managing Oneself

One quickly recognizes that one's most valuable resources are one's own time, energy and will. The job was so demanding of all of these that I was determined to manage them effectively. I did so with mixed success.

I realized from the start that if one was driving fundamental change, there was no substitute for hard work and the application of a great deal of concentrated attention. I also realized that, although I must concentrate on 'the big picture', and not be clouded and bogged down with a heap of minor, routine matters, there was no substitute for getting into the detail and into the implementation of policies and strategies.

Working with the Department was very time-consuming. In the Sir Humphrey Appleby mode, the Department would inundate me with paper in the form of 'briefings', which mostly sought my approval for some department proposal or other. In other than the merely routine matters, I insisted that the relevant officer actually make a verbal presentation to me so that I could question him or her and test out the assumptions and logic behind the proposal.

I found my most productive work time was in the early morning, either at home or in the office. This included Saturday and Sunday mornings. My best ideas came then, probably having germinated subconsciously overnight. Also, I found that by working early in the morning, one can get the jump on the bureaucrats, and be ready for them when they arrived at the office. This puts them at a disadvantage, even inducing a state of shock, especially if they are still suffering from caffeine deprivation. I liked to get some solid work behind me early in the day. This then gave me time during the day to deal with visitors, meetings and telephone calls in an orderly way, without a lot of paper work hanging over my head. Further, if one deals with matters early in the morning, it enables the Department to begin acting on one's instructions from the start of business.

A very important thing for me was coming to terms with information technology and using it. I had a personal computer behind my desk and I was able to use it to access information from the Department's information systems, and for e-mail.

There is no doubt that I was under constant personal pressure while implementing our reform agenda. This was aggravated by the fact that, by nature I do not enjoy confrontation, which was constantly being offered up by the opponents of reform. I vividly remember one incident when I had been invited to open an extension to a library in a secondary school in Reservoir, a northern suburb of Melbourne. As suggested by the school, my driver drove into the school yard, and parked near the rear of the main building.

I went into the school and was received in a friendly and hospitable manner. The usual speeches occurred, which were followed by morning tea, including very nice cakes made by some of the parents. At the appropriate time I bade my farewells and walked out of the rear of the building to where my car was parked. I discovered a change had occurred whilst I was at the ceremony. Whereas the school yard had previously been peaceful and nearly empty, it was now filled by a rowdy and unruly mob led by teacher union officials who, when I appeared, proceeded to yell personal abuse at me. I thought that the sooner I left this scene the better I would be. I therefore began to battle my way to my car, which I eventually reached after some difficulty. My driver started the car and began to drive slowly and gingerly through the mob towards the school gate. When we reached the gate, we discovered that someone had shut it and had chained and padlocked it. What's more, they had parked one of their cars across the outside of the gate as a further impediment. My car came to a halt and people started pounding on the roof and bonnet with their fists, yelling personal abuse all the time.

This was clearly an impossible situation, so I got out of the car and forced my way back into the school. Union officials had alerted television news crews of this exercise in attempted intimidation, and there was extensive coverage on news programs that night of me being jostled by this screaming mob. I finally got myself back into the school and went to the principal's office. I discovered that an Education Department bureaucrat had parked her car in a side street. I asked to borrow it, walked out through a side door and drove back to my city office.

When they saw the television coverage that night, many people, including teachers, were disgusted by the behaviour of teacher union officials and it did their cause no good. In fact, the reaction against them was so strong that they never tried these tactics against me again. It was reported to me that a teacher union official had said at a meeting that they wanted to 'give Hayward a heart attack'. I am happy to say that they did not succeed.

What helped me most to deal with the pressures of the job was the support of my family. My wife, our sons, our daughter-in-law (and out-of-law) and our grandchildren are a source of great joy to me, and constantly helped me to renew my spirit and energy.

Trying to keeping fit was also important. My objective was to walk for a total of at least forty minutes a day, although I did not always achieve this. I liked best to walk with my wife in the Royal Botanic Gardens that are close to our home in South Yarra. However, if this was not possible in daylight, we would sometimes walk around the streets of South Yarra in the dark. When I had no luncheon engagement, I would always walk at lunch time, buying a salad sandwich en route.

There were other things we did together which were always revitalizing. Both my wife and I love the bush and we would go bushwalking whenever we could, usually in the Otway Ranges near our house at Lorne. We also love the sea and swimming, and we would go swimming at Lorne as often as we could, and try to take a holiday of a week or more in the winter to go to Queensland and swim. We are both fond of the theatre and good movies and we would go to these as often as we could, usually the movies.

I like good orchestral music and I would listen to this at home, or sometimes take myself off to a concert at the Concert Hall of the Victorian Arts Centre, which is within walking distance of our home. However, I found that, even during a piece of orchestral music I really loved, my mind would keep wandering back to my work and my plans for the next phase of the reform program. It was not that I was thinking about operating problems in the Department, or even political problems; these I could let go. It was more the mission that was always in my mind and which I seemed to be thinking about all the time, even subconsciously.

I like reading, and I would always have a small pile of books alongside my bed. This was recreational, not business, reading. I would always read for about thirty minutes when I went to bed, no matter how late, and I never suffered from insomnia once during those three and a half years, despite the problems I would be facing the next day. On the other hand, I would sometimes not sleep very long, and I would often be up at 4.30 am working on my plans.

The most important sanctuary for me was our house at Lorne. We would go there in the winter as well as the summer, because in cold weather we love to go on long bush walks in the Otway Ranges, which begin just at the back of our house. After these long walks we would sit before a blazing log fire, reading and at peace with the world. Of course, what we liked in the summer at Lorne was the sea, and I especially enjoyed body surfing. To my mind, there is nothing more exhilarating than catching a wave and letting it power you into the beach. I make no claims to being a skilled body surfer. The fact that one misses many waves makes the one you catch all the more thrilling.

I tried to always eat healthy food. As the healthiest food was alway at home, I avoided meals elsewhere, except for essential official engagements. Even at official engagements, I tried to eat very little, and then have something to eat after I got home. I drank very little alcohol, and none at official engagements. I enjoyed a glass of good wine with my meal at home. Having said all this, I must confess that, ever since the bakery days of my childhood, I have a weakness for cakes, and I would sometimes find myself wolfing down homemade cakes during the afternoon tea that was invariably part of a school visit. My ever vigilant staff, no doubt with my welfare in mind, would usually report this to my wife, who then gave me a hard time.

I would like to refer back to something Bill Spooner said to me when I was a young man: 'If you want to be a really successful Minister, you have to believe in what you are doing. You have to have a personal commitment to it, and to be emotional about it. Then it doesn't matter what they say about you, you can shrug them off'. I think that was exactly the situation with me. I did believe in what I was doing and I thought it important to the future of our young people and of Australia. I had a personal, indeed emotional, commitment to it. That emotion, passion if you will, came out in everything I did and everything I said. That gave me the strength to carry on and to shrug off the opposition and the very nasty things they said about me personally. Although I have the reputation for being a very sensitive person, I just did not care what they said, and they really could not touch me. I also have the reputation for being an emotional person, which can be a drawback in politics, but in those three and a half years I let my emotions work for me and for my mission.

Dealing with the Budget Crisis and the Reforms Simultaneously

Commentators have remarked on the fact that we sought to deal with the budget crisis while at the same time implementing a major reform program. Ironically, I believed that it was advantageous to do both simultaneously. The process of implementing the budget reductions energized the Department and concentrated their minds wonderfully. They knew I was serious, and that I would brook no attempts to sabotage the budget cuts. When attempts were made to do this I came down hard on the people concerned, and heads rolled. Having activated the Department, and shown a strong determination to achieve the budget cuts, I then mobilized and focused this energy and sense of purpose to implement the reforms.

Further, the vested interest groups, especially the teacher unions, were so outraged by the budget measures, that they became preoccupied with them, and concentrated their attacks on them. As a result, they paid less attention to the reform process, and although they vigorously attacked each new initiative as a matter of course, they did not fully understand that a major revolution was under way. In particular, they did not fully realize that I was in the process of dismantling the centralized system, on which they depended for their relevance, and giving schools back to their local communities. In short, the budget cuts diverted the attention of the opposition from the reform process, and blunted their attacks on it.

Support of my Colleagues

After the Premier, Jeff Kennett, the most valuable and consistent support came from the Treasurer, Alan Stockdale, whom I will always regard as a friend. It is true that Alan Stockdale and I were at times at odds over budget allocations to the Department of Education, and some of our discussions on this matter were vigorous in nature. However, Alan Stockdale recognized the paramount importance of improving the learning levels of our students and on the pursuit of excellence in our schools, and at all times gave me the utmost support in my reform program. He gave that support around the Cabinet table, in his discussions with influential groups in the business community and in his comments to the media.

The life of a reforming Minister can often be a lonely one in a political sense. Reforms are never easy, and there are many well organized vested interest groups who oppose you. Inevitably the going gets tough as the debate hots up. Some of one's colleagues begin to wonder whether you will win, or even survive. Those who are not of stout heart then tend to distance themselves from you and to stay silent. This was not the case with Alan Stockdale. He stuck with me through thick and thin, and he gave me that public support that made me feel that I was not alone and helped to sustain my spirit when the battles were raging.

I realized that the success of the revolution depended to a significant degree on securing and preserving the support of the Government backbench Members of Parliament. They would be the front line troops. The radical changes would affect the schools in their constituency. They would have to help sell the changes to their school councils and to their local communities. When the teacher unions and other vested interest groups attacked the changes at local meetings and in the local media they would have to defend them.

I realized very clearly from day one that the Backbench Members of Parliament were of critical importance to the Government and deserved support. If the Backbench had not won their seats, some of which had previously been held by the Labor Party for a long time, we would not be in Government, and I would not be a Minister. What's more, if these Backbenchers did not continue to hold their seats in the next election, we would not stay in Government. It was incredible to me that some of my Ministerial colleagues did not understand this, and tended to forget the Backbench once they became a Minister.

I went to extraordinary lengths to keep the Backbench informed and to promote the changes to them. I did this by frequent briefing meetings at which I would make presentations to them about the Schools of the Future program and planned initiatives. I followed this up by a constant flow of information in the mail and by fax. We always advised them in advance of any major announcement. If it affected their constituency we tried to arrange for the Member of Parliament to make the announcement in his or her local media in advance of the announcement I would make in the general media.

Whenever a Member of Parliament contacted my office with a question I either spoke to the MP myself or the MP was immediately put through to a senior member of my staff. If the MP had a problem with a school in his or her constituency, we ensured that immediate action was taken by the Department to address it. If an MP asked me to visit a school or to attend a function at a school I always accepted. If I had a previous engagement, we would attempt to negotiate another time so that I could meet both commitments. I doubt whether a Minister has ever gone to greater length to communicate with MPs, or to service their needs in their local constituencies.

Conclusion

There is no question that the period from October 1992 to March 1996 was one of revolution in education in Victoria. The reforms undertaken in Victoria during those years were unprecedented, comprehensive, coherent and far-reaching, and they transformed education in the state.

The revolution essentially involved changes in culture and focus. Teachers and schools, perhaps for the first time, clearly saw that the only reason for their existence was to add value to a student's time at school. The attention and energies of teachers were focused on the pursuit of excellence by each student and on the school's mission of helping each student achieve his or her potential and give them the best chance for the future. Teachers grasped the new freedom provided by Schools of the Future to use their professional skills and creativity to help each student to advance.

The resources of the school and the talents and energies of its people are concentrated and focused on improving the learning of each student. Schools were given operating autonomy and control of their resources so that they would be better placed to achieve this mission. At the same time, they are held strictly accountable for such achievement through the Accountability Framework.

The leadership qualities of the school principal and his or her status were enhanced by effective leadership training, together with performance-based contracts incorporating an annual performance review. The professionalism of teachers was enhanced through extensive new professional development opportunities (Personal Professional Development Program) and a new professional career structure and performance based recognition system (Professional Recognition Program).

Schools were provided with rigorous and world-leading curriculum and learning standards (Curriculum and Standards Framework) and an advanced student assessment program (Learning Assessment Project).

Schools are being re-engineered to enable students to capitalize on the new learning opportunities through information technology and telecommunications that have the potential to significantly advance student learning, especially that of students with a background of disadvantage. Clearly information technology will have a profound influence on the nature of learning and teaching, and will give greater power to students and teachers at the expense of 'the system'.

At the end of the day, the only reason for all this was to improve the quality of learning of students so as to give them a better chance for the future. Of course, fundamental to this was improving the quality and motivation of teachers and making teachers and schools more accountable to parents through proper assessment of students' learning and communicating better quality information to parents. The challenge is how to continue this improvement in the quality of learning, and we will seek to give some answers to this question later in this book, and to try to paint a picture for education over the next twenty years or so.

It is important for future reformers to consider the lessons one can learn from this period of revolutionary reform in Victoria. The most compelling lesson I learnt was that, if you want to achieve fundamental and widespread cultural change, you need a simple action message. In our case, the message was helping each child to achieve his or her potential so as to give them the best chance for the future. Also, the leader has to drive the change, which, as Minister, I did.

Another important lesson I learnt was that you cannot do it alone. The partnership between Jeff Kennett, Alan Stockdale and me was crucial to the success of the revolution. Both gave me both official and personal support that helped to sustain me when the going was tough. A further lesson was that the revolution must be well planned. The planning that John Roskam and I did in the funny little upstairs room of my electorate office in Chapel Street, Prahran was critical. When we came to Government, we were able to hit the ground running, before the vested interests in the existing system could fully mobilize their opposition. Yet another lesson was that you have to carry people with you. The seemingly endless meetings I attended in draughty halls on winter nights to sell the Schools of the Future program to school communities were worth all the head colds and the sore throats.

The revolution in Victoria is the type of watershed development that happens rarely in education. In fact, it probably marks one of the most profound changes in direction in school education ever in Australia. There is no doubt that it is of enormous consequence to the future of young Australians, and has worldwide implications as well.

We have led the way to a new beginning in education where the focus is on better preparing students for the remarkable and different opportunities of the twenty-first century. In Australia these will come from the rapid development and application of technology that will result in sharp economic and social transformations. We also proved that fundamental and widespread change and refocusing of an education system are possible, despite virulent opposition from entrenched, vocal and previously powerful special interest groups.

Schools of the Future are just the beginning. If we are to give our young people the best chance to make the most of the new opportunities that will emerge in the twenty-first century, we will need to take the revolution to a further, even more radical stage. That will be discussed later in this book, after we appraise the process and its outcomes from a wider perspective.

4 Appraising the Outcomes

In this chapter we reflect on the process and outcomes of Schools of the Future in the light of research on what has transpired in Victoria and in other places where similar school reforms have taken place. We organize the chapter in four parts. The first part of the chapter considers the scale of the change itself, which must be considered an example of a successful large-scale policy initiative. We believe this success is explained by a model that has been described in the literature on policy-making to account for such an outcome. This model was proposed by James Guthrie and Julia Koppich (Guthrie and Koppich, 1993).

In the second part of the chapter, we compare the experience of Don Hayward, as Minister for Education, with the experience of a counterpart in a similar reform, who has also written of his work, in this instance, the reflections of Kenneth Baker, who served as Secretary of State for Education in the Thatcher Government in the United Kingdom. He held this position in the time leading up to and following the 1988 Education Reform Act that led to many changes that are similar to those that occurred in Victoria.

We turn then to research on the processes and outcomes of reforms such as Schools of the Future, commencing with a review of studies in the international arena, principally the United States of America, Canada and Britain. For Victoria, we consider in some detail the findings of the Cooperative Research Project, a joint endeavour of the Victorian Primary Principals Association, the Victorian Association of State Secondary Principals, the Department of Education, and the University of Melbourne. This cooperative effort began soon after the announcement of plans for Schools of the Future in early 1993. The findings of a parallel independent study by US scholar, Allan Odden of the Consortium for Policy Research in Education based at the University of Wisconsin–Madison are considered. Attention is also given to other studies that are generally critical of the process and its outcomes.

Accounting for the Success of Schools of the Future

How is it that the reforms in Victoria were implemented in so comprehensive a fashion in such a short time, especially in contrast to what has occurred in other states, especially in New South Wales, the most populous state in Australia, where an ambitious and in some ways similar program fell short of intentions? Internationally, a similar question may be asked: why is it that reforms in Britain have been so sweeping and almost certainly irreversible when a similar effort in a much smaller nation, New Zealand, has not yet been fully implemented? On an even larger scale, the elements of the Victorian program have been advocated or implemented in one form or another in different parts of the United States but, after a decade or more, the picture is fragmented, and it seems that hardly a day passes that a new agenda for reform is not proposed.

In this section, we offer an explanation for events in Victoria that responds to these questions. While serving as a policy analysis in retrospect, it will be of interest and value for policy-makers in other nations where similar reforms are being planned or implemented. It will be of ongoing interest, if our view is confirmed that what has transpired thus far is just the first of several stages of what in a decade or two will be seen as the years of transition in the transformation of public education. Will the same conditions be evident to allow this vision to come to realization?

To account for success to date, we draw on a model proposed by James W. Guthrie and Julia E. Koppich in their efforts to build a model of educational reform (Guthrie and Koppich, 1993). It was offered as a framework for consideration of the education reform efforts in a number of nations, as set out in the book edited by Hedley Beare and William Lowe Boyd on the theme *Restructuring Schools: An International Perspective on the Movement to Transform the Control and Performance of Schools* (Beare and Boyd, 1993). It was written before the irreversibility of events in Britain became apparent and before implementation got under way in Victoria. In other words, there were no large-scale reforms to test the model when it initially appeared in the policy literature. It is thus timely to re-visit the model, which we believe serves as a useful frame to account for events in both places, but especially Victoria, and as a guide to policy-makers everywhere.

The model advanced by Guthrie and Koppich contends that successful reform on the scale we have described is contingent on the existence of three pre-conditions: alignment, initiative and mobilization, expressed as 'AIM' in the title of their work. They offer the following account:

> In order for significant political system changes, including educational reform, to occur, a number of politically related phenomena must exist and be appropriately aligned. This critical alignment is itself contingent upon an initiating event, or series of events, which inject uncertainty or disequilibrium into a political system. These irritating or unsettling conditions or set of provocations initiate political alignment. Finally, enactment of a reform agenda depends crucially upon the existence of a political 'champion'. A motivating individual or catalytic group is necessary to take advantage of enabling conditions and predisposing events. This policy entrepreneur provides intention, direction, and sustains reform momentum. (Guthrie and Koppich, 1993, p. 12)

Considering these three dimensions in more detail, the first pre-condition involves the alignment of four phenomena: public policy preferences, the existence of a 'political problem', an alternative policy or plan of action, and a favourable political environment. An event or series of events are required to initiate this alignment, a condition which 'provokes dissatisfaction with the status quo, begins to move the populace toward a value disequilibrium, and initiates shifts in deep-seated value preferences and popular opinion' (Guthrie and Koppich, 1993, p. 23). While alignment is crucial, individuals and groups must mobilize to take advantage of the window of opportunity that has been created. Guthrie and Koppich contend that 'policy windows' open when 'three separate and independent streams — problems, policies, and politics — join and present opportunities for action' and that 'policy entrepreneurs' are ready to act when the 'policy window' opens, allowing them to promote their preferred policy (Guthrie and Koppich, 1993, p. 25).

It seems that the model accounts for experience in Victoria. The election of the Kennett Liberal National Coalition Government in October 1992 was the culmination of a series of events that contributed over time to public rejection of the predecessor Cain and Kirner Labor Governments that had been in office since 1982. These events amounted to a general view that gross mismanagement of the state had occurred, manifested in a state debt of grave proportions and large deficit in the annual budget. Development in the state had stalled and there was a sense of gloom and despair, within the state and beyond, where Victoria was the butt of seemingly endless jokes about the state of its affairs.

The alignment of the four phenomena described by Guthrie and Koppich was evident, generally in the broad program of the Kennett Government before and following the election, including the education reform agenda as it unfolded after the election. These phenomena — public policy preferences, the existence of a 'political problem', an alternative plan of action, and a favourable political environment — may be readily identified in the account of Don Hayward in Chapter 2. This is not to say that there was broad consensus across the community on these matters; the contentious nature of much of what was proposed is clearly evident in the public debates and differences of view within the educational community, but alignment was sufficient to carry the day. While unpalatable to many, there was broad public consensus on matters concerned with school closures and amalgamations, as well as reductions in staffing levels, as the public at large accepted that these were part of a larger strategy to manage the public sector in the face of crippling debt and disturbing deficit. While there may be debate about the detail, the concept of a curriculum and standards framework was broadly embraced when contrasted with the absence of such a framework over all of the primary and much of the secondary sectors.

The alternative plan of action was most evident in intentions for Schools of the Future, the key elements of which were widely canvassed before the election, especially with school principals, and which were made relatively explicit in the election policy of the Liberal National Coalition. A more detailed plan was released within a few months, with implementation under way on all fronts in 1993. That the Minister had correctly read the environment was graphically illustrated by the fact that more than 700 of about 1700 schools expressed interest in participating in the pilot phase of Schools of the Future, resulting in the larger than anticipated involvement of just over 300 schools from mid-1993 and the scheduling of remaining schools in batches of 500 at six-monthly intervals so that all were involved by 1996.

The favourable political environment in this alignment was made manifest in the election result of 1992, when the Coalition assumed power with sweeping majorities in both houses of parliament (Legislative Assembly and Legislative Council). Significantly as far as further reform is concerned, this same favourable environment is evident for the second term of the Kennett Government, which was returned with similar majorities in the election of April 1996.

Guthrie and Koppich suggest that the alignment triggered by events such as those described here results in, or is associated with, 'a value disequilibrium' and 'shifts in deep-seated value preferences and popular opinion'. There is evidence that this disequilibrium had been under way for some time and that shifts in value preferences and popular opinion in respect to school reform were gathering momentum. To some extent, the previous Labor Government had sensed these in allowing parents to choose the school that their children could attend, through the abolition of zoning arrangements for schools. The readiness of parents to exercise that choice became more evident as the years passed, so, in respect to choice, a significant shift in values had certainly occurred. Popular opinion would appear to have also shaped proposals for, and acceptance of, such initiatives as the Curriculum and Standards Framework and, more recently, the Learning Assessment Project. The latter, involving assessment of primary students at years 3 and 5 in key areas, was bitterly contested if the headlines of the day are an indicator, but experience in more recent times suggests that the majority of parents value the information that is provided. Further shifts in public opinion are evident, leading to proposals of a kind we make in Chapter 6.

Clearly, the 'policy window' was open, but a further condition was required to satisfy the elements in the model proposed by Guthrie and Koppich. They contend that 'enactment of a reform agenda depends crucially upon the existence of a political 'champion', and that 'a motivating individual or catalytic group is necessary to take advantage of enabling conditions and predisposing events. This policy entrepreneur provides intention, direction, and sustains reform momentum'. In a general sense, the 'champion' and 'policy entrepreneur' for the reform agenda of the Government was the Premier, Jeff Kennett, but it is clear from the account Don Hayward provides in Chapters 2 and 3 that, in education, the Minister himself played that role. His relentless pursuit of the Schools of the Future reform agenda is readily attested by those who worked closely with him, if not in the view of the public at large.

One can apply a similar analysis to parallel or similar reforms, or attempts at similar reforms in other times and in other places. In Victoria, aspects of an earlier attempt at reform by Ian Cathie, Minister for Education in the Cain Labor Government in 1986 were similar to the self-managing elements of Schools of the Future, namely, a provision to give schools more responsibility for their budgets and the selection of staff. Intentions in the report *Taking Schools into the 1990s* were thwarted when the reform was opposed by teacher unions, parent organizations and elements of the bureaucracy, and the scheme was rejected by Cabinet. Alignment was not achieved within the government and among forces that were generally sympathetic to government, and Ian Cathie, as political 'champion', was unable to carry the day (see Government of Victoria, 1986 for the outcome of this episode).

In New South Wales, the Liberal National Coalition Government in the late 1980s and early 1990s led by Nick Greiner assembled a comprehensive program of reforms that were similar in important respects to Schools of the Future following a review of the system by consultant, Brian Scott (New South Wales, 1990). Much was successfully implemented under Minister for Education, Terry Metherall, with a significant exception being provision for local selection of teachers that was trenchantly opposed by teacher unions. Terry Metherall fell from power on an unrelated personal matter and was replaced by Virginia Chadwick, whose main brief was to settle the system following the turbulence of the Metherall years. Significantly, however, the government of Nick Greiner, and that led by his successor, John Fahey, lacked the decisive parliamentary majority enjoyed by Jeff Kennett. Indeed, for much of this time, it was on a knife-edge, relying on the support of independents. Alignment was not achieved here, as it was not in Victoria when Ian Cathie was Minister for Education, because there was no overriding sense of crisis or recognition of need for change in the broader community, as was evident when Kennett and Hayward came to power in 1992.

In contrast to experience in Victoria, there has been little success to date with large-scale educational reform in the United States. Perhaps the heart of this failure also lies in the difficulty of securing alignment which is so important in the explanatory model of Guthrie and Koppich. The cause is, to a large extent, explained by the governance arrangements, with the United States comprised of about 15,000 school districts in the fifty states. The federal government has little power, except for funding arrangements for special purposes, through so-called categorical grants targeted mainly at students at educational risk or with special learning or physical impairment. While the individual states have primary responsibility for school education, the implementation effort is fragmented in the multitude of school districts, ranging from small single school arrangements to the large complex systems in Dade County (Miami) in Florida, New York, Chicago and Los Angeles. Only the state of Hawaii has a single school district, which makes it comparable to Victoria and where large-scale decentralization has been attempted.

While there is broad community concern about school education, it has not been possible to effect the alignment achieved in Victoria. The exception is in Kentucky, which has a counterpart to most of the elements of Schools of the Future, and where the existence of a crisis was marked by the Supreme Court of Kentucky ruling that the system of education in its totality violated basic guarantees under the Constitution. On the other hand, the diversity of the US experience has resulted in a number of promising initiatives such as those that made up the New American Schools Development Corporation, now referred to as New American Schools (NAS), in which a range of small-scale reforms in teaching, learning and school organization are under way, with efforts to achieve scale-up in districts and states across the nation (see Stringfield, Ross and Smith, 1986 for accounts of school designs in NAS). Several will likely be of interest in the next stage of reform in Victoria, which starts with an advantage over NAS as far as large-scale change is concerned, since the latter tends to involve a loose collection of schools and school districts, in contrast to the coherence of reform across a single relatively large system, as is the case with the former. We give further consideration to NAS in Chapter 6.

Some degree of consistency with the model is evident in Edmonton, Canada, with Michael Strembitsky, Superintendent of Schools serving as 'champion' and 'policy entrepreneur'; and in New Zealand, where these roles were played initially by David Lange as Prime Minister and Minister for Education, and Russell Ballard, as Chief Executive Officer (see Caldwell and Spinks, 1992 for an account of how these roles were exercised in Edmonton and New Zealand; see Macpherson, 1993 for an account of the New Zealand reforms that utilizes the Guthrie and Koppich model). In each instance, however, the reform did not have the sweep of that achieved in Victoria. That sweep is more evident in Britain following the 1988 Education Reform Act. The 'champion' and 'policy entrepreneur' in a general sense was, of course, Margaret Thatcher, in her role as Prime Minister. In a more specific sense, however, these designations fall most appropriately on Kenneth Baker who served as Secretary of State for Education in the months leading up to the passage of the ERA and in the crucial years of implementation. Baker has recorded his experience in an autobiography *The Turbulent Years: My Life in Politics* (Baker, 1993), with Margaret Thatcher also making reference to events in her book *The Downing Street Years* (Thatcher, 1993). We now turn to these accounts for a brief international comparison with the experience recounted by Don Hayward in Chapters 2 and 3.

An International Comparison of Ministerial Experience

Britain, comprising England and Wales as far as the reforms under consideration here are concerned, has about 25,000 schools in 104 local education authorities. The concept of a national system locally administered through local education authorities, that prevailed for much of this century, took on a different connotation with the introduction of the local management of schools in the 1988 Education Reform Act (ERA). Local education authorities were required to decentralize at least 80 per cent of their budgets to schools along the lines of Schools of the Future. This fraction increased to 85 per cent, although in most authorities, the figure is closer to or exceeding 90 per cent. The ERA also created a national curriculum and a national system of testing at primary and secondary levels, with each having similarity to the Curriculum and Standards Framework and Learning Assessment Project in Victoria, although the latter does not involve the publication of results on a school-by-school basis (the so-called 'league tables') as in Britain. Another feature of the reforms in Britain, not evident in Victoria, is the creation of grant-maintained schools, wherein a school on majority vote of parents may elect to leave its local education authority and receive public funds directly through the Funding Agency for Schools, a national entity.

James Callaghan's Ruskin Speech

The Conservative Party first came to power under Margaret Thatcher in 1979, but it was not until 1988 that the elements of reform described above came together. Earlier, the alarm bells for reform were rung by the Prime Minister of the previous Labour Government, James Callaghan, in his so-called Ruskin Speech at Ruskin College, Oxford in 1976. Callaghan referred in particular to the control over education that was wielded by those in the industry, notably teachers and bureaucrats, and to the broader influence that was needed if schools were to be responsive to individual and national need. He also called for rigorous education standards, greater accountability, and high priority for literacy. These themes were not taken up in any coherent way until the 1988 Education Reform Act, where they were made explicit, as they have been in Victoria in Schools of the Future. Thus, in the context of this book, some twenty years encompasses the call for reform by a Labour Prime Minister in Britain, sweeping action twelve years later by the Thatcher Conservative Government, and the end of the first term of the Kennett Liberal National Coalition in Victoria where counterparts in Australia were set in motion.

The Thatcher View

Margaret Thatcher wrote that 'The starting point for the education reforms outlined in our general election manifesto [of 1987] was a deep dissatisfaction . . . with Britain's standard of education' (Thatcher, 1993, p. 590). She, along with her Secretary of State for Education in the mid-1980s, Sir Keith Joseph, were keen to introduce school vouchers as a major reform but accepted that such a measure could not be introduced directly. She noted that intentions could be achieved through open enrolment and local management:

> An essential element . . . was per capita funding, which means that state money followed the child to whatever school he attended. Parents would vote with their children's feet and schools actually gained resources when they gained pupils. The worse schools in these circumstances would either have to improve or close. In effect we had gone as far as we could towards a 'public sector voucher'. (Thatcher, 1993, p. 591)

Kenneth Baker became Secretary of State in May 1986 and thus had responsibility for preparing for such reform. We take up his story, noting the parallels with the experience of Don Hayward as recounted in Chapters 2 and 3 (page references are to Baker, 1993).

Similarities in the Experiences of Kenneth Baker and Don Hayward

There are four points of similarity in the experience of the two ministers.

1   Overall objectives

Both ministers shared the overall objective of improving the quality of education for all children and of the need for a comprehensive approach. Baker sensed the urgency of reform, as did Hayward, indicating 'I realised that the scale of the problem could only be tackled by a coherent national program, and time was not on our side' (p. 164). He expressed the view that decisive action was required:

> To be successful, a politician has to have both a clear vision and the determination to pursue it. By the 1980s I believed that there was an overpowering need for educational reform. The English system had lost its way in the 1960s. (p. 164)

2   Inertia of the bureaucracy

Baker was also concerned about the inertia of the bureaucracy. He asserted that 'schools policy remained the fiefdom of those officials brought up and bred in the DES [Department of Education and Science] tradition. They had seen to it that key policy battles with Ministers had been won by civil servants' (p. 166). He cites the inaction following Callaghan's Ruskin speech to illustrate his point. Referring to the view of Bernard O'Donoughue, who had served as Head of Callaghan's Policy Unit:

> 'The education profession reacted, predictably, with less generosity than the public. The NUT [National Union of Teachers] was furious. The Department of Education was shocked'. The Green Paper which followed the Callaghan speech was 'sparse in content and complacent in tone'. The officials at the DES had seen to that. This was 'Whitehall at its self-satisfied, condescending and imaginative worst'. Labour too had been thwarted by 'the resistance of professional vested interest to radical change'. (p. 168)

It is little wonder that the Thatcher Government finally moved so comprehensively and so quickly. While the timeframe and context are different, there are parallels in the action of the Kennett Government. The decisive action of the Labour Government of David Lange in New Zealand (Government of New Zealand, 1988), implementing the Picot Report of 1988 (Task Force to Review Educational Administration, 1988) that called for essentially the same package of reforms, also reflected frustration that intentions for reform in that nation had been thwarted for more than a decade.

3   Key elements in the strategy for reform

The following accounts by Baker in respect to national curriculum, national testing and the local management of schools resonate with the Hayward account in Chapters 2 and 3:

National Curriculum

I was convinced that the key to raising standards across the country was the national curriculum. (p. 189)

National Tests

However, a National Curriculum was not sufficient by itself to improve education standards unless, during the children's time at school, their progress was measured at regular intervals. This meant introducing the sort of regular testing that was a feature of other countries like France and Germany . . . (p. 192)

The purpose of introducing regular testing to underpin the National Curriculum was not to try to fail children but to determine what they had actually been able to absorb and assimilate at a particular time in their education . . . I also wanted the results of the tests to be published, so that parents and the local community would be able to see how well a school was doing. These were the famous 'league tables'. Again that was anathema to most of the profession, but it was something which parents wanted to know. (p. 199)

Local Management of Schools

I also wanted to increase the range of choice for parents in the state system . . . I started first with the management of schools. The principle which we argued over was decentralization, and the metaphor which I coined and used again and again was the hub and the rim of the wheel. I wanted to disperse responsibility away from the hub and down the spokes to the rim. (pp. 210–11)

An essential second step was to establish per capita funding for each pupil so that if a school attracted more pupils it would receive more money, while a less popular school would lose money . . . but we soon discovered that there were wide variations between education authorities and that similar schools in the same authority received very different amounts of money. We had to establish a formula that would eventually iron out these differences and treat schools on an equal basis. It would, of course, have to take into account the extra costs of small schools and rural schools. (pp. 212–13)

With the exception of 'league tables', the issues and strategies parallel the Victorian experience. Taken together with the earlier excerpts from the Baker memoir, one senses the same urgency, the same frustration at the inertia of the bureaucracy, and the same configuration of policies to address similar issues that had emerged over roughly the same period in the second half of the twentieth century.

4 Dealing with the teacher unions

Whilst each of the Baker reforms drew fierce opposition from traditional opponents, including the Labour Party and teachers unions, it is noteworthy that, by 1997, there had emerged a broad consensus that the local management of schools had been a success story and was there to stay, regardless of the outcome of the national election. Despite a flawed start to the National Curriculum that necessitated its re-design and an initial teacher boycott of the testing program, it is now evident that these will be a feature of the British scene in the foreseeable future. While no account is offered here about grant-maintained schools, for there is presently no counterpart in Victoria, it is apparent that the major features of these entities will remain. While the Victorian program of reform followed some years after what occurred in Britain, research to date suggests that it too is largely irreversible.

Baker, like Hayward in later years, succeeded in marginalizing teacher union officials. In this sense, then, the ministers were successful in communicating their reforms directly to constituencies at the local level, namely, parents and teachers, so that despite initial opposition or scepticism, the reforms proceeded without disruption and eventually, broad acceptance.

Differences in the Experiences of Kenneth Baker and Don Hayward

There are, however, four important differences in the experiences of the two ministers.

1 Curriculum and Standards Frameworks

It is noteworthy that the Curriculum and Standards Framework in Victoria proceeded smoothly, in both design and implementation, compared to the National Curriculum in Britain, which essentially had to be re-designed at great cost. The explanation here lies largely in the way the schemes were conceptualized. In Britain, the National Curriculum tended to be too broad and, at the same time, highly detailed and prescriptive, and the manner of its initial design precluded extensive consultation with teachers.

In contrast Don Hayward required the Board of Studies to engage in extensive consultation with teachers, numbering in the thousands, so that a high level of ownership and commitment was soon built. He also required the Curriculum and Standards Framework to be what the last word in the title clearly conveys, a set of broad guidelines rather than a detailed and prescriptive document. In the final analysis, following the successful review in Britain by Sir Ron Dearing, the new and broadly accepted National Curriculum is remarkably like the Curriculum and Standards Framework in its scope, level of specification and degree of acceptance by parents and the profession.

2   Testing program

The most obvious point of difference in the area of tests is that the British tests were implemented at primary and secondary levels and that the results for each school were made public in 'league tables'. In contrast, the Victorian tests were at the primary level only and public release was explicitly rejected. The response in Britain was a damaging boycott by teachers. In Victoria, while many teachers refused to administer them and the unions were trenchantly opposed, the tests proceeded without large-scale disruption and, within two years, there was broad acceptance by parents and an increasing number of teachers.

The explanation for differences in the climate of acceptance lies in the assurance Don Hayward gave at the outset that the Learning Assessment Project was primarily a guide for parents, teachers and students about the achievement of a child in relation to standards in the Curriculum and Standards Framework. With this primary purpose in mind, the Board of Studies was able to consult with a large number of teachers about the nature of the LAP, with the design and analysis outsourced to others.

3   Relationships with Cabinet and Premier/Prime Minister

There are several differences in the relationships between the ministers and their respective cabinets and leaders. These are partly explained by the time at which they came to office. Kenneth Baker was not the first or even the second of Margaret Thatcher's Secretaries of State for Education. While he had worked with his leader on other occasions in the past, including on some policy-related matters in education, Don Hayward was, in contrast, Minister for Education from the outset. Also, as is clear from his account in Chapter 2, Don Hayward enjoyed a close relationship with Jeff Kennett during the years in Opposition and the two had developed together the key features of the intended reforms. There was a high level of trust between the two to the point that as Premier, Kennett never interfered or imposed his will or took a contrary stance. Kenneth Baker's memoir provides several illustrations of Margaret Thatcher taking a different or prior position to Kenneth Baker on a few matters of importance that made implementation difficult, at least in the short term.

Baker's account also illustrated how frequently he had to refer matters to the Prime Minister, to Cabinet and to Cabinet Sub-Committees. In contrast, Hayward rarely referred matters to Cabinet. An exception was on matters related to the budget, when reference to, and the approvals of, Treasurer and the Budget and Economic Review Committee were always required.

4   Complexity in the legislative process

Preparations for the 1988 Education Reform Act were long and complex as far as preparing and gaining approval for legislation were concerned. By contrast, implementing Schools of the Future required very little legislative change. Most changes were made through powers of the Minister for Education under existing legislation.

Other Views of the Introduction of Schools of the Future

Another view of the experiences of Kenneth Baker and Don Hayward was offered by John Gough and Tony Taylor of Monash University, who gave particular attention to similarities and differences in respect to curriculum reform (Gough and Taylor, 1996). Similarities include the sidelining of teacher unions and a determination to proceed quickly with comprehensive reform. Differences include the more extensive consultation that preceded the adoption of the Curriculum and Standards Framework in Victoria. These confirm the accounts of Baker and Hayward.

The analysis is astray in other respects, perhaps understandable given their generally negative stance to what has occurred in each setting, and they fail to acknowledge that, despite problems in implementation, there is a coherence to the reforms that has led to broad public acceptance, especially in Britain where all political parties now embrace the major features, including the national curriculum and, especially, the local management of schools.

An intemperate comment on the introduction of Schools of the Future was offered in the early months of the reform by John Smyth, formerly of Deakin University, now at Flinders University, in his edited book *A Socially Critical View of the Self-Managing School* (Smyth, 1993). The book is a robust scholarly discourse on the concept and practice of the self-managing school from a number of writers who draw on a range of perspectives and experiences in the tradition of critical theory, but Smyth's introduction to the book departs from such discourse:

> Since this book was completed, many of the predictions about what was envisaged as likely to happen under a conservative government in Victoria have come to pass ... It is interesting that perpetrators of policies like those behind that of the *Self-Managing School* are so arrogantly self-assured of the 'rightness' of what they are doing and the efficacy of their own narrow minded ideas that they are prepared to go to the extreme of closing off public debate by steamrolling them in without proper public discussion. Could it be that those who deem to 'know best' in respect of these matters understand that were their ideas allowed to be put under the light of careful debate and scrutiny, they would in all likelihood be exposed for the fraud that they are? What other explanations are there for governments who stoop to pushing through controversial measures like this in the dark of night? Far from actions like this being a sign of courage and leadership, they are a shameful and shallow reminder of what is coming to pass as 'democracy' in Western capitalist countries. (Smyth, 1993, pp. 8–9)

The reality is that the main elements of Schools of the Future had been widely canvassed in the public arena by Don Hayward prior to the election campaign of 1992, were spelt out in the election policy of the then Opposition in the weeks leading up to the poll, and were the focus of a ministerial statement in early 1993 (Hayward, 1993) that was the subject of wide consultation before the final form of implementation was determined. Implementation was more expansive than originally proposed because the number of schools seeking to enter the program was well above expectations. As Don Hayward made clear in Chapter 3, schools could choose the year they wished to join the program. Implementation occurred largely by Ministerial action, since little change to the existing Act set up by the previous Labor government was required. This sequence can hardly be described as 'a shameful and shallow reminder of what is coming to pass as "democracy" . . .' The actions in the 'dark of night' described by Smyth were late night debates in parliament on matters other than Schools of the Future.

Of course, many of the key elements of Schools of the Future were developed in the months and years following the events described by Smyth, including the Curriculum and Standards Framework, that was the focus of extensive consultation in 1993 and 1994, in contrast to the initially aborted British experience that involved relatively little consultation. Similarly for the development of a funding mechanism for decentralizing resources to schools, that came about in an orderly manner, shaped by recommendations of the Education Committee of the School Budget Research Project chaired by Brian Caldwell that met from early 1994 to the end of December 1996 (see Education Committee 1994, 1995, 1996 for accounts of the processes, consultations and recommendations arising from this work). The accountability framework was also developed in a methodical manner, with the approach to triennial reviews being trialed before full implementation in 1997, carefully balancing local responsibility with external validation.

The substance of the critique by other writers in the collection edited by Smyth is one that we do not share. Many of the issues raised are concerned with quite fundamental issues that are shaping public education and the profession of teaching, triggered in the main by the social transformation that is sweeping much of the world, but affected by the budget crises that are impacting the public school in many, mainly western nations. They are not a consequence of the self-managing school. We address these issues in Chapter 5. The irony in terms of a democratic tradition is that the concept of self-management or local management was embraced by all political parties in Britain in the election campaign of 1997, reflecting its broad acceptance, by the profession as well as by the public. In one of his first statements following the election, incoming Labour Secretary of State for Education, David Blunkett, made clear that 'We're committed to devolving a greater part of the budget' and set in train a review to help determine how this could be accomplished (cited by St. John-Brooks, 1997, p. 1).

Research on the Outcomes

There is a growing body of evidence about the processes and outcomes of reforms like Schools of the Future. For the most part they have failed to explain what impact, if any, there is on learning outcomes for students, although the logic of the reform suggests that they ought to have effects in this domain, especially in relation to planning and resource allocation, with a focus on building the capacity of staff to improve the quality of learning and teaching.

We provide an international perspective in the first instance, drawing on research from the United States, then from Britain. Unfortunately, the former consists of studies of school-based management, just one element of comprehensive reform of the kind we are considering, and it is understandable that evidence on impact is limited. The British research deals with a more comprehensive program, and while effects are discernible, there is little to illuminate the causal links between elements in the reform and outcomes for students.

Much of the chapter draws from research on the processes and outcomes of Schools of the Future as reflected in the Cooperative Research Project where significant benefits were identified, including analysis that suggests direct and indirect links between the major elements of the reform as experienced in schools, and perceptions of principals in respect to improvements in curriculum and learning. In brief, the evidence points to the value of a curriculum and standards framework, the focus that is afforded by the school charter, the resource flexibility that comes with decentralizing the budget to the school level, and the utilization of resources in patterns that respond to priorities in learning and teaching. Particular attention is given to staffing flexibility and professional development.

Problems of implementation are acknowledged and addressed, especially in respect to the increased workload, lack of administrative support, shortage of resources, and continuing constraints on action at the school level by the bureaucracy. These problems are, to some extent, endemic in the nations under consideration.

An International Perspective

United States and Canada

Research from the United States and Canada of greatest interest is on school-based management (SBM) or school-site management, being essentially the capacity for self-management (Schools of the Future in Victoria) and local management (Britain). There is now more than twenty years of experience with school-based management and the literature in the late 1990s contains several meta-analyses or syntheses of different investigations over the years. One of the best in our view is by Summers and Johnson (1996).

Summers and Johnson confirm the generally held view that school-based management has so many different meanings and has been practised in so many different ways that it is difficult to generalize from experience, the only common element and 'cornerstone' being the delegation of authority to the school defined on three dimensions: 'the areas of decision making to which the increased authority applies, the constraints limiting exercise of that authority, and the collection of individuals who receive the new authority' (Summers and Johnson, 1996, p. 77).

Summers and Johnson located seventy studies that purported to be evaluations of school-based management, but only twenty of these employed a systematic approach and just seven included a measure of student outcomes. They conclude, with justification, that 'there is little evidence to support the notion that SBM is effective in increasing student performance. There are very few quantitative studies, the studies are not statistically rigorous, and the evidence of positive results is either weak or non-existent' (p. 80).

A sustained positive view is presented in surveys of opinion in the Edmonton Public School District in Alberta, Canada, a city system of about 200 schools with nearly twenty years' experience. In the early stages, the focus of school-based management in Edmonton was the budget; hence its early designation as an initiative in school-based budgeting. All principals, teachers, students, system personnel and a representative sample of parents are surveyed annually. Brown's independent analysis of the evidence to the end of the first decade of system-wide experience led him to observe that:

> The Edmonton surveys reveal an increase in the form of satisfactions registered by large numbers of parents, students and personnel working in schools and district office. These results appear stable, significant, and superior to those observed in general surveys conducted in the rest of Canada and the United States. (Brown, 1990, p. 247)

Apart from the 'overwhelming obstacles' in the way of assessing the impact of SBM, Summers and Johnson draw attention to the fact that few initiatives 'identify student achievement as a major objective. The focus is on organizational processes, with virtually no attention to how process changes may affect student performance' (Summers and Johnson, 1996, pp. 92–3). For Eric Hanushek of the University of Rochester in New York, and Chair of the Panel on the Economics of Educational Reform, the findings are not surprising because of the absence of a purposeful link between SBM and student performance. He notes the review of Summers and Johnson and observes that 'Decentralization of decisionmaking has little general appeal without such linkage and, indeed, could yield worse results with decentralized management pursuing its own objectives not necessarily related closely to student performance' (Hanushek, 1996, p. 45). In establishing principles of reform that might provide incentives to reward performance, he concludes that 'Some form of site-based management is likely to be an important ingredient in new incentive systems' (p. 45).

Those familiar with the comprehensive reforms in Britain and Victoria will not be surprised by these findings, given that these reforms explicitly link school-based management to a curriculum and standards framework, with various testing and accountability mechanisms in place or under development. It is interesting that Marshall Smith, Under Secretary, US Department of Education, in commenting on the reform agenda of the Clinton Administration (Smith, Scoll and Link, 1996), draws attention to the importance of linkage by referring to the findings of an OECD study that parallels those of Summers and Johnson (OECD, 1994). The concluding sentence in the quotation below might well express the exasperation of those familiar with coherent reforms such as Schools of the Future.

School-based management may improve certain complementary aspects of schooling, not the least of which may be teacher morale and enthusiasm for the reform effort; however, little empirical evidence can be mustered to support the assertion that greater stakeholder participation directly improves student performance.

The OECD report goes on to suggest, however, that to the degree that a reorganization effort is conducted with a clarity of purpose to improve classroom teaching and learning, positive outcomes may accrue. In other words, to improve student learning, the content and instruction delivered to students must change as well as the organizational structure of the school. They complement each other.

This is not rocket science. (Smith, Scoll and Link, 1996, p. 21)

Research on charter schools in the USA will be worth watching as experience in this approach to reform gathers momentum. Charter schools, in their most powerful manifestation, are free of school district control, receive funds from the public purse but may charge no tuition fees, and may be established by individuals, organizations and even universities. In early 1997, it was too soon to draw conclusions. Bierlein and Bateman make the following assessment of progress to date:

In theory, charter schools attempt to break down the ingrained status quo elements of the system, and in reality, a great deal has been accomplished. Nearly 250 charter schools are already in operation. Many students who had not been successful in the traditional public school setting are now succeeding. Unique community and business partnerships are being formed, with many traditional 'outsiders' becoming intimately involved in the public education arena. Most importantly, ripple effects across the broader system are becoming visible as districts respond to pressures created by charter schools. (Bierlein and Bateman, 1996, p. 167)

However, Bierlein and Bateman identify forces that are working against the charter movement, and they conclude that 'Unless well-coordinated efforts are undertaken to battle the many opposing forces, we predict that the charter school concept will simply not be strong enough medicine to become a broad-based reform initiative' (Bierlein and Bateman, 1996, pp. 167–8). In our view, what these writers are raising is the issue of alignment, the phenomenon we described at the start of the chapter to account for the success of Schools of the Future. We return to the issue in the final chapter.

Britain

There is a growing research base on the impact of the local management of schools in Britain, where up to eight years' experience has been gained. Levacic (1995,

p. 190), a specialist at the Open University in the economics and finance of education, with a particular interest in local management, found that, of four criteria associated with intentions for the local management of schools (effectiveness, efficiency, equity and choice), 'cost-efficiency is the one for which there is most evidence that local management has achieved the aims set for it by government', especially through the opportunity it provides for schools to purchase at a lower cost for a given quality or quantity than in the past, and by allowing resource mixes that were not possible or readily attainable under previous more centralized arrangements. She found evidence for effectiveness to be more tenuous, although the presumed link is through efficiency, making resources available to meet needs not able to be addressed previously.

In Britain, as elsewhere, there has been no research to determine the cause-and-effect relationship between local management and discretionary use of resources and improved learning outcomes for students, although there is opinion to the effect that gains have been made. Bullock and Thomas (1994, pp. 134–5) reported that an increasing number of principals believe there are benefits from local management [LM] for student learning. In responding to the statement that 'Children's learning is benefiting from LM', the number of agreements among primary principals increased from 30 per cent in 1992 to 44 per cent in 1992 to 47 per cent in 1993. A similar pattern was evident among principals of secondary schools, increasing from 34 per cent in 1991 to 46 per cent in 1992 to 50 per cent in 1993. Among both primary and secondary principals, those in larger schools were more positive than those in smaller schools. For example, in 1993, among primary principals, 41 per cent of those in smaller schools agreed compared with 50 per cent in larger schools; among secondary principals, 30 per cent of those in smaller schools agreed compared to 80 per cent of those in larger schools.

Another finding in the surveys reported by Bullock and Thomas is related to whether principals would wish to return to arrangements that existed prior to the local management of schools. Principals were asked to respond to the statement 'I would welcome a return to pre-LM [local management] days'. Disagreement (indicating a favourable experience with local management) increased among both groups: with primary principals from 70 per cent in 1991 to 76 per cent in 1992 to 81 per cent in 1993; for secondary principals from 85 per cent in 1991 and 1992 to 93 per cent in 1993. These findings are of interest in the light of a similar question asked in a survey in the Cooperative Research Project on Schools of the Future reported later in the chapter.

On other outcomes, while her research did not explicitly address these elements, Levacic cited the case study research of Ball, Bowe and colleagues in respect to distributive equity and choice:

> . . . the indications are that socially disadvantaged parents are less able to avoid ineffective schools for their children. There is also ad hoc evidence that schools in socially deprived areas have suffered a loss of pupils to other schools . . . (Levacic, 1995, p. 195)

Such effects raise the stakes in ensuring that all schools develop a capacity for school improvement, drawing on much sturdier 'theories of learning' derived from research on school and classroom effectiveness than have existed in the past. Also indicated is an approach to marketing that ensures all parents have information about schools that their children may attend.

In general, the critiques of research on school-based management in Canada and the United States can be applied just as powerfully to research in Britain, even though reform in the latter has the coherence advocated by Summers and Johnson; Hanushek; and Smith, Scoll and Link in their commentaries on the North American literature. No meta-analyses or syntheses of research on the British experience have been attempted at the time of writing.

Hong Kong

Research on school-based management in Hong Kong, led by Y.C. Cheng and W.M. Cheung, is arguably at the forefront internationally, not only conceptually and methodologically, but also in the manner in which it is beginning to illuminate the links between the practice of school-based management or self-management and outcomes for students. The conceptual framework set out in an award-winning paper (Cheung and Cheng, 1996) and in a book by Cheng (1996) asserts that there are three levels of self-management or school-based management that are important: school, group and teacher. If one seeks an impact on learning, it is not sufficient simply to decentralize authority and responsibility to the school; it must penetrate the classroom. Confirmation of the model was secured through research by Cheung, reports of which are now making their appearance at international conferences such as the International Congress of School Effectiveness and Improvement (Cheng and Cheung, 1997).

The schools in which Cheung conducted his research were participating in the School Management Initiative (SMI) established by the Education Department of Hong Kong in the early 1990s following a review of management in Hong Kong Schools conducted as part of a larger Public Sector Review. The SMI called for schools to volunteer their participation in an approach involving higher levels of local participation in decision-making, more resource flexibility, a deeper planning capacity and more accountability. By 1997, almost all government schools and a small fraction of schools in the aided sector had joined (in Hong Kong, only about 8 per cent of schools are government schools, with most of the others being aided schools that are privately or corporately owned but receiving grants from government to meet a major part of their recurrent costs).

It is interesting that the Education Commission in Hong Kong, established in 1984 to make recommendations on education policy, has called for full implementation of the SMI approach in all schools by 2000, referring to it more generically as school-based management but, significantly, proposing that it be integrated with a range of practices in pursuit of quality schooling for all. The linkages that emerge as so important in the review of research on school-based management are intended for Hong Kong. The Education Commission observed that:

With the implementation of the School Management Initiative in 1991, the Education Department has introduced certain arrangements which provide School Management Initiative schools with a more accountable framework for school-based management with teacher, parent and student participation. After several years of implementation, the experience from School Management Initiative schools suggests that such management is helpful in achieving school goals and in formulating long-term plans to meet student needs. The Commission therefore recommends that all schools should by the year 2000 practise school-based management in the spirit of School Management Initiative so that they can develop quality education according to the needs of their students. (Education Commission, 1996, xi)

Cooperative Research Project

In Victoria, Schools of the Future was the focus of a major investigation known as the Cooperative Research Project, established in early 1993 as a joint endeavour of the Department of Education, Victorian Association of State Secondary Principals, the Victorian Primary Principals Association and the University of Melbourne. Its purpose was to monitor the processes and outcomes of Schools of the Future. The project was managed by a Steering Committee of two representatives of each of the four participating organizations and chaired by Fay Thomas.

The project was a five-year longitudinal study with several components, including broadly framed surveys and highly focused investigations, with the former conducted by the Steering Committee, and the latter by post-graduate research candidates at the University of Melbourne. There were several related projects and international links with similar work were established.

Scale of the Project

Reported here are the findings from the sixth survey of principals of Schools of the Future. The first three surveys were conducted shortly after schools in the first three intakes completed their charters: intake 1 in late 1993, intake 2 in early 1994, and intake 3 in late 1994. A fourth survey of intake 1, twelve months after introduction, was also conducted in late 1994. A fifth survey was conducted in late 1995 with principals in a representative sample of schools in intakes 1, 2, 3 and 4, after implementation in all but three schools in the state, and after all features of Schools of the Future had been introduced. The sixth survey was completed in late 1996, again in a representative sample of schools, after intake 1 schools had completed three years in the program and were about to undertake their first triennial review.

The findings of the first survey were published as *The Base-line Survey* (Cooperative Research Project, 1994). The findings of the second survey of principals of intake 1 schools, twelve months after the base-line study, were published as *One Year Later* (Cooperative Research Project, 1995a). The findings of the first four surveys were published as *Taking Stock* (Cooperative Research Project, 1995b). The fifth report was titled *A Three Year Report Card* (Cooperative Research Project, 1996), reflecting its publication three years after the commencement of the project and as the Kennett Government finished its first term. The report of the sixth survey was titled *More Work to Be Done . . . But No Turning Back* (Cooperative Research Project, 1997), for, as is evident in the findings summarized below, it became clear that principals, by an overwhelming margin, preferred the new arrangements to the old, even though there were issues to be resolved in implementation.

In addition to the foregoing, by the start of 1997, fifteen more focused invest-igations by post-graduate research students at the University of Melbourne had been completed or were in progress. Topics included the early adoption of school charters, leadership styles of female principals, attitudes of teachers to Schools of the Future, principals' perceptions of their roles, professional development needs of primary principals, leadership among secondary principals, stressors and coping mech-anisms among primary principals, strategic leadership by principals, leadership and the management of change, secondary schools as exemplary learning organizations, cost-benefit analysis of principal professional development programs, links between elements of the reform and improved learning outcomes for students, creation of leadership teams, and the Professional Recognition Program. New insights into leader-ship theory were obtained in the doctoral research of David Gurr (see Gurr, 1996a, 1996b and 1996c).

Links were established with other major research efforts, notably with the work of Allan Odden, Director, Consortium for Policy Research in Education, University of Wisconsin at Madison, whose parallel but independent study of Schools of the Future is reported later in the chapter (Odden and Odden, 1996).

We are not aware of such a comprehensive research effort on a similar reform in any other country. Readers can have a measure of confidence in the findings that may be difficult to achieve with one-off surveys, especially where there has been no systematic sampling or low response rate, and or in case studies in selected schools on a one-shot basis.

Scope of the Survey

The sixth survey in 1996 included items on confidence in the attainment of object-ives of Schools of the Future; sources of information and support for principals; support for involvement in Schools of the Future; role of the principal, including time devoted to the principalship and job satisfaction; benefits experienced thus far; improvements in areas of school charter and each element in the framework of Schools of the Future, namely, Professional Recognition Program, full staffing flexibility/workforce planning, school global budgets, accountability; curriculum and standards frameworks, and teacher professional development planning. These items had all been asked in 1995 and, with the exception of those concerned with elements of the framework, had been asked in earlier surveys. Comparisons of responses across all years was thus possible.

In 1996, there were six new questions that are important to the title of the research report, namely, whether principals preferred the new arrangements or conditions that prevailed before the introduction of Schools of the Future. The Steering Committee had considered such questions earlier in the reform but determined to wait until all schools were involved and there was a 'critical mass' of schools with at least three years of experience. These conditions were satisfied in 1996.

Sample Size and Rate of Response

A representative sample of 500 schools was drawn from all schools that had joined Schools of the Future, these numbering about 1700. This was a structured, representative sample reflecting differences among schools according to type, size, geographical location, and year of entry in Schools of the Future.

A total of 339 useable responses was received from the 500 principals surveyed, representing a rate of response of 67.8 per cent compared to rates in earlier surveys of 69.2 per cent for intake 1 (base-line), 66.2 per cent for intake 1 (one year later), 53.0 per cent for intake 2, 41.4 per cent for intake 3 and 57.0 per cent for the first survey across all intakes (1995). This is a noteworthy achievement given that the survey was conducted in Term 4 soon after a further round of school amalgamations was initiated and that the survey was the most complex yet constructed.

Summary of Findings

Except where indicated, the findings reported here are taken from the report of the sixth survey (Cooperative Research Project, 1997). They were also reported at the Annual Meeting of the American Educational Research Association in March 1997 (Caldwell, Gurr, Hill and Rowe, 1997). The reader is referred to the full report (Cooperative Research Project, 1997) and its counterparts in previous years (Cooperative Research Project, 1994, 1995a, 1995b, 1996) for the rich range of findings and analyses, with interesting commentary on differences among the perceptions of principals when classified according to such variables as age; gender; type, size and location of school; and length of experience as a principal. Most of the data analysis for the sixth survey was conducted by Dr David Gurr, Department of Education Policy and Management at the University of Melbourne. Ken Rowe at Melbourne's Centre for Applied Educational Research undertook the structural equation modelling.

In general, principals across all intakes in 1996 were confident that the objectives and purposes of Schools of the Future will be attained in their schools and reported moderate to high realization of expected benefits or capacities in most elements of the reform, especially in planning and resource allocation, but also in personnel and professional matters and, also, in curriculum and learning. These confirmed the 1995 findings, with evidence of a higher level of benefit in 1996 in the personnel and professional domain. The sense of direction provided by the school charter and opportunities for professional development in areas related to reform, especially the Curriculum and Standards Framework, are identified as 'success stories'. Principals valued above all other sources the information provided by and support of their colleagues. There was evidence that the deeper culture of the system is changing, with a focus on the school rather than on the region and centre.

Problems of workload and frustration at constraints on flexibility were significant and consistent with those identified in earlier surveys. Mean workload was 59 hours per week, the same as in 1995, but 69 per cent indicated that the workload was higher than expected, also a consistent finding in recent years.

Mean job satisfaction was down, to a mean of 4.3 on a 7-point scale, compared to 5.3 on the base-line survey and 4.6 in the 1995 survey. The modal rating of job satisfaction was 5, the same as in 1995, but down from 6 in the earlier surveys. Principals were asked to compare their job satisfaction with that twelve months earlier, with 18 per cent reporting higher, 38 per cent reporting the same, and 44 per cent reporting lower, these proportions being similar to those found in 1995.

There are some consistent differences in view when the responses of the least and the most satisfied groups of principals are compared. Across most of the questions asked of principals, the least satisfied group of principals were the most negative respondents. To a lesser extent, the most satisfied group of principals were the most positive respondents. What is clear is that there are at least three different groups of principals: those that are highly satisfied and generally positive about Schools of the Future, a middle group in terms of satisfaction who have mixed views about Schools of the Future, and a highly dissatisfied group who are generally negative about Schools of the Future.

Overall, compared to 1995, a higher level of realization of benefits was reported and there was a levelling off in depth of concern on a range of problems. Workload seems to have peaked. In contrast, there was a slight weakening in confidence in the achievement of objectives and there has been a decline in levels of principals' job satisfaction. It may be that the latter was due in part to a generally negative view of the principal performance management scheme, including the accreditation process and annual performance planning, the outcomes of which lead to differential bonus payments of up to 15 per cent of salary.

The most noteworthy findings relate to the views of principals about whether they would wish their schools to return to previous arrangements, prior to the implementation of Schools of the Future. They were asked to give five ratings, four related to each of the four elements in the framework for Schools of the Future, the other an overall rating. The overwhelming majority of principals would not wish their schools to return to pre-Schools of the Future arrangements, being 82 per cent for the curriculum framework, 89 per cent for the resources framework, 77 per cent for the people framework, 77 per cent for the accountability framework, and 86 per cent in an overall sense. Principals who had served as principals under both arrangements were asked to indicate their personal preference. In this instance 70 per cent indicated their preference for being a principal since the implementation of Schools of the Future.

These findings indicate a preference for the framework of self-management at a similar level to that reported for Britain cited earlier in the chapter. Bullock and Thomas (1994) reported a preference for new arrangements, with a trend for primary principals from 70 per cent in 1991 to 76 per cent in 1992 to 81 per cent in 1993; and for secondary principals from 85 per cent in 1991 and 1992 to 93 per cent in 1993. This suggests the same broad acceptance for self-management under Schools of the Future in 1996 as developed by mid-decade in Britain for the local management of schools. There are, however, some interesting differences when the Schools of the Future findings are broken down on a primary and secondary basis. In Victoria, overall, 87 per cent of primary principals in 1996 would not wish their schools to return to pre-Schools of the Future arrangements, which is higher than the 81 per cent preferring local management in Britain, whereas 82 per cent of secondary principals in 1996 would not wish a return, compared to 93 per cent in Britain. In both instances, the surveys were taken about three years after most schools had entered the reform program. It appears that primary principals in Victoria are more accepting of the new arrangements than their counterparts in Britain and than their secondary colleagues.

Acknowledged here are the consistent findings in reports of the Cooperative Research Project related to workload, the rate of change, levels of 'bureaucratic interference' and perceived shortcomings in implementation. These indicate that there is indeed 'more work to be done'. But one must be struck by the preference principals have for the new arrangements despite these concerns, a point made also by Tony Misich who, while serving as President of the Western Australia Primary Principals Association, received the Australian Primary Principals Association 1995–6 Telstra Research Award to study developments in Australia and New Zealand. He observed that:

> . . . one common variable is that all Principals, having gone down the path of devolved decision making, do not wish to return to a more centralized system, regardless of the extra work and responsibility. There is far greater satisfaction in schools being 'in charge' at the local level. (Misich, 1996, p. 3)

> Principals everywhere have hailed the devolved budget as the most concrete tool to affect any real decision for school improvement. (Misich, 1996, p. 7)

Findings Related to Outcomes

The findings for those aspects of the survey that focused on, or included, items related to learning outcomes for students are reported in this section of the chapter.

These are concerned with levels of confidence that the objectives of Schools of the Future will be attained, the extent of realization of expected benefits, and the impact to date of the Curriculum and Standards Framework.

1   Confidence in the attainment of objectives

A key component in each survey has been an invitation to respondents to rate their confidence that the objectives and purposes of Schools of the Future will be attained in their schools. These objectives and purposes are those contained in the ministerial statement on Schools of the Future of January 1993 (Hayward, 1993). A confidence scale from 1 ('low') to 5 ('high') was provided. The distribution of responses is shown in Table 4.1, with mean ratings of confidence for each of the surveys conducted to date.

A feature of the ratings is the moderate to high levels of confidence across all items for each of the five surveys, with mean scores in the range 3.0–4.3. For the 1996 survey, at least 80 per cent of respondents provided a rating of 3 or higher for five of nine items. The modal rating was 4 for all but one item. While there has been a slight weakening of confidence over the life of the project for all objectives, it is fair to conclude on the basis of the mean, mode and distribution of responses that, overall, principals have sustained a moderate to high level of confidence that the objectives and purposes of Schools of the Future will be attained in their schools.

The two items with the highest mean ratings in 1996 were the same as those in each of the previous surveys, but the order was reversed, with the 'accountability' objective supplanting the 'good schools' objective:

- Schools of the Future are accountable to the community for the progress of the school and the achievements of its students (mean of 3.8 in 1996 compared to 4.1 in base-line survey of 1993 and 3.8 in last annual survey in 1995).
- Schools of the Future actively foster the attributes of good schools in terms of leadership, school ethos, goals, planning and accountability (mean of 3.7 in 1996 compared to 4.3 in base-line survey in 1993 and 3.9 in last annual survey in 1995).

2   Realization of expected benefits

Principals in the base-line study in 1993 were invited to list the benefits they expected from their schools being Schools of the Future. Twenty-five benefits were classified in four areas — curriculum and learning, planning and resource allocation, personnel and professional, and school and community — and included in the survey of intake 1 principals one year later. Essentially, the second survey asked of principals: 'You expected these benefits when you were surveyed in the early stages of Schools of the Future, to what extent have these benefits been realized twelve months later?' As in the second and subsequent surveys, principals were asked to indicate the extent to which these benefits had been realized in their

Table 4.1:   Confidence that objectives and purposes will be attained in schools as perceived by principals in 1996 survey

Objective/Purpose	Lo 1	2	3	4	Hi 5	Mean all intakes 1996	Previous surveys[1] 1	2	3	4	5
Schools of the Future . . .											
• encourage the continuing improvement in the quality of educational programs and practices in Victorian schools to enhance student learning outcomes	3	9	28	**47**	14	3.6	3.6	3.8	3.7	3.7	3.6
• actively foster the attributes of good schools in terms of leadership, school ethos, goals, planning and accountability process	1	8	20	**58**	13	3.7	4.3	4.2	4.1	4.0	3.9
• build on a statewide framework of quality curriculum, programs and practices	4	14	34	**39**	9	3.4	3.4	3.6	3.4	3.5	3.5
• encourage parents to participate directly in decisions that affect their child's education	6	22	30	**32**	10	3.2	3.5	3.5	3.4	3.4	3.3
• recognize teachers as true professionals, able to determine their own careers and with the freedom to exercise their professional skills and judgments in the classroom	11	22	**30**	28	9	3.0	3.2	3.2	3.2	3.3	3.2
• allow principals to be true leaders in their school with the ability to build and lead their teaching teams	6	16	28	**39**	11	3.3	4.1	3.8	4.0	3.7	3.4
• enable communities, through the school charter, to determine the destiny of the school, its character and ethos	5	14	34	**36**	11	3.3	3.8	3.8	3.7	3.6	3.4
• within guidelines, enable schools to develop their own programs to meet the individual needs of students	6	16	24	**42**	12	3.4	3.9	3.8	3.6	3.8	3.5
• are accountable to the community for the progress of the school and the achievements of its students	2	6	24	**51**	18	3.8	4.1	4.1	4.0	3.9	3.8
Overall Mean						**3.4**	**3.8**	**3.7**	**3.7**	**3.6**	**3.5**

Source: Cooperative Research Project, 1997, pp. 25–6

Note: [1] Key to previous surveys: 1 = intake 1 (pilot),   2 = intake 1 (one year later),   3 = intake 2,   4 = intake 3,   5 = all intakes, 1995

Table 4.2: *Extent to which expected benefit has been realized in school as perceived by principals in 1996 survey*

Expected benefit	Level of realization (%)					Mean all intakes 1996	Mean all intakes 1995	Mean intake[1] 1994
	Lo 1	2	3	4	Hi 5			
Curriculum and Learning								
More relevant and responsive curriculum	5	13	**39**	36	6	3.2	3.1	3.1
Improved learning outcomes for students	4	11	38	**43**	4	3.3	3.2	3.1
Opportunity to innovate	8	17	30	**38**	8	3.2	3.2	3.5
Planning and Resource Allocation								
A higher level of self-management	2	11	18	**52**	17	3.7	3.6	3.6
Better resource management	3	8	25	**49**	15	3.6	3.5	3.7
Clearer sense of direction through school charter	3	4	23	**50**	20	3.8	3.9	4.1
Increased accountability and responsibility	1	2	12	**52**	33	4.1	4.1	4.2
Greater financial and administrative flexibility	5	12	24	**41**	18	3.6	3.5	3.7
More resources	19	**32**	27	15	7	2.6	2.5	2.5
Improved long-term planning	6	10	29	**43**	11	3.4	3.5	3.9
Improved school policies	5	9	**40**	38	9	3.4	3.3	3.3
Better administrative support	13	19	**32**	29	7	3.0	2.7	3.0
Personnel and Professional								
Better personnel management	4	11	32	**49**	5	3.4	3.0	3.5
Increased staff job satisfaction	18	**35**	30	15	2	2.5	2.4	2.7
Enhanced professional development	2	4	26	**51**	17	3.8	3.6	3.3
Shared decision-making	3	9	35	**44**	9	3.5	3.2	3.4
Improved staff performance	3	10	**46**	34	7	3.3	3.1	3.2
More effective organization following restructure	12	24	**40**	20	5	2.8	2.9	3.1
Enhanced capacity to attract staff	24	20	**29**	19	7	2.7	2.4	2.8
School and Community								
More cohesive staff and community	7	16	**49**	25	3	3.0	2.9	3.2
Increased community involvement	10	25	**45**	16	4	2.8	2.8	2.9
Higher community profile	6	14	**38**	35	7	3.2	3.2	3.2
Less bureaucratic interference	26	27	**28**	15	4	2.4	2.6	2.8
Enhanced school identity	3	12	**42**	36	8	3.3	3.2	3.3
Improved cooperation between schools	18	21	**35**	18	7	2.7	2.9	2.8
Overall Mean						**3.2**	**3.1**	**3.3**

Source: Cooperative Research Project, 1997, p. 30

Note: [1] Intake 1 principals surveyed one year after base-line survey.

schools. Responses are summarized in Table 4.2, with mean ratings for 1995 and for the survey of principals of intake 1 schools one year after implementation. Responses were provided on a 5-point extent of realization scale from 1 ('low') to 5 ('high').

Mean scores in 1996 exceeded 3.0 for 16 of the 25 items. The modal rating was 4 for 11 items, 3 for 12 items, and 2 for 2 items. These were an improvement

Table 4.3: Extent of improvement in building a school's capacity through the Curriculum and Standards Framework

The Curriculum and Standards Framework improves school's capacity to . . .	Extent of improvement (%)					Mean
	Low 1	2	3	4	High 5	
• plan the provision of the curriculum program	6	12	29	**45**	9	3.4
• establishes levels and standards for your students in the eight learning areas	5	12	34	**40**	10	3.4
• focus attention on the Key Learning Areas	3	8	18	**49**	23	3.8
• incorporate initiatives such as early literacy programs, programs for gifted students and physical and sport education into the school's curriculum plan	11	15	**34**	33	8	3.1
• move towards a curriculum planning model based around learning outcomes for students	4	8	29	**44**	14	3.6
• report to parents on student achievements	9	14	34	**35**	7	3.2
• meet the needs of range of students	11	16	**41**	27	5	3.0

Source: Cooperative Research Project, 1997, p. 50

on the 1995 survey when only 7 items received a modal rating of 4 and all but one lay in the area of planning and resource allocation. There was a substantial improvement in the ratings of 5 of the 7 items in the personnel and professional area, indicating a higher level of coherence is emerging in the elements in the framework of Schools of the Future.

Noteworthy as far as outcomes are concerned are responses for the three items related to curriculum and learning, for which mean ratings are close to the mean ratings for all items related to realization of benefits: more responsive and relevant curriculum (mean of 3.2), improved learning outcomes for students (mean of 3.3) and opportunity to innovate (mean of 3.2). For the second of these, improved learning outcomes for students, 85 per cent of principals (up from 82 per cent in 1995) have provided a rating of 3 or more on the 5-point scale. Assuming this is a considered response, it is an important finding that is worthy of closer examination, as is done later in the chapter in the structural equation modelling of the 1996 findings.

3 Curriculum and Standards Framework (CSF)

The Curriculum and Standards Framework (CSF) adopted by the Board of Studies is intended to serve a range of purposes such as those listed in Table 4.3. Principals were invited to rate the extent to which the CSF had improved the school's capacity to achieve these purposes. A 5-point extent of improvement scale was provided, ranging from 1 ('low') to 5 ('high').

The ratings of improvement set out in Table 4.3 are noteworthy given the often expressed view that such reforms do not have impact on curriculum or on the learning needs of students. Mean ratings exceed 3 on the 5-point scale in each instance with about three-quarters of respondents giving a rating at this level. The focus on students is evident in ratings for three items:

The Curriculum and Standards Framework improves school's capacity to:

- move towards a curriculum model based around learning outcomes for students (mean of 3.6)
- establish levels and standards for your students in the eight learning areas (mean of 3.4)
- meet the needs of a range of students (mean of 3.0)

Specifying the Links Between Reform Elements and Outcomes in Curriculum and Learning

An important issue in this review of research, in Victoria and in other places, is the relationship between the capacities that come with school-based management and improved outcomes for students. It became abundantly clear in the review of research in the United States that these capacities alone may have no impact on the latter (see Hanushek, 1996; Smith, Scoll and Link, 1996; Summers and Johnson, 1996), and that linkages must be established with other initiatives that address student learning. The coherence of the elements in Schools of the Future and the comprehensive nature of the survey instruments in the Cooperative Research Project enabled the research team in Victoria to gain an understanding of these links and confirm their importance.

As summarized in Tables 4.2 and 4.3, the distribution of responses indicated a view among the majority of principals that there have been gains in the areas of curriculum, teaching and learning, either in improved outcomes or improved capacities to carry out the work of the school. For example, 85 per cent of principals gave a rating of 3 or more on a 5-point scale of 'low' to 'high' on the extent to which the expected benefit of 'improved learning outcomes' had been realized in their schools.

These are, of course, opinions or perceptions. Analysis on the basis of actual achievement scores could not be conducted for two reasons. First, because these achievements were not systematically monitored at the time Schools of the Future was initiated, hence there were no base-line data on achievement. Second, because the unions placed a ban on teachers furnishing information to researchers when an attempt was made to monitor profiles of student achievement in intake 1 Schools of the Future and in schools that had not yet entered the program.

Analysis of Direct and Indirect Effects on Perceptions of Curriculum and Learning Benefits

It is possible to undertake analysis of responses in the survey to determine the direct and indirect effects of selected factors on learning. The approach known as structural equation modelling was employed, using LISREL 8 (see Jöreskog and Sörbom, 1993). This approach allows the analysis of ordinal-scaled variables such as those utilized in the items of this survey.

Figure 4.1:   Explanatory regression model showing interdependent effects among factors influencing perceived Curriculum and Learning Benefits showing standardized path coefficients

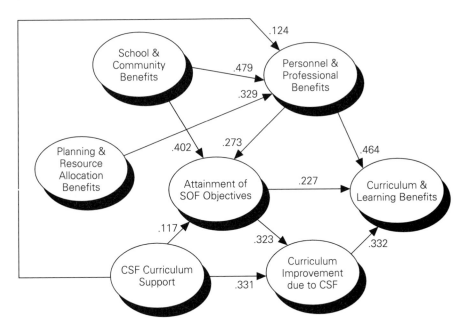

Source: Cooperative Research Project, 1997, p. 80

The first step was to take clusters of related items in the survey and to treat these as constructs. These clusters are essentially the different areas reported in Table 4.1 (achievement of objectives), Table 4.2 (progress in realization of benefits) and Table 4.3 (capacities deriving from the Curriculum and Standards Framework). Further analysis was conducted to determine the 'goodness of fit' between the data and a model formed by these constructs: *Curriculum and Learning Benefits, Planning and Resource Allocation Benefits, Personnel and Professional Benefits, School and Community Benefits, Curriculum Improvement due to the Curriculum and Standards Framework, Curriculum Support through the Curriculum and Standards Framework*, and Confidence of Principals in the *Attainment of Schools of the Future Objectives*. These constructs contain virtually all of the elements of the Schools of the Future program. Explanations for why reforms such as Schools of the Future should impact on student learning invariably refer to these elements; for example, through an enhanced capacity to attract staff (*Personnel and Professional Benefits*) and greater financial and administrative flexibility (*Planning and Resource Allocation Benefits*).

Figure 4.1 contains the explanatory regression model that shows the interdependent effects among variables (in this instance, latent variables that represent the constructs) on the variable *Curriculum and Learning Benefits*. Standardized path coefficients are shown, representing the direct effects (all paths are statistically significant beyond the $p < 0.05$ level by univariate two-tailed test). The fit between data and model is very good indeed, with an Adjusted Goodness of Fit Index of 0.947, indicating that almost all (94.7 per cent) of the variances and co-variances in the data are accounted for by the model.

The path coefficients may be interpreted in this manner. The direct effect of *Personnel and Professional Benefits* on *Curriculum and Learning Benefits* is indicated by a path coefficient of 0.464. This indicates that an increase in the measure of *Personnel and Professional Benefits* of 1 standard deviation, as reflected in the ratings by principals, produces an increase in the measure of *Curriculum and Learning Benefits* of 0.464 of a standard deviation.

The factors having direct effects on the *Curriculum and Learning Benefits* are *Curriculum Improvement due to Curriculum and Standards Framework* (0.332), *Personnel and Professional Benefits* (0.464) and confidence of principals in *Attainment of Schools of the Future Benefits* (0.227). The remaining three factors have indirect effects on *Curriculum and Learning Benefits*, being mediated through other factors. The indirect effects of *School and Community Benefits* are mediated through *Attainment of Schools of the Future Objectives* and *Personnel and Professional Benefits*. The indirect effects of *Planning and Resource Allocation Benefits* are mediated through *Personnel and Professional Benefits*. The indirect effect of *Curriculum Support through the Curriculum and Standards Framework* is mediated through *Curriculum Improvement due to the Curriculum and Standards Framework* and *Personnel and Professional Benefits*.

Discussion

While these findings are based on the perceptions of principals, the direct and indirect effects are consistent with expectations for the successful implementation of coherent programs of reforms such as Schools of the Future, especially taking account of the critiques of school-based management as a single reform initiative. The structural features of such reforms such as the shift of authority, responsibility and accountability to the school level are unlikely, by themselves, to have either a direct or indirect effect on curriculum and learning unless the capacities that may be nurtured within such arrangements are developed. Clearly, the principals who report curriculum and learning benefits tend to be those who have reported benefits in other domains that have emerged with the Schools of the Future program, including the capacity to select staff, increased flexibility in the use of resources, and involvement of the community.

The explanatory model derived from findings in the 1996 survey is similar to that derived one year earlier, that is, there is a high degree of stability in the explanatory model. A noteworthy difference is the stronger effects of the three constructs that impact directly on *Curriculum and Learning Benefits: Personnel and Professional Benefits* (0.464 in 1996 compared to 0.217 in 1995), *Curriculum Improvement due to the CSF* (0.332 in 1996 compared to 0.271 in 1995) and confidence in the *Attainment of SOF Objectives* (0.227 in 1996 compared to 0.195 in 1995). Also noteworthy is the low correlation between individual and school characteristics of respondents and the various dimensions of the model. In other words, the explanatory model stands independent of the nature of respondents and their schools.

An Independent Assessment: The Odden and Odden Research

The Cooperative Research Project is an example of an 'insider–outsider' collaboration, with the initiative in the first instance taken by the two principals associations (Victorian Association of State Secondary Principals, Victorian Primary Principals Association), who invited the employing authority, the Department of Education, and a third party, the University of Melbourne, to join it for a five-year longitudinal study of Schools of the Future. All parties to the project were, however, involved in some way in the design and implementation of the program, including the key representatives for the third party — Professor Hedley Beare, Professor Brian Caldwell and Professor Peter Hill.

A parallel but independent four-year longitudinal study was conducted by Professor Allan Odden, Director of the Finance Centre of the Consortium for Policy Research in Education (CPRE) in the USA. Odden has been at the forefront of education policy in the USA for many years, including a period at the professional level for the Education Commission of the States. His research and writing on policy matters has been influential, initially in the finance area but with a broader perspective in recent years to forge a link between resources and outcomes of schooling.

Odden's study of Schools of the Future was sponsored by the CPRE, with grants from the Carnegie Corporation and the Office for Educational Research and Improvement, US Department of Education. This investigation involved annual visits to Victoria, commencing in 1993 and continuing to 1996. For most visits, and in the preparation of reports, Allan Odden was joined by Eleanor Odden, from whose joint report in 1996 some excerpts are drawn below (Odden and Odden, 1996). Data were gathered from interviews with key stakeholders, including the Minister and senior staff of the Department of Education, the Australian Education Union, and academics, with most gathered through questionnaire surveys, structured interviews and observations in case study schools, usually four in any one year, with most of these in districts with relatively high levels of disadvantage.

Odden and other researchers frequently refer to a 'high involvement approach' to decentralization, drawing on a framework established by Edward Lawler of the University of Southern California. The four elements in this framework are concerned with decentralization of power, information, skills and rewards. Conclusions after four years are described in the following terms:

In sum, Victoria, Australia has made major strides towards local management of schools. Victoria has included most components suggested by the high involvement approach to decentralized management and has created a rich and ambitious instructional guidance framework for the task of decentralization that now includes both performance standards and a system of measuring student achievement. Although the Victorian approach needs to be studied further, both to see how the approach evolves over time and to document more validly and reliably its impacts on student achievement, it currently represents one of the world's most comprehensive, well designed, and promising approaches to decentralized school management. (Odden and Odden, 1996, pp. 61–2)

Odden and Odden recognized that time was now required 'for implementation and solidification', and also for participants in schools to 'learn' the new approaches, especially new personnel and assessment practices (p. 62). They note the increase in workload at the school level and 'hope efforts are soon exerted to find ways to work smarter rather than harder as a result of the new conditions' (p. 63). They conclude with a statement that concurs with our view, suggesting that:

the first stage of Schools of the Future may be ending — the design of its various elements and their initial implementation. The second stage might need more re-engineering or restructuring to continue implementation and to produce the results that are desired — all students achieving to high standards. (Odden and Odden, 1996, p. 63)

Other Research on Schools of the Future

Other research has been conducted on Schools of the Future and we comment on three studies, each of which is broadly critical of the reform. Jill Blackmore and others at Deakin University reported case studies in four schools (Blackmore *et al.*, 1996). While the authors do not claim that one can generalize, the work is set in the context of wider research and the contributions of other scholars who write in a critical theory tradition, as illustrated in the work of Smyth (1993) cited earlier.

Expressed simply, these researchers found evidence to support their conclusion that the workplace for teachers under reforms such as Schools of the Future are profoundly different in form and value from those that have prevailed in public education:

While devolution is seen to be an efficient administrative solution to wider political, social and economic problems, its effect in the form of the self-managing school is to construct new sets of relationships in them that are often antithetical to long-held values in public education. In that context teachers do change, but in order to do the maintenance work needed to retain what they value in public education as much as in response to the new policy initiatives. (Blackmore *et al.*, 1996, p. 217)

We believe that the analysis and conclusion fail to appreciate the implications for schools of the societal transformation that has been under way for some decades, a transformation at least as important and far-reaching as the industrial revolution that changed almost every aspect of work, including that in schools, and the values that underpinned the way that work was conducted. The same is occurring now and the concept of public education and the profession of teaching are changing in dramatic fashion. The authors are certainly aware of the scale of change, but their commentary suggests that schools and teachers ought not change too. Reforms like Schools of the Future, which are much broader than 'devolution' and 'the self-managing school', are just one manifestation of these changes and the challenge for researchers and policy-makers is to understand the nature of those changes and to show leadership in the transition, and that includes attending to personal and professional needs of those whose work is affected. That challenge has been taken up in Britain, for example, where all political parties have accepted that the local management of schools was one of the success stories of the 1988 Education Reform Act (a story that included elements of 'devolution' and 'the self-managing school') and where scholars at the forefront of research on school and classroom effectiveness are positively and constructively helping to shape further reform in a new view of public education and the profession of teaching. We also take up this challenge in Chapters 5 to 7.

A study reported by Pamela Bishop and William Mulford of the University of Tasmania (Bishop and Mulford, 1996) takes a similar tack to the research of Blackmore and colleagues. Drawing on masters research by Bishop completed in 1995, the investigation was carried out in just four schools chosen for their similarity (providing 'the study with the capacity for cross-comparisons'), namely, four female principals in inner Melbourne primary schools. Drawing mainly from interviews, the authors show principals and teachers to be cynical of the reform, with increased workload and feelings of powerlessness in the face of change they do not approve. The merit of the report lies in its reference to other research that highlights the limitations of school-based management that is not connected to strategies to improve student learning. Ironically, becoming 'connected' is precisely the intention of Schools of the Future, through the school charter, curriculum and standards frameworks, professional development that focuses on school-determined priorities, budget flexibility, and school annual reports. Not one of these strategies is mentioned by the authors. Respondents seemed to be commenting on budget measures in train at the time rather than to the Schools of the Future program. The authors and their subjects seemed unaware of the difficult context, namely, a Government having to curtail public expenditure, including education, because the previous Government was borrowing to pay the interest on borrowing to sustain staffing levels out of kilter with comparable states and with no discernible benefit as far as outcomes for students were concerned.

Survey research has been conducted on Schools of the Future by Tony Townsend, who is Director of the South Pacific Centre for School and Community Development at Monash University. He provided a comprehensive account of his own research and a comparison of his findings with those of the Cooperative

Research Project in a paper published in late 1996 (Townsend, 1996). He has reported two studies, one of opinions of parents, school counsellors and teachers on aspects of Schools of the Future; the other of revenue of schools analysed according to community characteristics.

Townsend found that parents and counsellors tended to be more positive about the impact of Schools of the Future than teachers, and that each tended to have moderate to high levels of satisfaction or confidence in most matters, especially those over which the school had control. These findings were generally consistent with those in the Cooperative Research Project, as were those concerned with workload and limited resources. He took issue with aspects of the design and inter-pretation of findings of the Cooperative Research Project. Even though his sample is unclear and only one such survey was reported, compared to the representative sampling over six surveys in the Cooperative Research Project, his findings on both gains and shortcomings are consistent with those in the latter.

Townsend is critical of the structural equation modelling based on the 1995 survey results in the Cooperative Research Project that show how the linked capacit-ies across many elements of Schools of the Future may, directly or indirectly, have an impact on learning outcomes, even though school-based decision-making of this kind is generally associated with, or is advocated, if there is to be meaningful reform, as discussed earlier in this chapter in the context of research on school-based management. His criticism is related in part to the failure to use achievement data, a somewhat empty criticism since base-line data do not exist and a union ban was placed on furnishing other information. It was the best analysis on offer at the time.

In his other research on the resourcing of schools, Townsend draws attention to the different capacities of communities to raise funds for their schools, a con-dition that has prevailed for decades and which is becoming acute, given the resource needs of schools and the limits of funding from the public purse. It was 'the size of the cake' that concerned him rather than 'how the cake is cut'. Indeed, on the latter, he is very positive in his appraisal of efforts in Schools of the Future to develop a formula or index to match resources allocated to schools to the learn-ing needs of students: 'The index is possibly the fairest of any in the world and can seriously be considered as "world's best practice"' (Townsend, 1996, p. 189) (see Education Committee, 1994, 1995, 1997; Caldwell, 1996; and Hind, 1996 for an account of the resource allocation mechanism described by Townsend).

It is his concern about resources that inclines Townsend toward his final conclusion, the sweep of which is not consistent with much of his own data:

> Is the self-managing school the miracle educational reformers need or a myth designed to divert attention away from the massive reduction in resources over the past few years? Given the evidence we would have to conclude the latter. (Townsend, 1996, p. 191)

Apart from a false dichotomy on a need never claimed and an insensitivity to a budget and debt crisis that any responsible government must address, his conclusion is at odds with another he offered in a public commentary on Schools of the Future shortly after the paper cited above was published. Writing in *The Age*, he claimed that:

> After four years it is obvious the Victorian system is at or near the cutting edge of educational thought. The Government has implemented self-managing schools. It has introduced computer technology into administration and multi-media and satellite technology into teaching. It has put more educational resources into the hands of schools than any comparable system and sought to tie resource levels to the needs of students. But many concerns remain. (Townsend, 1997, p. 11)

It is hard to credit that such different conclusions could be drawn by the same person on the basis of the same research data. Tony Townsend is a respected scholar who has made an important contribution in the field of school and community education. He has played a leading role in the networking of research findings on school and classroom effectiveness through the International Congress for School Effectiveness and his books and other publications. His statements reflect the dilemma of many academics who have advocated the empowerment of schools and their communities and who now balk when such empowerment is implemented with accountability in difficult times for resourcing public sector services. Clearly, we feel his balanced and constructive public commentary in the second citation above is more on target. Rather than offer a sweeping rejection on the basis of unresolved concerns that warrant further work, we take up in Chapter 5 issues that now need to be addressed and identify the pre-conditions for lasting school reform, a policy framework for which is offered in Chapter 6. We go to the heart of the issue of resources and the role of government.

In Summary

Our review of research on the processes and outcomes has covered much territory. We demonstrated at the outset how the success of the large-scale reform that is Schools of the Future is explained by the model for such an outcome proposed by Guthrie and Koppich (1993). Essentially, there was a relatively rare alignment of a number of conditions that allowed the Kennett Liberal National Coalition to proceed with sweeping change on a number of fronts, including education and Schools of the Future. This was contrasted with circumstances that have thwarted similar attempts at large scale change that have been only partly successful or are fragmented or incomplete, as in New South Wales, or generally across the United States. We compared the ministerial experiences of Don Hayward in Victoria and Kenneth Baker in Britain, noting similarities in their determination to proceed, sidelining the teacher unions and being wary of the bureaucracy, tending to appeal to and involve the profession more directly. They differed in important respects, notably in the extent to which they consulted on the important matter of building curriculum and standards frameworks, with the outcome being a need to 're-start' the British effort. Some academic comment on the introduction of Schools of the Future was taken apart and shown to be premature and intemperate.

International research on school-based management was reviewed, and this highlighted the not surprising finding that such practices by themselves cannot be expected to have impact on learning outcomes for students, even if they have other effects that may make the effort worthwhile, as have been reported in some places. A tight link must be established between the authorities, responsibilities and accountabilities of school-based management and the implementation of strategies that target improvement toward clear goals and standards. Schools of the Future has made such a linkage in what, by international standards, is a remarkably coherent package of reforms. Findings in the five-year multidimensional Cooperative Research Project were reviewed, and these revealed a consistently high rating by principals as far as confidence in the program and realization of benefits are concerned. Despite these ratings, principals report a number of concerns related to their roles, resources and workloads, and these are acknowledged; there is more work to be done to improve the implementation. Despite these concerns, as in Britain, the overwhelming majority of principals would not wish to return to previous arrangements. A model showing direct and indirect effects on curriculum and learning was determined using constructs of elements of Schools of the Future. This model is consistent with theory and intuition for reforms of this kind.

Research that has drawn more negative conclusions was also reviewed. While some scholars remain ambivalent, others see reforms such as Schools of the Future as a cause of many deep-seated problems in public education and the teaching profession. We reject this view and contend that Schools of the Future was a necessary but insufficient reform. To achieve lasting school reform, we must understand the nature of these deep-seated problems, and consider the options for further change that will achieve that end. That is our task in Chapters 5 and 6.

5   Pre-conditions for Lasting School Reform

In Chapter 5 we present our view of the pre-conditions for lasting school reform. We believe that reforms to date, such as those in Schools of the Future, were a necessary but insufficient stage along the way and that much remains to be done. The critics of those reforms have, for the most part, missed the point of it all, or have remained trapped in an industrial frame of thinking, although in some instances, often without realizing it, they have simply highlighted what more needs to be done to advance the cause.

Our starting point is a set of assumptions about schooling and society which makes clear our commitment and conviction that the school has a vital role to play for the future of society and for the satisfaction and success of its citizens. We then address five issues which we believe must be resolved if there is to be lasting school reform. These issues are complex and inter-related, with analysis directed, in turn, to teachers and teaching, learners and learning, the relationship between education and the economy, the resourcing of schools, and the role of government. This forms the major part of the chapter. We conclude by proposing the pre-conditions for lasting school reform, thus providing the basis for a policy framework in Chapter 6.

Assumptions about Society and Schooling

We start with twelve assumptions about society and schooling for the dawn of the third millennium. Most concern the impact of technology. Our interest is not only in nations in the West but also the dynamic societies in the East, the 'tigers', nations we have described in our assumptions as 'developed'. The implications are profound as far as schools are concerned, helping us to shape the issues to be addressed in the next stage if school reform is to be lasting.

1   That because of the explosion of knowledge and the pervasive and penetrating influence of information technology, the world in the twenty-first century will be fundamentally different from the past.
2   That most of the opportunities for our young people in the future will be in knowledge-based work.
3   That for the developed nations, many of their future opportunities will come through complementing, not competing with, the rapid growth of developing nations.

4   That many of these opportunities will be through the provision of knowledge-based services to firms and government agencies in developing nations, using the creativity and innovation of their young people.

5   That the key economic resources for the developed nations will be the knowledge and intellect of their young people, being even more important than commodities and natural resources.

6   That much of the conventional employment in existing industries in developed nations, especially process work in manufacturing industries, will disappear.

7   That technology will continue to drive change at a rapid rate, and diversity will be the order of the day.

8   That many of the opportunities for young people will be in industries and activities that have not yet been thought of, or invented, and these opportunities will continue to change.

9   That it will be essential for young people to be flexible and responsive to new opportunities as these occur.

10 That the most important capacity for our young people will be the ability to learn, and to continue to learn throughout their lifetime.

11 That information technology, including multimedia, will be an important learning aid in the future, and much of the learning will occur in informal settings, such as at home, or at work.

12 That the school will lose its monopoly in the education of our young people.

The further reform of public education ought in our view reflect these assumptions about society, learning and school education. Whilst there are a host of issues to be addressed in such reform, most are sharply focused by these assumptions, and the imperative for further change becomes even more apparent.

Issues to Be Addressed if Reform Is to Be Lasting

In this section we identify and analyse the issues we believe must be resolved if there is to be lasting school reform. They are complex and inter-related, with analysis directed, in turn, to teachers and teaching, learners and learning, the relationship between education and the economy, the resourcing of schools, and the role of government. These issues emerge as unresolved matters of concern in the ongoing implementation of reforms such as Schools of the Future. In some instances, they have been argued in negative fashion by the critics of reform some of whom have, in our view, taken shortcomings in implementation or difficulties in transition or an unfinished agenda as grounds for dismissing long overdue and necessary change.

Teachers and Teaching

We start our analysis by considering teachers and teaching because the role of the teacher is central to the success of current reforms and, in the longer term, to the future of public schooling. Expressed another way, reforms that have seen the establishment of curriculum and standards frameworks, with associated measures to provide teachers, parents and students with information about achievement in relation to standards; and the creation of systems of self-managing schools, with the capacity to plan and allocate resources, including staff; will make no difference if teachers do not teach differently or students do not learn differently, with improved outcomes. These reforms may, of course, be worth implementing if they achieve the same outcomes as before, but at less cost (that is, they result in a more efficient system), or if they respond to parental or corporate concerns to effect a closer match between curriculum and teaching on the one hand and the economic needs of the individual, family and society on the other. But we should strive for more, in the current wave of reforms and in those that follow, to ensure higher levels of achievement for all students, especially those who are not achieving well through failure in literacy in the early years or who are turned off by schooling in later years.

In some respects, we ought to have begun this section with consideration of the needs of students, and approaches to learning, considering especially the role of the new information technologies. Surely the starting point for system design should be the student! However, we believe we cannot make progress in doing just that until we address some fundamental concerns about teachers and teaching and the notion of teacher as professional in the years to come. More generally, of course, we should be considering not only teachers but the full range of educator professionals, for in the future, there ought to be a richer range of skilled professionals who provide service in or to the public school.

We address five concerns about teaching that have been expressed by teachers themselves: low morale, ensuring a supply of teachers, declining levels of academic standing on entry to the profession, the need for improved training to deal with the demands of the contemporary curriculum, and decay in the fabric of schools.

1 Low morale

It seems to us that concern about teacher morale has been around in the countries under consideration for many years. It has become almost a cliché that 'morale has never been so low'. While no doubt there are many examples of high levels of morale in schools that are doing exceptionally well, we suggest that the general level of concern is warranted. Recent evidence from Britain comes from a survey of teachers in about one-third of schools (about 8500) by the Local Government Management Board, as reported in *The Times Educational Supplement* (Dean and Rafferty, 1997, p. 1). The survey indicated that early retirements in late 1996 were at their highest level since 1990, with only one in eight reaching retirement age, and with resignations now exceeding recruitments. A parallel telephone survey of almost 1000 teachers, conducted for *The Times Educational Supplement* (TES), revealed that 41 per cent of primary teachers and more than 25 per cent of secondary and independent teachers wanted to quit. Discussions in focus groups indicated that teachers wanted greater investment in schools, smaller class sizes, a rise in the status of the profession and improvement in training and professional development, a review of salaries, an inspection system based on support and advice, and a program to address the backlog of building repairs and maintenance. Most of these call for a dramatic increase in the resourcing of public education, an issue we consider later in this section.

We note from the report of the TES survey that teachers told surveyors that 'they wanted a complete change of career, preferably working for a charity, or in writing, broadcasting or PR. But the most popular choices were posts in management, industry, commerce or retirement'. It is interesting that the preferred alternatives lay mainly in areas that teachers have traditionally been wary of, at least in respect to their influence on schooling. They now appear more attractive than teaching.

2   Ensuring a supply of teachers

Evidence of a looming shortage of teachers was presented in a report in early 1997 by the Australian Council of Deans of Education (ACDE) which estimated a shortfall of 7000 teachers across Australia by 2003. The ACDE called for state education authorities to 'significantly increase the attractiveness of teaching as a career' through paying higher salaries and other measures (Armitage, 1997, p. 3). Similar projections have been made in other nations.

The report is based on projections of increases in student enrolments and assumptions that schooling in the future will be similar to schooling at present. We accept the former but not necessarily the latter, if this assumes that students will still work in traditional class settings with teacher–student ratios as they are now. Utilization of new information technologies, learning in places other than on the traditional school site, especially for senior secondary students, and greater variety in the range of learning groups, from individual and small teams to large, lecture-style settings, will all confound predictions made in the absence of a vision for schooling in the new millennium.

Another variable in making predictions is the length of a teacher's career, which has traditionally been seen as life-long. It may be that we ought no longer expect teachers to devote a whole career of more than forty years to the classroom. The demands of teaching combined with the need to bring education and the economy closer together, as presented below, suggests that much shorter periods of service, with greater mobility to and from other fields of work, may be the most attractive way in the future. The implication is not so much a teacher shortage, as we traditionally understand this term, but mobility between the professions or across different sectors of the work force, and providing more flexible approaches to teacher training to allow entry to the profession that takes account of prior learning and experience.

3 Declining levels of entry to teacher training

Tertiary entrance scores for students entering undergraduate programs in education continue to fall and, in Australia at least, tend to be among the lowest of any faculty at the university level. This phenomenon may realistically be taken as evidence of the relative unattractiveness of teaching as a profession, despite the increasing number of reports of imminent shortages of teachers that ought normally provide assurance of security of employment in times of uncertainty.

It seems to us that another factor is the extent to which careers advisers, and teachers in general, are prepared to recommend to senior secondary students that they select teaching as a career. A consequence of low teacher morale, and unwillingness to 'talk up' the profession, is a declining interest by students in becoming teachers. Similarly, for those who work in other fields who may be attracted to teaching, but are discouraged when confronted so regularly with reports of teacher dissatisfaction.

4 Need for improved training

We include in this analysis of concerns about teachers and teaching the level of knowledge and skill in critical areas such as early literacy and the adoption of new information technologies. We note, in Australia and comparable nations, that there is broad acceptance that about 20 per cent of students leave the early years of primary school unable to read well. The issue is not that this number is greater or the same as a decade or so ago, but the fact that these levels prevail despite the growing research evidence that strategies can be employed to ensure all students read well. Given this evidence has been around for some time, we are confronted here with a failure in teacher training programs, a failure in professional development, and a failure in commitment. There is a lag in teacher training and teacher professional development in the adoption of skills in new information technologies. While this lag is partly a consequence of the rate of adoption of hardware and software in schools, it seems that many teachers do not give a high priority to development in this area. We note the cliché that many students know more than their teachers as far as information technology is concerned.

More generally, however, expectations for schools are probably higher now than ever before and arguably higher than they ought to be in an important respect. A curriculum and standards framework ought to be helpful to the extent that it removes the expectation that each school develop its own curriculum. With careful setting of local priorities within a curriculum and standards framework, there ought to be less stress on teachers than that associated with trying to meet impossible expectations. Such a framework ought to guide efforts in the pre- and in-service training of teachers.

5 Decaying fabric of schools

The decaying fabric of schools was a factor in the account of Don Hayward in Chapter 3 and it surfaced again in reports of focus groups of teachers in Britain. In the case of Victoria, Don Hayward came to office to be confronted with a massive backlog in building repairs and maintenance. He described how little had been devoted to this area in the previous decade as funds were spent, and borrowed, and borrowed again to pay interest on the borrowing, to build a work force in excess of requirements, taking account of relative need as judged by the Commonwealth Grants Commission and the Audit Commission. Some progress was made from 1992 until the time of writing but more, much more needs to be done. It is evident that the same situation has emerged in Britain.

In effect, we see teachers in large numbers of schools being forced to practise their craft in buildings designed on a factory model, with students progressing from year to year in batches, in boxes laid end to end as in a production line, with little flexibility to respond to the needs of learners and learning in the late twentieth century, all made worse by a backlog in maintenance and repairs that mean leaking roofs and disintegrating floors and walls, especially in buildings of light timber construction that were built with a life expectancy barely one half of the time that has elapsed since they were erected.

In summary

Taking these five areas of analysis together, it seems palpably clear that profound changes are needed if teachers and other professionals in public school education are to have the high levels of buoyancy that one should expect in a highly skilled and empowered profession. This cannot be achieved if we expect solutions to current concerns by simply doing better the things we did in the past or moving incrementally on small-scale change. We have broken the mould in some respects, as illustrated in Schools of the Future, but we must now plan more dramatic change. We address some other issues before proposing pre-conditions to achieve lasting school reform that will include this new sense of professionalism.

Learners and Learning

There are several critically important issues associated with the theme of 'learners and learning'. We address three here, namely, frameworks and standards and how students are achieving against standards; strategies for ensuring that all students learn well in areas of learning where state-of-the art knowledge tells us that success for all may be achieved; and utilization of new information technologies to support, extend and challenge students.

1 Frameworks and standards

Concern about quality in schooling has been a major issue for several years but has now reached almost crisis proportions in some nations. Among those we have referred to in this book, these concerns appear strongest in the USA and in Britain. Developments in the USA are of particular interest because there seems to be consensus about the existence of a crisis. It is also the nation where there seems to be a wider range of initiatives in school design and approaches to learning than in comparable nations, yet large-scale implementation is proving difficult, and states and districts seem bound to inaction because flexibilities and a capacity for school level planning now evident in Britain and in Victoria, in Schools of the Future, have not made their appearance to any great extent, despite the momentum that is building for charter schools and school-site management through waivers of regulations that constrain.

A graphic illustration of concern about quality in the USA may be found in an extraordinary issue of *Education Week*, a weekly journal of news and commentary on developments in schools across the nation. Working in collaboration with The Pew Charitable Trusts, a 238 page 'Report Card on the Condition of Public Education in the 50 States' was released in early 1997, with national overviews and state-by-state reports. Of particular interest in the context we are addressing in this section is the opening statement:

> Public education systems in the fifty states are riddled with excellence but rife with mediocrity. Despite fifteen years of earnest efforts to improve public schools and raise student achievement, states haven't made much progress.

> As the new millennium approaches, there is growing concern that if public education doesn't soon improve, one of two outcomes is almost inevitable:

> - Our democratic system and our economic strength, both of which depend on an educated citizenry, will steadily erode; or,
> - Alternative forms of education will emerge to replace public schools as we have known them.

> This will not happen next year or perhaps even in the next ten years. But in time, if our education system remains mediocre, we will see one of these two results. Either would be a sad loss for America. (*Education Week*, January 22, 1997, p. 3)

The second is the most likely of these two alternatives, given that there are so many other sturdy supports for democracy and economic strength in the USA. Frankly, we feel the second alternative is a refreshingly honest view of the state of affairs in that nation, but we feel that the same statement could or should be made about likely scenarios in Australia, Britain and comparable nations.

More generally, however, we note the intense interest generated by the findings of investigations such as the Third International Mathematics and Science Study, or the high profile reports of relatively high achievement of students in some nations, for example, Taiwan compared to Britain and Australia as featured, respectively, in a BBC *Panorama* program in late 1996 and a Channel 9 *60 Minutes* segment in early 1997.

Locally, of course, professional and parental concern about standards, which was initially rather nebulous because of the unavailability of data, is now highly focused with the publication of test scores and 'league tables' in Britain, the more constrained Learning Assessment Project in Victoria, and the range of approaches across the states in the USA. Whilst professional concerns are still evident about the efficacy and validity of these data, there is no doubt that they have led to the heightened concern illustrated in the *Education Week* report cited above.

2   Ensuring that all students learn well

Curriculum and standards frameworks as well as new mechanisms for data gathering and accountability are yielding a mountain of information about student achievement. These developments provide a more powerful focus on areas where student achievement is not as it should be than ever before, and making that information accessible to the public as well as the professional. Examples include the approximately 20 per cent of students in the early years of primary school who leave this stage of schooling unable to read well, with consequences for later schooling and chances of life success that are very serious indeed. The levels of achievement of particular groups, such as those in family or social circumstances that mitigate against success in schooling, or of boys in comparison to girls, have also been highlighted.

Some may say that these levels of achievement have always been known, at least to teachers, and that matters are no better or no worse than a decade or two ago. This may be true, but the point is we all know about it now; it is now in the public domain and the public is concerned about it. Expressed another way, all the rhetoric of educationists about responding to the needs of every child and the whole child is being challenged.

3   Utilization of new information technologies

The issue of quality of learning and teaching and the issue of incorporating the new information technologies should not be considered mutually exclusive. Indeed, in important respects, they are interdependent. We illustrate by referring to situations that are not only relatively well endowed in respect to technology but also, and especially, to those that most would agree represent some of the most difficult circumstances for learning, namely the acquisition of literacy skills and a love of learning in poor inner-city areas and in schools that cater mainly for indigenous students.

Some schools have made remarkable progress in the adoption of new technology, and these include schools in the public as well as private sectors. Governments are setting targets for relatively high numbers of computers in schools, as many as one to every four students or more, and arrangements are being made with providers in the telecommunications industry to make special plans for including schools in the 'roll out' of their information networks. How technology may transform the school is evidenced by the experience of one school, Methodist Ladies College in Melbourne, a private school that made a flying start in the late 1980s under former principal David Loader. Less than a decade later, about 2000 of about 2200 students have their own notebook computers, including those at senior grades of the junior (primary) school.

Virtually every aspect of learning and teaching has been transformed at Methodist Ladies College, as it has in other schools that have the same density of information technology. The teacher is now as much a facilitator of learning as a formal instructor, the timetable has been changed to include longer classes; furniture has been changed to accommodate the new ways of working, especially in teams, that contrasts with the stereotype of learning with computers as being a lonely activity; and buildings have been refurbished so that they no longer look like a collection of boxes for classes of standard size, they are now more warm and caring, accommodating a range of learning styles, from students working alone or in small groups on self-directed activities to more-or-less standard teaching space to small theatres for larger groups. There is a 'connectedness' across curriculum areas that the use of information technology encourages and there is a blurring of learning location across the school and the home, with the latter being more than routine 'home work'. A visit to the school gives the impression of a new dimension of empowered learning in a setting that is as rich as ever in respect to learning in the arts, defined broadly, and in sports.

But settings such as Methodist Ladies College are more favourable for the adoption of new information technologies than most schools, given that it is a private school serving relatively well-to-do families. Nicholas Pyke's account in *The Times Educational Supplement* provides a graphic illustration of what can be achieved in a blighted inner city area of London:

> A project equipping seven-year olds with executive-style 'pocket book' computers is reversing the inner-city reading blight in two of the London boroughs officially savaged for low standards of literacy. The Government's National Literacy Project and the Labour party's Literacy Task Force are already showing keen interest in the £1 million scheme which, crucially, has produced startling improvements irrespective of children's social background. The scheme, which operates in three of the poorest boroughs in the country — Newham, Tower Hamlets and Southwark — has seen a 700 per cent jump in the number of schools hitting the national reading average. All 600 pupils in the Docklands Learning Acceleration Project, run by the National Literacy Association, are making progress at close to national average levels, despite the low expectations habitually associated with inner-city areas. Professor David Reynolds, one of the academics who assessed the project and a member of Labour's task force on reading, has described the results as 'phenomenal'. The Dockland's project has also, significantly, used a regime of 'target-setting', the Government-backed approach to helping schools raise their standards according to national norms. (Pyke, 1997, p. 1)

The British experience supports our view that matters related to learning and teaching, including the use of the new information technologies, lie at the heart of further school reform in the years ahead, and that a consensus across the political spectrum is likely to emerge on the importance of the issue. This follows the broad support that can now be found in Britain for the major features of structural reform over the last decade, notably, a curriculum and standards framework and the local management of schools, which have their counterpart in Schools of the Future.

Evidence that involvement in interactive learning technologies can make a significant contribution to student learning in challenging circumstances is also furnished in the experience of Koorie education in Victoria, cited earlier in the account of Don Hayward in Chapter 3. This evidence does not simply mean increasing the amount of knowledge to which a student has access, for example, through the Internet or the CD-rom. It goes to the heart of the learning process itself: student attitudes to learning.

The reader will recall that our evidence comes from the Woolum Bellum Koorie Open Door Education (KODE) campus in Morwell, a country town in Gippsland, Victoria. Its Aboriginal students had previously demonstrated a lack of interest in learning, as indicated by their high absence rate from school, their poor attention span, and their sense of alienation.

When the Woolum Bellum campus was established, the teachers knew that the task of engaging the interest and attention of these students was a formidable one. They realized that a very special approach was required. After extensive discussions with the local Koorie community, it was decided that the best way to achieve a breakthrough in the learning of the Koorie students was to quickly and significantly incorporate cutting-edge interactive learning technologies into the learning process. With the enthusiastic support of the Koorie community, the use of these technologies became a priority for the school, as set out in its charter.

As an initial step, a site on the worldwide web was created. Students were able to communicate by e-mail and to engage in collaborative projects with indigenous students in other nations. Essays were published on the web. Students used scanners and digital cameras and incorporated static and moving images into their publications. They accessed vast amounts of information on the internet for their projects and their discussions with counterparts around the world.

Students who previously showed no interest in school now came early and went home late. Students who previously had poor literacy skills now became very interested in learning to write and spell properly. Students who previously had a very limited information base found they had access to the knowledge of the world. After a year, there were observable and measurable improvements in students' attendance, literacy, risk-taking and general learning.

Among other things, the worldwide web publishing has provided the drive for students to re-discover the local Koorie heritage and language. They are now considered a global resource on local Aboriginal culture and are engaged in a collaborative project with indigenous students in other countries on the re-discovery of their languages.

Computers on the campus were networked, allowing interaction within and between classes and the internet. Not every student had a computer; indeed, this was thought to be counterproductive. Students worked in a group in using the computer. The teacher, rather than using a 'stand and deliver' approach, became a leader and manager of the learning process, with team teaching further enhancing the collaborative approach to learning and teaching.

In the acquisition and utilization of knowledge, these Koorie students may be moving ahead of many of their non-Koorie counterparts in regular schools. Perhaps the most valuable aspect of the use of the new information technologies is the way they ignited the interest and curiosity of students in their learning. It was as though a switch was turned on in their minds. With the turning on of this switch came a quest for knowledge and learning from within the student, as distinct from learning being driven by the teacher. This student drive, in turn, seemed to 'infect' the teacher, who then became more 'active' in the educative process, thus commencing a cycle of mutually reinforcing behaviour.

Generalizing, the significance of the experience of Aboriginal students at the KODE campus at Morwell is that it has proved that the use of interactive learning technologies can dramatically improve learning and attitudes to learning of some of the most disadvantaged students in Australia, with that improvement likely to be enduring. The same improvement would appear possible for students in comparable settings anywhere.

Hardware and software are expensive, but the cost will decline. In the short term, we note that improvement does not demand one computer for each student; one for each classroom will enable progress to be made. In the first instance, the key seems to be to engage the interest of the teacher in the potential of new information technologies. The teacher must initiate these new approaches to learning and, before that can happen, the teacher must be convinced of their value and feel confident in their use. Teacher professional development is vital; building a substantial skills base will thus require a teacher driven grass roots approach.

Relationship between Education and the Economy

We believe that the relationship between education and the economy is a significant issue to be addressed if there is to be lasting school reform. We take two perspectives, one in a substantive sense in that the theory and practice of education on the one hand and economics on the other have diverged in recent decades after an extended period of convergence; the other in matters of perception, especially on the part of educators who generally do not see the relevance of the economy and economics to their work, and hence are suspicious if not antagonistic to reforms that endeavour to link the two. Our starting point in understanding these two perspectives is a reflection on the great social transformations of the twentieth century.

1   A century of social transformation

We take our lead from Peter Drucker (1995), the eminent writer on matters of economics, management, policy and society whose work spans much of the twentieth century. He refers to 'a century of social transformation' in western society and reminds us that, at the start of the century, the largest single groups of workers were agricultural workers and domestic workers. As the effects of the industrial revolution took hold, these groups were displaced by another group, the industrial workers, with the invention of machines reducing the need for many workers on farms, who left for the cities, and for servants in homes, much of whose work could be done by machines.

For this period of history, over nearly one hundred years too soon after World War II, it is fair to say that links between education and the economy were strong. We took it for granted that schooling prepared students for the world of work, and for the most part this was in the local community, on a farm or in a factory, or for many women, in the home. A few went on to higher education. Education and the economy were also linked through widespread apprenticeship schemes. It was also accepted that schooling was a means of transmitting from one generation to another all that was good about civilization and of inculcating values, on both counts a role that schools shared with the family and the church.

Links between education and the economy were particularly close in the last few decades of the nineteenth century, the period in western history when most systems of government or public schools were created, and this was the period when the industrial revolution gathered momentum. Schools were needed, especially in towns and cities, to prepare children to work in factories that were the new sources of employment, starting to displace farms as the dominant workplace in many communities. This was also the time when modern systems of government took shape, with the rise of the public service to support government that took on a wider range of functions than in the past. Management practices in the new industrial domain had their impact on school systems and the public service, a point made clear in books on educational administration that trace modern approaches to their foundations in the factory model, usually expressed as a matter of regret.

Theories of economics and public finance were rudimentary throughout the period we are considering here. Indeed, the practice of having a national budget is a phenomenon of the twentieth century. These theories have evolved to their present level of complexity as the role of government has become more complex and as the economy of nations has grown from local agriculture and industry, through building of a national economy, to the present era of globalization.

In summary, we recall an era of almost one hundred years when the relationship between education and the economy was close, understood and unquestioned.

2 The need for convergence

The relationship diverged as the local economy became a national economy, and places of work became increasingly remote from the local school and its community. Theories of economics were developed and public finance became more complex, as did government. Education and economics diverged.

This divergence became more acute in the next great societal transformation as the industrial worker was displaced by the knowledge worker as the largest single group in the workforce, and schools began to prepare their students for a place in the knowledge society. We have not yet given a name to this transformation; it may be the knowledge revolution but more likely the information revolution, but its impact on schools is now and will continue to be profound.

Drucker spells out the opportunities and the threats to school education in the 'knowledge society':

Paradoxically [in the knowledge society], this may not necessarily mean that the school as we know it will become more important. For in the knowledge society clearly more and more knowledge, and especially advanced knowledge, will be acquired well past the age of formal school- ing, and increasingly, perhaps, in and through educational processes that do not centre on the traditional school — for example, systematic continuing education offered at the place of employment. But at the same time, there is very little doubt that the performance of schools and the basic values of the schools will increasingly become of concern to society as a whole, rather than be considered 'professional' matters that can safely be left to the 'educator'. (Drucker, 1995, pp. 204–5)

He sets six priority tasks for society in the twenty-first century, and three of these involve knowledge and education:

- We will have to think through *education* — its purpose, its value, its con- tent. We will have to learn to define the *quality* of education and the *product- ivity* of education, to measure both and manage both (p. 236).
- We need systematic work on the *quality of knowledge* and the *productivity of knowledge* — neither even defined so far. On those two, the perform- ance capacity, and perhaps even the survival of any organization in the knowledge society will increasingly come to depend (pp. 236–7).
- We need to develop an *economic theory* appropriate to the primacy of a world economy in which knowledge has become the key economic resource and the dominant — and perhaps even the only — source of comparative advantage (p. 237).

It is reassuring to those with an interest in schools that three of Drucker's items in a social agenda concern education. It is equally reassuring that it is theory in economics that must change to embrace the work of schools, namely knowledge, though there is a sharp edge to this in his challenge to the primacy of schools in the knowledge society. In any event, he calls for a convergence of education and economics, and that is good news!

The promise of a convergence of economics and education reverses a trend described by Stehr (1994) in his analysis of knowledge societies:

... sociological discourse, in the past few decades, has been increasingly separated from economic discourse ... Economics lost interest in the ana- lysis of social institutions, while sociology conceded the study of socio- economic phenomena to economics ... Finally, both economic analysis and sociology lost interest in the study of the societal and socio-economic impact of science and technology. (Stehr, 1994, p. 122)

One illustration of how this convergence is occurring is in the recognition of how the capitalized value of some companies exceeds their book value due to the intellectual capital of their staff (see Dawson, 1997 for an account of this). For example, software giant Microsoft is capitalized at over fifteen times its book value. Management writer Charles Savage contends that 'the currency of traditional assumptions, principles and values of the industrial era is bankrupt. Knowledge management is laying the foundation for a whole new economy'. Australia, according to Savage is 'moving from the extraction of natural resources to the extraction of human capital' (cited by Dawson, 1997, p. 47). The Royal Melbourne Institute of Technology is the first institution in Australia to offer a graduate diploma in knowledge management, with studies in the subject also included in its MBA program.

3 A problem of perception

A significant aspect of divergence has been a perception on the part of some teachers that education and the economy are incompatible, and that decisions about education and training that link their work to success in the economy are regrettable or a distraction from their most important endeavour.

We do not dwell on this because we prefer the more optimistic though challenging perspective of Drucker. It may be helpful, however, to account for the problem. Whereas the relationship between education and the rudimentary local economy was understood and accepted by teachers in the past, suspicion grew as the economy became more remote, in the sense that the world of work for graduates lay beyond the immediate community, and the economy of the nation and matters of public finance became more complex. However, teachers observed and felt the impact of economic change that accompanied social change, as has been the case with the displacement of the industrial worker by the knowledge worker. In many communities, large-scale unemployment and social deprivation have followed the collapse of local industry that can no longer compete in a national economy, let alone a global economy.

Suspicion has been accentuated by two aspects of the professional life of teachers. The first concerns career paths. In the past, the work of teachers and work in the local community were closely connected, and it did not matter that a teacher had little if any experience in employment other than teaching. Today, the world of work is remote from teachers who in most instances still follow the path from school to university to teaching. The second concerns the challenge to teachers of keeping pace with changes in technology. These changes are, of course, central to the societal transformation now under way, and the fact that many teachers are now de-skilled in terms of the technology of their work leads to suspicion of that transformation, and the apparently connected efforts of those concerned with economics and public finance.

Problems of perception also derive from the financing of education and the role of government, two issues that are taken up in more detail below. Suffice to observe that terms like efficiency and effectiveness have been anathema to those in schools, especially after an era of expanded resourcing such as occurred in the 1970s and 1980s, and in the face of constraints or cutbacks in the 1990s. Some awareness and understanding have followed reforms such as the Local Management of

Schools in Britain and Schools of the Future in Victoria, as teachers have been part of school decision-making when scarce resources have to be targeted at locally determined priorities and where inefficiency is not countenanced. These are, of course, the same issues that are faced by governments in their efforts to resource the public sector and it is to this issue that we now turn our attention. We simply conclude this section by applauding efforts to achieve convergence in the relationship between education and the economy, and by noting that teachers and others who work in, and support, schools are now appreciating that matters of economics and finance in public education are an inevitable aspect of achieving lasting reform.

Resourcing of Schools

Resolving issues related to the resourcing of schools is critically important for lasting reform in public school education. There seems to be consensus across the political and educational spectra on the seriousness of these issues, but the manner in which they will be resolved is contentious. The options we explore and the preferences we express in Chapter 6 are centrally concerned with resources.

We address three aspects here. First, that current levels of resources are inadequate and are likely to remain so, unless dramatically new approaches are adopted. Second, that exclusive reliance on public funding is no longer realistic if we are to be serious about lasting reform that will ensure a high quality of schooling for all. Third, that there is a range of alternatives as far as mixes of revenue sources are concerned, and that failure to select or adapt these in some nations is to maintain an ideological stance that is needlessly impairing the effort to achieve reform and doing grave harm to current and future generations of students.

1 Inadequacy of current levels of resources for public education

The evidence for our contention that current levels of resourcing are inadequate has largely been presented. We have highlighted the decaying fabric of the majority of schools in the countries to which we are giving major attention, whether it be because they are literally falling apart through years of neglect or because, if sturdy, they are obsolete, and neither humane nor appropriate for learning in a knowledge society. The cost of rebuilding or refurbishing most of the school plant is staggering. We have also highlighted the requirements for technology, both hardware and software. Whilst costs are decreasing rapidly, fairness demands that all students have reasonable access to adequate technology if they are to benefit. Governments around the world are giving this matter priority, often in partnership with the information technology industry, but progress is slow and much remains to be done. To these costly items we should add the resources required to re-skill a teaching force that has failed to keep pace with technological advance and to achieve higher levels of salary to attract and keep a well-qualified and highly professional workforce.

Re-setting priorities in the broader education and training sector has little to recommend it, given parallel concerns about a shortfall in resources in higher education and in vocational education and training. There is little scope for re-setting priorities within the schools sector, given that needs identified in the last paragraph fall across all levels in primary and secondary schools.

Re-designing the nature of learning and teaching presents some possibilities for savings and reallocation to the aforementioned, but these tend to be either unacceptable in settings under consideration or long term in their potential. An example of the former is to return to much larger classes, perhaps more like what may be found in many nations in the East where levels of student achievement are high, such as in Japan and Taiwan. We acknowledge that high levels of achievement for all students have been attained under these conditions, but accept that the cultural supports for such practices in these countries cannot be replicated in the nations we are considering in this book. Included here are community support for schools, esteem in which teachers are held, and high levels of motivation among students. Larger classes are possible in some subjects employing some modes of teaching, especially at the senior secondary levels, but across-the-board re-design along these lines is not feasible in our view, and the extent to which it can be achieved still leaves a substantial shortfall in resources. Longer-term possibilities in respect to the re-design of learning and teaching include the wider adoption of information technology and more learning at home and in the workplace. The nature and extent of any savings that might help redress the resource needs we have highlighted is speculative at best, and certainly not of a kind that can resolve the issue in the short term.

Having made these observations about class size and the limitations of comparisons of East and West, there is no doubt in our minds that serious questions can be asked about the impact of allowing class sizes to fall so dramatically in some nations. The analyses of the distinguished Panel on the Economics of Educational Reform in the USA which met from 1989 to 1993 noted the steady increase in real expenditure on schools in that country over a century, with most targeted at reducing class size and increasing teachers' salaries. A key member of that panel, Eric Hanushek of Rochester University, who is at the forefront of efforts to bring a rigorous econometric perspective to improve school education, summarizes the impact of these increases on student achievement in recent decades:

> Schools currently have record-low pupil–teacher ratios, record-high numbers for completion of master's degrees, and more experienced teachers than at any time at least since 1960. These factors are the result of many specific programs that have contributed to the rapid growth in per-pupil spending but have not led to improvements in student performance. (Hanushek, 1996, p. 39)

Hanushek is careful to point out that there are some circumstances where class size is important, and the consensus of scholars is that this should be in the early years of schooling, especially for programs that focus on special needs such as literacy where one-to-one tutoring is important, as in the outstanding Success for All program, but his overall conclusion is striking:

Perhaps the most dramatic finding of analyses of schools is that smaller class sizes usually have had no general impact on student performance, even though they have obvious implications for school costs. Moreover, the basic econometric evidence is supported by experimental evidence, making it one of the clearest results from any extensively researched topic. Although some specific instruction may be enhanced by smaller classes, student performance in most classes is unaffected by variations in class size in standard operations of, say, 15 to 40 students. (Hanushek, 1996, p. 38)

In summary then, our recognition of the need for additional resources is not one that is inspired by calls for further reductions in class size, except where there is clear and incontrovertible evidence of a link to student performance, as in the early years and especially in literacy, but is connected to the capital and infrastructure costs associated with restoring the fabric of schools, providing for new information technologies, and the large-scale re-training of teachers to ensure that further efforts at school reform can be targeted at raising student performance through strategies that are known to be effective. It may be that class sizes ought to increase in certain areas of learning and stages of schooling; indeed, productivity gains along these lines may be necessary to secure an increase in salaries that might attract and maintain a highly qualified teaching force, working in improved buildings and with state-of-the-art technology.

2   Exclusive reliance on public funding is no longer realistic
We do not believe that increases in levels of resourcing of the magnitude implied in the foregoing analysis can be achieved by exclusive reliance on public funding. Indeed, in some places, notably Australia, including Victoria, there is an increasing dependence on 'voluntary' contributions by parents and other forms of private effort to maintain schooling as currently construed, with associated inequity from community to community in terms of capacity to supplement public funds.

Why not simply increase levels of taxation to meet the shortfall is the position taken by many. While increases at the margin may be possible, they go nowhere near maintaining the status quo let alone addressing the needs we have identified. In reality, a major increase in levels of taxation is neither adequate nor feasible. Consider three cases. In our own state of Victoria, Australia, all the needs we have identified are present, but the citizens of the state are already, on a per capita basis, at the highest or second highest level of taxation in the nation. The art of government includes addressing simultaneously the resource needs of school education and the needs of other sectors in the public domain, including health, transport and law enforcement. With an aging population, the needs of school education are more difficult to sustain compared to the 1970s, when resourcing for schools was at its high point and the majority of voters had children in schools. In the current environment, there is pressure to reduce levels of taxation coming from the citizen-at-large; from opposition parties, who simultaneously call for increases in resources for schools without explaining the trade-offs; or from international credit rating agencies such as Moody or Standard and Poor.

In the case of Britain, the 1997 election saw Labour, now in government, promising to maintain current levels of taxation but calling for a reallocation of funds to achieve smaller class sizes in the early years at the primary level, with the transfer occurring at the expense of the Assisted Places Scheme that funded some students from disadvantaged backgrounds to attend the more exclusive schools in the country such as Eton. The Liberal Democrats went to the election promising a 1 per cent increase in personal income tax to fund its program in school education. In neither instance can inroads be made to meet the resource requirements for schooling as we have envisaged it.

In the United States we recall the declaration by President Clinton in his 1997 State of the Union speech, following re-election to a second term, placing education at the top of his priorities. While part of his agenda referred to higher education, he also set high expectations for all students in elementary and secondary schools learning well, with a sound foundation in literacy, and a revolution in the adoption of new information technologies. He declared these intentions despite the federal government in the United States having a minimal role in school education and despite a promise to achieve a balanced budget in his second term, which means significant reductions in public expenditure, given that an increase in taxation is politically out of the question. Some school districts in the United States are adequately resourced, reflecting the substantial tax base that the more affluent suburbs can maintain, but the trend is against reliance on local property tax toward statewide reform and state-based resourcing that will level the playing field to some extent, but leave schools in general under-resourced along the lines we have argued in this analysis. One state has targeted significant additional resources to an aspect of school reform, and that state is California which set a policy in 1996 of achieving a reduction across the state in class sizes for elementary schools. While there is some evidence to support the measure as far as its impact on student learning is concerned, especially in the early years, the initiative is likely to be a one-shot effort as far as raising levels of resourcing is concerned, leaving the needs we identified at the outset in need of funds.

Hanushek presents the plight of schools in the USA in the starkest of terms, especially in the urban districts:

> As rising student populations combine with growth in real spending per student, aggregate spending will be up at a much higher rate than over the past decade. These prospective expenditure increases are likely to collide with public perceptions that school performance is not rising. If this happens, local taxpayers, who continue to play an important role in American school finance, are likely to resist future expenditure increases with unprecedented insistence, perhaps putting schools into a real fiscal squeeze. Moreover, many major urban districts face fiscal pressures from competing demands for public revenues, such as welfare or police funding, suggesting that the worst of the fiscal crisis might appear in the already pressured schools of major cities. (Hanushek, 1996, p. 35)

Taken together, these are illustrations of nations where commitment to an exclusive reliance on public funding will leave schools far short of resources to achieve lasting school reform. Resolving this issue requires that we tackle another issue, and that is the current largely ideological barrier to using other sources of funds to secure that achievement.

3   Being pragmatic rather than ideological in the interests of students
Clearly, in the short term at least, additional funds for public schools can only come from two other sources, from the contributions of families and from the corporate sector, and we contend that both should now be embraced more systematically, providing that appropriate mechanisms are in place to ensure equity in access to quality schooling. The manner in which this might be done is examined in Chapter 6.

Most western nations have embraced the view that public education should be free and compulsory to a designated level of schooling. Such intentions were enshrined in legislation at the time of formation of the great government or public school systems toward the end of the nineteenth century. Governments committed themselves to providing free schooling for all, no matter how remote or disadvantaged the setting, and this was mostly achieved. Similar intentions were declared for health care, although the concept of a private contribution was accepted for other services such as public transportation. Voluntary contributions and local fund-raising were encouraged from the outset and are not recent developments, although the extent to which there is reliance on these has increased in recent times.

We argued in the last section that exclusive reliance on public funding is no longer feasible. We reinforce that point in our analysis on alternative sources by reflecting on the conditions that prevailed in schools and hospitals in the late nineteenth century compared to those that are now required for quality schooling. A school at that time consisted of little more than classrooms, teachers, blackboards, chalk (or slates and slate pencils), and a few basic books, maybe one or two for each student. Classes were large and there was little equipment other than maps and globes. Teachers' salaries were low. Similarly for hospitals, where the local institution consisted of wards and an operating theatre, doctors and nurses, and some basic equipment. It was not difficult to sustain a fully funded system of public schooling and health care under these conditions.

Conditions in both settings have changed profoundly in the intervening years, especially in health care. Consider the personnel and equipment needs of the modern hospital where there is now the expectation that all citizens will have access to the full range of services including treatment of life-threatening illness and sophisticated elective surgery. Doctors and nurses are supported by an extraordinary array of professionals and para-professionals, machines are very costly, often in the millions for single items, and drugs for treatment are similarly expensive on a unit basis. Public health care has been in crisis for some time and, difficult though the decision may be, it is clear to governments of all persuasion that placing such hospitals in every community is no longer possible and that some form of private contribution is needed if immediate access to the best services is to be assured.

We now realize that schools have not kept pace with hospitals in respect to their utilization of advanced technology and their deployment of a wide range of professional and para-professional services, a point made in dramatic fashion by Seymour Papert in the opening lines of his book *The Children's Machine* (Papert, 1993). Imagine, writes Papert, time travellers from the 1890s visiting hospitals and schools of the 1990s: surgeons would not recognize the modern operating theatre, but teachers would be immediately familiar with their surroundings and could likely take over the class! Apart from helping make the case for what needs to occur for lasting school reform, when combined with our analysis of resource needs and capacity or willingness to meet the costs from the public purse, Papert helps make the argument for private effort that parallels the manner in which governments everywhere are seeking to cope with the crisis in health care.

A similar analysis can be applied to efforts to sustain a fully government owned airline, as in the case of British Air and Qantas. It became palpably clear in the 1970s and 1980s that these airlines could not remain competitive if there was exclusive reliance on the public purse to purchase and maintain a fleet of modern planes and provide the public with the services expected in modern times. The solution was delayed until an ideological commitment to the notion that a government should fully own and resource an airline was abandoned, giving way to the notion that private capitalization was necessary while maintaining a key role for government as a major or minor shareholder. Similarly in the case of banks. In these and other instances, the public interest was sustained through standards enshrined in charters.

The reality is that public education has not been free, almost from the outset, but it is especially evident now that there is increasing reliance in some settings on the contributions of parents. It is a significant public issue, notably in most states in Australia, including Victoria where voluntary private effort, through non-compulsory non-instructional 'fees' or through local fundraising, forms about 5 per cent of the operating budget of most schools. To maintain a strictly ideological stance on the matter is to maintain the current haphazard, unsystematic and opaque approach that leaves public schools short of much needed resources, to the detriment of current and future generations of students.

Role of Government

Central to our analysis has been the role of government. We acknowledged in the opening lines of the book that public education has been one of the success stories of the century. We are not advocating a retreat from the concept of the public school, although as will be clear in Chapter 6, we call for a re-conceptualization. We have shown that, with initiatives such as Schools of the Future (Victoria, Australia) and the Local Management of Schools (Britain), a public system can be transformed from one that is highly centralized in almost all of its operations to one with a relatively lean but powerful centre that furnishes curriculum and standards frameworks, accountability schemes and mechanisms for the allocation of resources, but in all other respects leaves management decisions to schools that are responsive to the needs and priorities of students in unique local settings. There is wide acceptance of such a transformation and, though it is difficult to obtain because of the absence of base-line data, there is evidence of a contribution to improved outcomes for students. We have then argued that the next and lasting stage of school reform should focus on achieving improved outcomes for all students in schools that are well-resourced in terms of technology and other requirements for learning in a knowledge society. Our analysis so far suggests that exclusive reliance on public funding to sustain a system of public education is no longer possible and that there should be systematic provision for a private contribution. How this should be done is taken up in Chapter 6.

There are three other matters that relate to the issue of the role of government that we address here. These concern the secular nature of systems of public education, parental choice and access to public schooling, and markets and equity.

1 Secular nature of systems of public education

Maintaining an exclusive reliance on full public funding is connected in some places with a commitment to the secular nature of systems of public schooling. This commitment is part of the ideological rigidity that is holding back further reform. Among the nations we have drawn on for analysis, this stands out most in the United States and Australia. In the former, there is a constitutional bar to prayer in the public school so that public funds cannot be directed to Catholic or Jewish schools, for example. These must be fully funded by private (fee) and community (church) effort. Parochial and independent schools in the USA form a small minority of all schools in that country where most students are in public schools that are more or less fully funded, but under-resourced in the sense we have argued earlier.

In Australia, the absence of a constitutional bar has allowed significant resourcing of non-public, independent or private schools from the public purse, most from the Commonwealth (national) Government but also from state governments. Various indices of need have been established so that Catholic schools in deprived areas, for example, are almost fully publicly funded, with low levels of student fee, and independent schools in well-endowed communities draw some public funding, with most revenue from the fees of their students. These are relatively recent developments in Australia, mostly deriving from the late 1960s and the early 1970s and the great 'state aid' debates in the political arena. The particular mechanisms for funding non-public schools are of special interest and relevant to the proposals we present in Chapter 6.

In Australia and the USA there remains an ideological barrier to embracing the concept of private effort to help resource public schools and resistance remains to the notion that public funds ought to help resource non-public schools. These barriers are not so evident in some other countries and account should be taken of practice elsewhere in determining how the issue of the role of government should be resolved to help sustain lasting reform. We note, for example, that most church schools are integrated into the system of public schools in New Zealand, although there are a number of truly independent schools. Similarly in Britain, where schools owned by the churches are 'aided' schools in the sense of their recurrent resourcing from the local education authority (Local Management of Schools) or the Funding Agency for Schools (Grant-Maintained Schools). In Canada, several provinces have systems of public and separate school districts, with the former being the schools of choice of the majority of electors and the latter of the minority, either Catholic or Protestant. A significant feature of the Canadian approach is that electors direct the 'school portion' of their local property taxes to the system of their choice, with each type of system receiving identical funding from provincial (state) governments. Hong Kong provides an interesting mix of government and non-government schools, the former being the minority but fully funded from the public purse, the latter being a mixture of privately owned, corporately owned or church schools that receive government funds on virtually the same basis as government schools. The almost seamless integration of all kinds of schools in The Netherlands is also of interest.

Our point here is that what constitutes a public school, and what constitutes a government school, and how resources are allocated across these types of schools, varies from nation to nation and the distinctions are blurred and more pragmatic than ideological, although the particular pattern that now prevails in each instance was the outcome or settlement of a debate in earlier times that was intensely ideological, as in the case of the Canadian arrangements and the 'state aid' issue in Australia. These practices illustrate how all kinds of schools can be embraced under the concept of 'the public school' and that various resourcing arrangements are possible. We believe it is timely to re-visit the issue, no doubt with vigorous debate, with a new settlement to lay the foundation for lasting reform and a new or re-defined role for government in some settings.

2   Parental choice and access to public schooling

We embrace the primacy of parental choice in matters of schooling. By this we mean that parents should have a virtually unfettered right to choose a public school for their children, and that past practice of zoning schools in the public sector so that parents were required to send their children to a particular school has no place in the scheme of things. Fortunately, most systems around the world, at least in nations we are considering in this book, have abandoned the practice. There are, of course, a number of qualifications. First, that this right should extend to the right to attend the local or nearest school, so in managing enrolments or registrations in the exercise of parental choice, school authorities should give a first preference to local parents and thus assure this right. Second, that not all schools can provide the same programs or provide the particular programs that a parent may seek for their children. This is most evident in the case of schools for students with disabilities and impairments, and the nearest school is unlikely to be able to provide what is needed. Similarly, for schools that offer specialist programs such as the arts. In these matters, considerations of efficiency in the use of public resources require a limitation on the exercise of parental choice. Third, that some choices will require a parent to provide a substantial personal effort by way of fee to secure the kind of schooling that is sought. This is, of course, the condition for those who seek private, non-government, non-public or independent schooling.

If these rights are accepted, along with the qualifications, and if there is acceptance that public education should be broadly defined as we have illustrated across a range of settings in the last section, then private entitlement to a share of public resources should be assured. We propose mechanisms for achieving this in Chapter 6.

3   Markets and equity

Advocacy of parental choice in these terms is not advocacy of a perfect market in public schooling. The qualifications we have provided help ensure that it is not a perfect market. There is not now, never has been, and likely never will be a perfect market in school education, and certainly not in public education. Nevertheless, conditions have changed in recent times and there is clearly more of a market situation now than in the past. It was not Schools of the Future or the Local Management of Schools that triggered this situation but the abandonment of zoning arrangements that, in one stroke, gave dramatic effect to the exercise of parental choice. Similarly, the new funding arrangements in self-managed or locally managed schools so that 'the money follows the student' is simply a financial translation of the de-zoning mechanism that facilitates parental choice rather than a new market-driven ideologically based arrangement.

The issue of equity is important in two respects. One arises out of the exercise of parental choice and a stronger market orientation. There is no doubt that in Britain, for example, de-zoning arrangements, per capita driven funding, and greater public awareness of school performance as reflected in the publication of test results, have led to a shift in student enrolments, so that some schools are perceived as being better than others and tend to be over-subscribed and other schools, perceived as failing, have rapidly declining enrolments. If the latter phenomenon occurs as a result of poor schooling, through ineffective approaches to teaching and learning as confirmed in valid assessments, then strong and immediate corrective action ought to be taken and the necessary mechanisms should be in place, though they have not yet been used to any great extent. If only some parents have the interest or capacity to exercise this choice, then there is no point in hand-wringing and seeking to curtail parental choice; the answer is to help more parents gain access to understandable and valid information about schools and help them exercise their choice. The inequities in the past have arisen in part because only the better informed parents have been able to exercise their choice. There is also a concern that shifts in enrolments of this kind might denude some schools of their more able students, resulting in a climate that is not conducive to setting and achieving high expectations for those students that remain. While there is not widespread evidence of this occurring, the response is not to abandon the exercise of parental choice, but to take measures to ensure that all schools, including small schools, provide schooling of the highest quality to retain their best students or at least maintain a high quality of schooling for all who attend. The issue simply raises the stakes in efforts to achieve the lasting reform of schools.

The second aspect of equity is the more important, given our view that lasting reform in public education cannot be achieved by exclusive reliance on public funds and that some private contribution is required. Clearly, there are differences in the capacity of parents to make such a contribution and the prospect of entrenching existing inequities in voluntary contributions and local fund-raising will understandably be a concern. That such an issue can be resolved is evidenced in arrangements for systems of Catholic schools in Australia that draw significant public funding on an index of capacity to resource and that charge what amounts to a sliding scale of fees according to the community setting of the school. Parents in some settings pay minimal fees, others in other settings pay high fees. We consider but reject such an arrangement in Chapter 6, but the point we make here is that there are mechanisms in place that ensure that issues of equity can be addressed in mixed public and private funding arrangements. The Catholic example is a good one, for the system is explicitly driven by values of equity and social justice.

Pre-conditions for Lasting School Reform

Analysis of these five issues sets the stage for the presentation of our view of the pre-conditions for lasting school reform in nations of the kind we are broadly considering in this book.

1   Reforms such as Schools of the Future are a necessary but not sufficient condition
For the foreseeable future, frameworks such as those constructed in Britain and in Victoria, under Schools of the Future, are necessary but not sufficient. There are some matters to be taken up in the detail of implementation and ongoing refinement, but essentially, the first of the pre-conditions is that there exists a curriculum and standards framework for all schools, with a central authority responsible for its maintenance as well as with the provision of resources to schools, which are then able to manage their own affairs as they pursue the highest possible standards of achievements for their students. This capacity for self-management or local management or school-based management is primarily concerned with ensuring that schools can make their own plans, taking account of the needs of their students, to select staff to meet that unique mix of needs and priorities, set targets for achievement, allocate resources to support these efforts, and report to the community and the school system about how well they are doing. The accountability mechanism is important, whether it be the system of testing and public reporting with inspection as in Britain, or the more constrained approach to monitoring achievement and conducting school reviews as in Victoria.

For nations like the United States of America, the challenge is to provide a framework that has this coherence, a task that is proving difficult with a national government that has few direct powers in school education and about 15,000 school districts in fifty states. The reform effort is highly fragmented. Progress has been made in states like Kentucky, starting from a low base as far as standards are concerned, that achieved coherence in its reforms following a crisis that essentially threw out the existing approach to public education and literally re-invented the system.

2   Public policy and school effort must be tightly focused on the achievement of high standards for all students
Re-structuring schools and school systems along these lines is just a starting point. Every aspect of public policy thereafter must be focused on setting standards and providing a framework for helping schools achieve them. This framework will have many elements, including policies on resourcing schools, selecting and maintaining a highly qualified work force of teachers and other professionals, providing buildings and other infrastructure that ensure learning occurs in settings that are consistent with requirements for a knowledge society, and gathering information about student achievement to guide further policy development and inform the public about what is being accomplished in schools.

For schools, this means high levels of knowledge and skill among teachers and other professionals about how students learn, and how to design and deliver programs to ensure that students achieve at the highest levels possible. Teachers must be comfortable about measuring and monitoring student achievement for a range of reasons, the most important of which include helping to set targets for improvements, furnishing evidence of progress toward achievement of those targets, and informing parents and others with an interest about how well the school is doing. Taking up capacities for self-management calls for high levels of professionalism by all, including principals and other school leaders who must become 'educational strategists' in energizing these efforts.

3   High levels of professionalism must be achieved among teachers and others who work in schools
Low levels of morale are apparently endemic in the profession at this time, although highly motivated and well satisfied teachers are doing great things in schools that have embraced a reform agenda. Measures to address this state of affairs, and in other ways to achieve high levels of professionalism, include ensuring a supply of highly qualified entrants to the ranks, including greater mobility with other sectors of the workforce; providing initial training and continuing professional development to give all the knowledge and skill to design and deliver state-of-the-art approaches to learning and teaching, including utilization of the new information technologies; and building or re-building the physical plant and the furnishings of schools to make them exciting places of work for skilled professionals and their students. Higher salaries and improved working conditions along these lines will likely be necessary.

4   Education and the economy should converge after decades of divergence
With the aid of eminent writer Peter Drucker, we traced the manner in which the workplace changed so dramatically over more than one hundred years since systems of public education were built in many nations. We showed how school

education, like other fields of social endeavour, grew apart from the workplace, and the expanding field of economics. We are greatly encouraged by calls for new theories of economics that afford a greater place for education in the knowledge society, but we contend that those who work in school education must also gain greater understanding of the economy and the world of work. This convergence is necessary if teachers and others who work in schools are to understand, be committed to and be full partners in efforts to achieve lasting school reform. Achieving it calls for high levels of leadership in the profession and for new themes in the preparation and ongoing professional development of teachers.

5   Higher levels of resources and formal recognition of private effort on the revenue side are required to energize and sustain the enterprise
Higher levels of resourcing will be required for public education in the nations that seek further reform in the direction we are proposing. These resources are not to reduce class size, for we are persuaded by the evidence that this will not likely lead to significant gain, although we acknowledge that smaller classes, even one-to-one tutoring, are required for some purposes. They are required primarily for re-building the run-down infrastructure of school education, for equipping schools with the new information technologies, and for massive re-training of the profession to ensure that teachers have the knowledge and skill to design and deliver programs to achieve high standards for all. Increases in salaries are also indicated.

We are also persuaded that only improvement at the margin can be gained through increases in taxation, given public resistance to further increases of any kind for any purpose, let alone winning the battle against competing areas such as health, law enforcement and public transport. Private contribution to public effort will be necessary, in some instances confirming the unsystematic approaches to 'voluntary contributions' or 'non-instructional fees' paid by parents, long evident in places like those with which we are most familiar, in Victoria and other states in Australia. Other personal, charitable or corporate effort should be encouraged, perhaps along the lines that has long been a strong part of the culture in Hong Kong, or that is now starting to have impressive effect in the United States of America.

Incorporating other sources of revenue for public education clearly calls for a more pragmatic approach to funding by those who hold to the notion that such education should be free in all respects. This was an appropriate stance in the nineteenth century, when the task was to provide a basic education, essentially a school house, a teacher, blackboard and slates, basic readers and a few maps and globes, to a widely dispersed community, just as it was under the same conditions for basic health care. It is no longer possible for schools at the dawn of the twenty-first century, just as it is no longer possible for health care, for which a private contribution is now generally required. Just as we have abandoned long and fondly held beliefs that governments should fully own and operate airlines, post offices and banks, even provide us with free pure water, so we should recognize that private effort is required to create and sustain a system of public education. To maintain rigid ideological opposition to such a course is to limit the quality of schooling we provide to future generations. We are, of course, mindful of the attendant issues of equity and capacity to pay, and we take this up in the last pre-condition, and canvas the options in Chapter 6.

6   For public education, government should establish the framework, set standards, provide infrastructure and other resources, support schools and monitor outcomes, allowing self-managing schools to respond to parental choice, with due account in the framework for matters of access and equity, particularly in respect to private effort for additional resources

We see no reason not to give full effect to parental choice of schooling, continuing a trend that was given a major boost in most settings with the decision to de-zone schools, that is, allowing parents to send their children to a school of their choice, not necessarily the closest. This is not advocacy of a perfect market, for we should also provide for parents to send their children to the nearest school, if that is their wish, and acknowledge that not all schools can provide the particular facilities and particular programs that will meet the needs and interests of all students.

Some of the barriers that remain in Australia and the United States, for example, must still be removed. We are thinking here of the way church and other private schools are part of the public or aided sector in other places, notably, Britain, Canada, Hong Kong, The Netherlands and New Zealand. A distinction between government and non-government, public and private, is still maintained in Australia in a way that restricts our thinking about the role of government, thinking that has long since been freed in these other countries, although public debate may have been vociferous at the time current arrangements were settled. Such freedom may be more problematic in the USA, given the constitutional barriers to public funding for private schools.

Giving full effect to parental choice has led to fears of some schools facing decline as parents respond to information about achievements in other schools, and the former are left with a critical mass of under-achieving students. Our response is not to deny parental choice but to ensure that all parents have access to valid information and that all schools have the capacity to provide a quality education for all their students.

In Summary

In this chapter we provided our view of the pre-conditions for lasting school reform, based on assumptions about schooling in the twenty-first century, being schooling for a knowledge society in nations such as Australia, Britain, Canada, New Zealand and the United States, which furnish the main readership for this book, as well as other nations with advanced or developing economies, including the 'tigers' of the East. This was intended to be a positive and up-beat view of the role of school, even though the school will likely be challenged as the exclusive provider of education for young people. For public education, our pre-conditions may be summarized in this manner:

- Reforms such as Schools of the Future are a necessary but not sufficient condition.
- Public policy and school effort must be tightly focused on the achievement of high standards for all students.
- High levels of professionalism must be achieved among teachers and others who work in schools.
- Education and the economy should converge after decades of divergence.
- Higher levels of resources and formal recognition of private effort on the revenue side are required to energize and sustain the enterprise.
- For public education, government should establish the framework, set standards, provide infrastructure and other resources, support schools and monitor outcomes, allowing self-managing schools to respond to parental choice, with due account in the framework for matters of access and equity, particularly in respect to private effort for additional resources.

There are several options for a policy framework. Exploring these options and expressing our preferences are tasks for Chapter 6.

6 A Policy Framework for Public Schools of the Third Millennium

In this chapter we propose a policy framework for public schools of the third millennium that responds to the issues addressed in Chapter 5. We make clear at the outset our vision for public schools in a manner we hope will reassure readers of our commitment to an enduring institution, the achievements of which we saluted in the first pages of the book. We then start building the policy framework, using as a starting point the pre-conditions for lasting reform that were presented at the end of the last chapter. We cannot address every national setting so we illustrate the essential features in our own country, taking every opportunity to draw ideas from and suggest applications in other places. We pay particular attention in our framework to the role of government and how public schools should be resourced.

A Vision for Schools of the Third Millennium

We have a vision for public schools, indeed all schools, that has the following elements. These should be read in association with our assumptions about society and schooling at the beginning of Chapter 5. We have a picture in our minds, and a commitment to schools where:

- all children learn the basics well;
- schools do well in their traditional role as 'centres for communicating civilization' (imagery suggested by D'Arcy, 1989), rich in learning of history, language, literature and the arts;
- formal schooling starts earlier and continues lifelong;
- while the concept of a curriculum and standards framework will endure, there will emerge a global view of curriculum and this will be achieved by consensus among the key stakeholders rather than formal prescription;
- monitoring and demonstrating achievement through the use of tests and other devices will continue, with technology allowing a global framework to be utilized;
- a place called school will continue to be important but much learning will occur in other locations;
- schooling at the upper secondary level will become more complex and diverse, with multiple providers; combined with advances made possible by technology, the concept of a 'virtual school' will emerge at this and higher levels of education and training;

- the nature of teaching and other areas of professional work will change in dramatic ways, with much more fee for service like for other professionals; the packaging of work into 'a job', with tenure, will be rare in schooling as in almost every other field of work;
- there will be little need for a bureaucracy in the traditional sense although a strategic core for resourcing and accountability frameworks will continue, since the public purse will continue as the major source of funds in the foreseeable future; and
- schools, parents and students will utilize a highly sophisticated network of student and school support, largely privatized or outsourced, to use the quaint jargon that crossed the scene in the mid 1990s.

It is beyond the scope of the chapter to describe this vision in more detail. Much of that detail is presented in another book in this series, co-authored by Brian Caldwell, being the third in a trilogy with Jim Spinks (Caldwell and Spinks, 1998). The earlier books with Spinks provided, first, the concept of 'the self-managing school' and some approaches that were helpful in many countries as local management or school-based management was introduced (Caldwell and Spinks, 1988) and second, a revised model for self-management that took account of the increasing complexity of schooling in the 1990s and outlined four dimensions of transformational leadership in the self-managing school (Caldwell and Spinks, 1992).

In *Beyond the Self-Managing School*, Caldwell and Spinks (1998) acknowledge the reality of local management or school-based management or self-management, reiterate their earlier call for linkage with learning and teaching, now powerfully supported in the research literature as set out in Chapter 4, and then outline a vision or *gestalt* that is likely to take shape in the first decade of the third millennium. The focus is on learning. The elements in our vision set out above are consistent with that *gestalt*, as illustrated in Figure 6.1 and described briefly below.

Caldwell and Spinks describe their vision as a *gestalt* in the sense of it being 'a perceived organized whole that is more than the sum of its parts' (Concise Oxford Dictionary). It cannot be described in detail but may be presented as a *gestalt* (g1–g7 in Figure 6.1). The detail will be clearer as the years advance, as opportunities are sensed and seized, as new factors come in to play, and as exemplars emerge.

- Dramatic change to approaches to learning and teaching is in store as electronic networking allows 'cutting across and so challenging the very idea of subject boundaries' and 'changing the emphasis from impersonal curriculum to excited live exploration' (Papert, 1993, p. 39). At risk is the balkanized curriculum that has done much to alienate children from schooling, especially in the middle years of the transition from primary and secondary (g1 Connectedness in curriculum).
- Schools as workplaces will be transformed in every dimension, including the scheduling of time for learning and approaches to human resource management, rendering obsolete most approaches that derive from an

Figure 6.1: A vision for schooling for the knowledge society presented as a gestalt

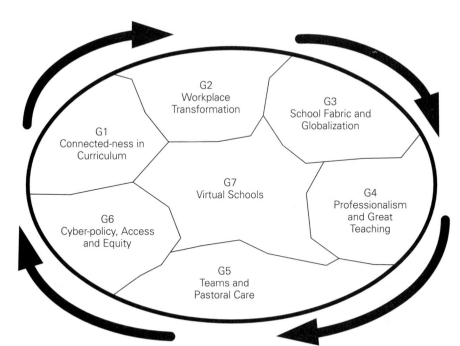

Source: Caldwell and Spinks, 1998

industrial age, including the concept of 'industrial relations' (g2 Work-place transformation).

- The fabric of schooling will similarly be rendered obsolete by electronic networking. Everything from building design to the size, shape, alignment, and furnishing of space for the 'knowledge worker' in the school will be transformed. In one sense, of course, the school will have no walls, for there will be global learning networks, and much of the learning that calls for the student to be located at school will occur in many places, at home and, at the upper years of secondary schooling and for life-long learning, in the work place (g3 School fabric and globalization).

- A wide range of professionals and para-professionals will support learning in an educational parallel to the diversity of support that may be found in modern health care. The role of teacher will be elevated, for it will demand wisdom, judgment, and a facility to manage learning in modes more complex and varied than ever. While the matter of intellectual capital must be resolved, the teacher will be freed from the impossible task of designing from their own resources learning experiences to challenge every student: the resources of the world's great teachers will be at hand (g4 Professionalism and great teaching).

- A capacity to work in teams will be more evident in approaches to learning, given the primacy of the work team in every formulation of the workplace in the knowledge society. This, of course, will confound those who see electronic networking in an outdated stereotype of the loner with the laptop. The concept of 'pastoral care' of students will be as important as ever for learning in this mode, and in schools that will quite literally have no boundaries (g5 Teams and pastoral care).
- Dale Spender's challenge to formulate 'cyber-policy of the future' (Spender, 1995) will be a priority. The issues of access and equity will drive public debate until such time as prices fall to make electronic networks as common as the telephone or radio, and that may soon be a reality, given trends in networked computers (NCs) (g6 Cyber-policy, access and equity).
- The concept of the virtual organization or the learning network organization will become a reality in the knowledge society. Schools will take on many of the characteristics of such organizations, given that learning will occur in so many modes and from so many sources, all networked electronically (g7 Virtual schools).

Pre-conditions for Lasting School Reform

In Chapter 5 we described pre-conditions for achieving lasting school reform, presented here for easy reference.

- Reforms such as Schools of the Future are a necessary but not sufficient condition.
- Public policy and school effort must be tightly focused on the achievement of high standards for all students.
- High levels of professionalism must be achieved among teachers and others who work in schools.
- Education and the economy should converge after decades of divergence.
- Higher levels of resources and formal recognition of private effort on the revenue side are required to energize and sustain the enterprise.
- For public education, government should establish the framework, set standards, provide infrastructure and other resources, support schools and monitor outcomes, allowing self-managing schools to respond to parental choice, with due account in the framework for matters of access and equity, particularly in respect to private effort for additional resources.

Building the Policy Framework

Our framework has four dimensions, each built around a key concept. For the concept of 'public', we propose that the public school should encompass virtually all schools, and that distinctions in some countries between government and non-government, public and private, state and independent, locally managed and grant-maintained, and the like, should cease to exist and that all receiving funds from the public purse should be considered 'public schools'. There will, of course, be differences among public schools according to 'foundation arrangements'. For the concept of 'entitlement', we extend the notion of the public school by adding the notion of choice, to define an entitlement to public resources that should attach to each student attending a public school. For some states and nations, this will remove the complexity of funding arrangements that are neither fair nor transparent. For the concept of 'contribution', we acknowledge that current reliance on so-called voluntary contributions or levies is leaving many schools under-resourced. We propose a scheme for a school education contribution, with provisions for some parents to be exempt and some schools in disadvantaged areas to have increased grants from the public purse. For the concept of 'design', we suggest how different approaches to restructuring learning and teaching should be encouraged and supported, building on an idea that gathered momentum in the 1990s.

The Concept of 'Public'

The concept of a 'public school' varies from nation to nation. In the USA it is restricted to those schools that are publicly funded, which excludes schools that are operated by churches and private fee-charging independent schools. The two sectors are described by some as 'public' and 'non-public'. The distinction arises from a constitutional ban on the use of prayer in public schools that effectively bars the use of public funds for church schools. Noteworthy is the fact that in most states that allow charter schools, the charter school leaves the school district, assumes ownership of its property and employs its teachers, and is still considered a public school. The concept of 'public' is thus tied to the use of public funds.

In Britain, the concept has often proved elusive since it has been reserved in one usage to the most exclusive of private schools but, more recently, it refers to schools that receive support from the public purse, so it now has the same meaning as in the USA, except that it applies to a much wider range of schools. There are those schools that are funded by a local education authority (LEA) but are locally managed and there are two kinds, authority operated and 'voluntary schools', with the latter including schools that are operated by churches or private foundations or trusts which own the property but receive grants to meet recurrent costs, including salaries, along the same lines as schools operated by the authority. Voluntary schools are either 'aided voluntary', receiving grants from the LEA covering part of recurrent costs, or 'controlled voluntary', receiving grants from the LEA covering all recurrent costs, with the difference between the two depending on the extent to which the foundation body, usually religious, maintains a controlling role in determining the (religious) program of the school (Halls, 1994, p. 6518). The other kind of school receiving public funds is the grant-maintained schools, which were formerly operated by the local education authority but which left, following a majority vote of parents. Grant-maintained schools receive funds from the public purse at a slightly higher level than locally managed schools, with the addition being the value of services previously provided by the local education authority. Funds for grant-maintained schools are disbursed by the Funding Agency for Schools, a body established by the national government for this purpose. There are very few schools that receive no funds from government and that are therefore described as private (an Assisted Places scheme in private schools for students of low income families is to be abolished by the Labour Government).

The situation in New Zealand is similar to that in Britain as far as the inclusion of church schools in the public sector is concerned, and there is no difference between the levels of recurrent funding received by church and non-church schools. These arrangements followed the Private Schools Conditional Integration Act of 1975 that provided for the voluntary integration of private schools into the state system (Barrington, 1994, p. 4106). In New Zealand there are no grant-maintained schools and there is a relatively small number of private schools enrolling fewer than 5 per cent of students.

In some provinces of Canada, the term 'public' is reserved for schools of the majority of tax-payers, while the term 'separate' is reserved for schools of a minority of taxpayers, but each is funded from the public purse to about the same level. A designation of 'separate' is made on the basis of the tax-payer being 'Protestant' or 'Catholic'. In Edmonton, for example, the minority give their support to the Edmonton Roman Catholic Separate School District, so the majority are associated with the Edmonton Public School District. In the neighbouring city of St Albert, the reverse applies, and the minority support the St Alberta Protestant Separate School District. In financial terms, support translates to specifying which system shall receive that proportion of local property tax that is to be directed to schools. This level of tax may differ between systems, but the province, in this instance, Alberta, provides the major part of funds to support schools, and levels are the same, regardless of the type of system. More recently, the province has moved to collect the school proportion of local property tax and disburse the total to school districts around the province on an equitable basis. The point to be made in the Canadian experience cited here is that, while the word 'public' is being used in a special sense, schools of different types based on a religious classification receive the same treatment when it comes to funding from the public purse and it is the decision of the tax-payer as to which system a part of these public funds shall be directed. Fewer than 5 per cent of schools in Canada are private schools.

Another system where there have been ambitious proposals for school reform is Hong Kong. Here there are three types of schools: government schools owned and operated by government (about 8 per cent); aided schools owned and operated by churches, foundations, trusts or some other private organization or agency (just over 80 per cent); and private schools which, unlike the first two, receive no support from public funds (just under 10 per cent). For the aided sector, while ownership of the school resides with a body other than government, funding for recurrent expenditure is virtually the same as for government schools. A Direct Subsidy Scheme introduced in the early 1990s enables aided secondary schools to become private schools and receive substantial government grants.

The approach in The Netherlands is also of interest here, with schools owned and operated by public authorities attracting about 30 per cent of students, with the rest mainly denominational, either Catholic or Protestant (about 65 per cent), and non-denominational (about 5 per cent). The funds for the operation of these schools are provided by the state, with the distinguishing feature of the private schools being that they are governed by an independent board or council. The financial equality of public authority and private schools is guaranteed in the Constitution (Vuyk, 1994, p. 4071).

A different arrangement prevails in Australia. Until recently, the term 'public school' was reserved in general usage to the exclusive private school, as was traditionally the case in Britain, so there were government or state schools, Catholic schools operated on a systemic basis, and independent or private schools. More recently, people have started to refer to government or state schools as public schools.

While usage of the word 'public' will continue to vary from nation to nation, and will likely continue to evolve in different ways within nations, we think it is timely for there to be a new agreement on the concept of 'public'. The emerging common theme across nations is that such a concept should apply to schools that receive funds from the public purse. The primary interest of the authors is Australia, and it is in our country that a major shift in usage should occur as a result of this conceptualization. Essentially, we propose that, in Australia, as in each of the other countries we have mentioned, except for Canada although the spirit is the same, all schools that receive funds from the public purse should be considered public schools and, consistent with practice in other places, the basis for the recurrent funding of all such schools should be the same. We return to the funding arrangements in our consideration of the concepts of 'entitlement' and 'contribution'.

In nations such as Australia, where such a change in usage should occur, there will be similar arrangements as in Britain and New Zealand in terms of 'foundation arrangements' as these apply, in particular, to the ownership of the school, including the land, buildings and other capital items, and to the employment of staff. Clearly, ownership of land and employment of staff shall continue to lie with the church, council, board or trust that established the school, so there shall be no disturbance of these foundation arrangements with the proposal we are making.

We acknowledge that the proposal may be viewed by a few as the manifestation of some ideological bent. This can hardly be the case given that we are simply accommodating the concept of the public school in the same spectrum that exists in other nations and that has no particular ideological connotation in these places even though, in earlier times, the establishment of some arrangements may have been controversial, as it was in Canada when matters related to the practices described above were settled. No doubt there will be vigorous public debate in Australia, as there was as recently as the 1960s, when the first public funds began to be directed toward non-government schools, but we expect this will soon be settled with wide public acceptance.

We also propose that schools that are currently called government or public schools should have the opportunity to become more autonomous, along the lines of grant-maintained schools in Britain or charter schools in the USA. In our view, there are many schools in Australia where there is sufficient community interest and commitment, and where principals and staff have the skill and the will to move in this direction, and they should have the opportunity to do so. We recall in this regard the findings of the Cooperative Research Project that a relatively large number of principals see 'bureaucratic interference' as a shortcoming in the implementation of Schools of the Future, and the time is certainly appropriate in Victoria to move in this direction. This may mean transfer of ownership and employment of staff from the state to the school. Mechanisms along the lines adopted for these arrangements with grant-maintained schools (Britain) or charter schools (USA) might be employed but it is beyond our scope to address these in detail.

These elements of the policy framework are, of course, already in place in Britain, including those related to more autonomous schools, designated grant-maintained under the previous Conservative Government, maintained by the Labour Government but re-named with some changes to governance arrangements. We propose the following for nations such as those we have discussed in this chapter, including the USA, even though the concept of 'public' is constrained in that nation by the constitutional bar referred to earlier.

Elements in a Policy Framework Based on the Concept of 'Public'

- That all schools that receive funds from the public purse should be designated 'public schools'.
- That existing 'foundation arrangements' shall continue in respect to ownership of the school and its resources and the employment of its staff.
- That schools whose communities and staff have the commitment and capacity should have the opportunity to change their 'foundation arrangements' from government owned and employed to privately owned and employed, with transition arrangements established to ensure such a change is a valid expression of intention and is feasible.

The Concept of 'Entitlement'

We use the concept of 'entitlement' in two senses, first, the entitlement of a public school to public funds and, second, the entitlement of parents in terms of the nature of schooling to be received by their children.

We propose that all public schools receive funds to cover recurrent expenditure from the public purse on the same basis, regardless of the nature of the school. Recurrent expenditure refers to operating costs, including staff, supplies, equipment and services. For schools that remain government owned, public funds shall be provided for capital expenditure, including the construction and maintenance of buildings and major items of equipment, including information technology. For nations like Australia, this will mean dramatic change, but for nations like Britain,

Canada, Hong Kong (China), The Netherlands and New Zealand it will mean no change, for all schools funded from the public purse receive grants to cover recurrent expenditure on more-or-less the same basis, including those that in Australia would be regarded in 1997 as non-public.

An important change for Australia is that non-government or private schools will no longer receive different per student grants from Commonwealth and State Governments according to their placement in a classification of schools based on an assessment of their resource capacity. For Australia, we are simply proposing that, if one accepts the same concept of 'public' that is widely embraced elsewhere, and if one accepts the principle of choice, then the concept of 'entitlement' means an equitable basis of support from the public purse.

Two issues arise from this proposal. First, what shall be the level of entitlement and how shall it be delivered? Second, how shall arrangements be made, given different levels of responsibility for providing resources? For the first issue, we note the important progress made in Britain and Victoria in determining a mechanism for distributing resources to schools under conditions of local management or self-management that prevail in each place. Difficulties in Britain include a mechanism that leaves a larger than warranted difference between per capita funding at the upper primary and lower secondary levels, and the wide disparity across the country in levels of per capita support from one local education authority to another. Even attempts to determine a common funding formula for grant-maintained schools through the Funding Agency for Schools were confounded by the latter. In Victoria, things are more straightforward on both counts, assuming implementation of recommendations for allocating resources on the basis of stages of schooling, smoothing the transition from primary to secondary (see recommendations in Education Committee, 1997) and because differentials in costs across the state are not so high and can be accommodated in one element of the mechanism for determining the levels of resources in school global budgets.

Victoria is close to being able to specify a core element in per capita allocations to schools at different levels according to stage of schooling, with additional elements for special needs of students and location of schools, that could be applied to all schools in the new conceptualization of public schooling, providing funds from Commonwealth and State are 'pooled' for allocation to schools. This second issue shall require new agreements between levels of government, and an opportunity is presented in the case of Victoria. In 1996, Victoria ceded the exercise of its powers in industrial relations to the Commonwealth. A new arrangement for schools might involve the Commonwealth providing funds that it normally disburses itself. In other words, a special arrangement is struck with Victoria, and any other state that wishes to enter into such an agreement. Victoria is specified because it is at the leading edge in respect to self-managing schools. In time, of course, the arrangements would apply across the nation.

For a few, this proposal, like that on the concept of 'public', will have more than a hint of ideology that departs from long-held values that underpin public schooling. As before, we reject this. Others may be concerned that this is the introduction of a voucher in school education. The original connotation of a voucher as a piece of paper given to a parent to be 'cashed in' at a school of choice has rarely been implemented for, apart from objection in principle, it was seen in practice as inefficient if not unworkable. However, the concept of a fairly determined per capita allocation, with additional elements where there are special education needs, following the student, as it were, and being paid to the school in the form of a grant, is now widely embraced and no longer has any particular ideological connotations. This is especially the case in Britain where all political parties embrace this approach to the resourcing of schools. We note too that the original meaning of voucher has to some extent been lost, as evidenced in a recent report for the World Bank that used the term to cover virtually every variant of decentralization in public education (West, 1996).

We see no reason why the concept of 'entitlement' cannot be implemented in a way that captures the core intentions of the voucher, which are to tie the resources to the student and to facilitate parental choice. We have the technology now to keep track of entitlements in most other spheres, as in the sophisticated information systems for medicare, so the argument about feasibility no longer applies. Moreover, the amount of the entitlement that will appear on a statement for each student will take account of such factors as stage of schooling, special education needs, disabilities and impairments, with a school location component. This contrasts with a view that some have held or feared that a voucher provides a uniform amount for each student.

This proposal should not result in government-owned schools in disadvantaged communities receiving fewer resources from the public purse. Indeed, when combined with our proposal on the concept of 'contribution', we expect that such schools will be resourced at a much higher level, consistent with the pre-conditions for lasting reform set out in Chapter 5. We address this in the next section. Along with the expectation that this approach entitlement will serve to drive down fee levels in many non-government or private schools.

Elements in a Policy Framework Based on the Concept of 'Entitlement'

- That to cover recurrent expenditure, all public schools should receive funds from the public purse on the same basis, payable as an entitlement that attaches to the student.
- That the basis for funding schools in this manner be determined through an extension of current work on funding mechanisms for resourcing schools under conditions of decentralization, taking into account such matters as stage of schooling, special education needs of students and school location.
- That where there are several levels of government, new funding agreements be established to facilitate the disbursement of grants that are currently managed separately.
- That parents are entitled to expect an education for their children that is offered within a curriculum and standards framework and to receive information about how well their children are achieving against standards.
- That existing arrangements in respect to entitlement to attend the nearest school shall be maintained.

We turn finally to the entitlement of parents. We propose that parents who enrol their children in a public school, as we have conceptualized it and that is funded in the manner we have described above, are entitled to expect an education that is offered within a curriculum and standards framework and to receive information about how well their children are achieving against the standards in that framework. More fundamentally, of course, the expectation should be for an education of high quality, consistent with the vision we articulated at the start of the chapter. We also propose that existing entitlements in terms of access to a government school shall be maintained, that is, subject to limitations that currently apply, each child has the right to attend the school nearest their home.

The Concept of 'Contribution'

In this section we refer to contributions to the funding of education other than from the public purse. Our proposals in respect to the concept of 'contribution' may be the most contentious, at least as they concern parents for, at first sight, they call for a departure from the tradition if not a legislative requirement that public education shall be free. Such a tradition and requirement applied to government or state schooling and, by definition, these are violated with our proposed concept of 'public'.

We presented the argument in Chapter 5 that this is no longer a realistic position given the nature of schooling at the dawn of the third millennium compared to conditions that prevailed in the nineteenth century when systems of public schools were created. In some places, like Australia, the present reality is that parents pay a contribution, but it remains voluntary and all manner of euphemism is adopted to avoid calling that contribution a fee. Expressed simply, schools need these additional resources, and expectations for further increases from the public purse to minimize or eliminate them are simply unrealistic, given the current burden of taxation. The same analysis may be applied in other nations where levels of 'voluntary contribution' are lower, indeed minimal or non-existent in some settings, but where additional resources are sorely needed and the willingness of the public to provide additional resources has clearly reached its limit. Some nations have the good fortune to have rapid economic growth, relatively low levels of taxation and extraordinarily high commitment to public education, and they do not now and may not need in the future to require a significant contribution along these lines. Australia and comparable nations do not enjoy these circumstances and should adjust their policy framework accordingly.

We are acknowledging here that the entitlement that attaches to a student, payable from the public purse, may not cover all of the recurrent expenditure required for the operation of the school. In some cases, of course, where schools desire to offer a costly service, a relatively high fee should be charged, as is the case now for many private schools. We propose that all schools be able to set fees on a scale to be determined by the council or governing body. For a school owned and operated by the government, this fee shall not be applied to cover the costs of tuition. This preserves the ethos of public schooling that has prevailed since the formation of government schools in nations like Australia.

Experience in systems of Catholic schools will reassure those who contend that the payment of such fees is inequitable, for these schools cater for the full range of students as far as socio-economic circumstance is concerned, and their commitment to equity and social justice is embedded in their mission and beyond reproach. The example of the primary school is used here. In 1997, one such system in Australia received grants from the Commonwealth Government and from the State Government on a per capita basis according to school placement on a resource index of sixteen categories, reflecting different socio-economic circumstances of schools and their communities, amounting overall to about A$1,800 and A$650 per student, respectively. Most of these funds were then distributed to schools through a needs based formula. Schools were permitted to charge a fee for recurrent expenditure ranging from about A$100 per student to about A$400 per student per student, dependent on a school's placement on a ten category socio-economic index. There was provision for families unable to pay the fee.

This represents one approach to the payment of a contribution, but it is one that we do not propose in our policy framework. We have already made clear that entitlements to cover recurrent expenditure should be the same for all students in all schools in the new concept of public education, so a school should receive the total of entitlements for all students who choose to attend, to which shall be added revenue from grants that are not determined on a per capita basis, such as certain premises-related costs for schools that continue to be owned and operated by government, and the total of private effort, which includes the contribution we are describing here. Most importantly, however, we do not advocate a sliding scale of fees according to the socio-economic circumstances of the community in which a school is located. We decline to do so for two reasons. First, because increasingly students do not come from the communities in which a school is located. De-zoning and increasing exercise of choice means that students come from a range of settings. The approach may have been valid in the past, when zoning applied, and one could define the socio-economic condition of a school's community, but that is no longer the case. Our second reason is more fundamental, and that is that resources should attach to a student because of educational circumstance and not socio-economic circumstance. We appreciate that socio-economic circumstance may create a special education need that then determines an educational circumstance, but it is the latter that should be diagnosed precisely, as it is now possible to do, and a resource provision made accordingly.

We proposed above that the level of fee should be determined by the school council or governing body. This is a serious and responsible task and account must be taken of the capacity of parents to pay. One element of our framework was that 'existing arrangements in respect to entitlement to attend the nearest school shall be maintained'. This applies to government owned and operated schools, so levels of fees shall be set to take account of capacity in a particular community. There will need to be a simple means-tested provision to exempt parents on low incomes from paying a fee.

We conclude this section by noting that the overall level of public resourcing for some schools will need to be at a level that is considerably higher than at present, given the level of educational need that exists and the relatively low levels of fees that may feasible. We are mindful of the case made in Chapter 5 that the overall level of resourcing for schools will need to be raised if we are to take seriously the needs of schools, especially in respect to fabric and infrastructure. This will require a determination by an expert panel that looks at the needs of all such schools and we expect this will be mainly related to capital expenditure. We also note that the approaches to entitlement and contribution, taken together, should serve to drive down fee levels in many schools currently classified as private or non-government.

> *Elements in the Policy Framework Related to the Concept of 'Contribution'*
>
> - That all public schools should be permitted to charge fees, determined by the school council or governing body, taking account of the kind of schooling to be offered and the capacity of parents to pay, but that such a fee for schools owned and operated by government shall not include a charge to cover the costs of tuition.
> - That fees for government owned and operated schools should take account of the policy of entitlement to attend the nearest school, with means-tested arrangements to accommodate parents whose incomes will not meet the level of fee.
> - That schools in some communities should be funded from the public purse at a higher rate than at present, especially in respect to capital and infrastructure, to take account of the overall high levels of resourcing needed for lasting school reform.

The Concept of 'Design'

The concept of 'design' is familiar to those involved in the planning and implementation of new products. It is now starting to make its appearance in the creation of a new service or a new approach to providing existing services, in this case, the public school. It has a high profile in the USA following the formation of the New American Schools Development Corporation (NASDC) in 1991. NASDC was the initiative of business and foundation leaders who were prepared to invest in efforts to transform schools, free of government funding in the design phase of five years, after which schools and school systems were to take charge as efforts were made to achieve scale-up on the basis of lessons learned. The effort is now known as New American Schools (NAS). Partnerships were established with school systems toward the end of the initial phase. Nine designs were approved on the basis of a Request for Proposal, each taken further in NAS through the work of a Design Team (detailed accounts of NAS are contained in Stringfield, Ross and Smith, 1996).

The NAS designs include one that focuses on the core purpose of schools such as literacy and numeracy. This is Roots and Wings developed by Robert Slavin at Johns Hopkins University, with the former referring to the outstandingly successful reading program in elementary schools and the latter to a secondary counterpart that extends the approach to mathematics. A more comprehensive program involves the Atlas Communities near Boston that build on the work of Comer, Gardner and Sizer to create unified, supportive communities of learners in a K-12 pattern. Another is the National Alliance for Restructuring Education that involves whole states and districts engaged in standards driven reform.

We return in a moment to NAS, but note that, on an international scale, other reform efforts fall in the category of a 'design', although they differ in important respects on some features. For example, the local management of schools in Britain may be considered a new design for the operation of a public school system administered by the local education authority. The initiative in this case was taken by government, building on successful pioneering efforts in local financial management of schools in authorities such as Cambridgeshire. Scale-up was achieved to the point where all British schools are locally managed, and the new design is so widely embraced as to be irreversible. The extension of the locally managed school to the grant-maintained school may also be considered a government initiative in school design that did not achieve the scale-up to the extent intended. Similarly with City Technology Colleges, that called for a partnership between industry and government in the design of technology-oriented secondary colleges in urban areas in Britain. Scale-up was not achieved with fewer than twenty schools set up across the country.

Schools of the Future in Victoria is also an example of a government initiative in school design that achieved rapid scale-up in an initial decision to move beyond a relatively small-scale pilot project to phased implementation over all schools in three years, assisted by a much higher number of initial expressions of interest than anticipated. Some promising work has also been done in Australia with the National Schools Project where innovative approaches were encouraged with some Commonwealth funding, with dissemination of outcomes on a moderate scale, but without substantial take-up across the nation (see Louden and Wallace, 1994; Walker, Bradley and de Kantzow, 1996 for accounts of the National Schools Project).

Returning to the 'bold plans' for New American Schools (Stringfield, Ross and Smith, 1996), there is certainly a high measure of coherence if the nine designs are taken as a whole. These designs must have the following features in common, with a Memorandum of Understanding the basis for action by states and districts as scale-up proceeds:

- The willingness to give schools wide authority and autonomy to make decisions regarding all aspects of schooling, including staffing, budgeting, curriculum and scheduling.
- Common publicly supported standards for achievement for virtually all students, accompanied by institutional mechanisms through which schools or systems of schools can petition for the acceptance of self-developed standards as equivalent to or exceeding the established standards.

- Rich and reliable systems of assessment that help schools demonstrate that they are meeting the standards and help teachers make improvements in their programs.
- Sources of assistance in choosing and developing curriculum and instructional strategies that are consistent with the standards and responsive to individual students' needs . . .
- A system for professional development and certification that is responsive to the needs of schools and school professionals, and assures that their instructional staff can help students meet high standards.
- Technology that supports teachers and students in the instructional process, assists in the management of schools, and generally supports the restructuring of schools to provide students with the individual attention and opportunities they need.
- A services and support system that strengthens community and family engagement in the school, reduces health and other non-academic barriers to learning and promotes family stability.
- A multifaceted plan to engage the public in the transformation in serious and meaningful ways and to develop a broad and deep public understanding of, and support for, the transformation.
- A capacity and willingness to allocate and reallocate the resources necessary to transform individual schools, at both the system and school level.
- A management and governance system that ensures that schools have the broad guidance, individual autonomy, and support necessary to achieve their mission. (Kearns and Anderson, 1996, pp. 18–19)

We note that most elements in the aforementioned are a feature of Schools of the Future, suggesting that what has occurred in Victoria should be of wide interest to those in the USA and elsewhere that now seek large-scale take up. By the same token, Victoria and other places that have achieved a necessary but still insufficient stage along the way to achieving lasting school reform, such as Britain with its highly successful local management of schools, ought now embrace the concept of school design.

A range of initiatives, each with a design team, ought to be established in these settings using the New American Schools' terminology, some may be a 'core design', focusing on the core aspects of schooling like curriculum, learning, standards, assessments, student groupings, community involvement and professional development. Others may be a 'comprehensive design', adding the elements of integrated services, governance arrangements and approaches to school organization and staffing. Some may focus on the system itself, the so-called 'systemic design', that involves external matters that impact on a system of schools as well as systemwide matters such as changes in authorities, responsibilities and accountabilities (see Stringfield, Ross and Smith, 1996, pp. 7–8 for these classifications). In both Victoria and Britain, there is no particular need to wait for a government or system initiative, for schools have the authority to proceed, although an impetus may be given from the centre. Promising developments were under way in Victoria at the time of writing, with several approaches to middle school education (Years 5–8) that drew in part from earlier work in the National Schools Project, and on the integrated service or full-service concept of school support that involved high levels of cooperation among government and municipal government in the areas of education, health and other human services.

In general, however, the next stage of school design in places like Victoria is to extend local management to create more autonomous schools, perhaps along the lines of grant-maintained schools in England, or charter schools in the USA, and we addressed this possibility in our discussion on the concept of 'public' earlier in the chapter. Each school must then develop a capacity for school design, utilizing where appropriate the services of a consultant, and it is here that experiences of single schools in the private sector can be a guide. Brewster Academy in New Hampshire is an example of the latter that is attracting interest among schools in public as well as private sectors (see Bain, 1996; Brosnan, 1996 for accounts of school design at Brewster).

One aspect of the NAS that has no counterpart in Australia and most other nations is the extensive involvement of the corporate and foundation sectors, and a major transformation of culture in these nations ought to be nurtured to broaden the base of commitment and resourcing. There are few incentives to become engaged. We hope this will change, acknowledging that some of the reticence is likely due to lack of confidence that current arrangements are likely to lead to lasting school reform. Tax incentives may be helpful to encourage these and all forms of private effort that add resources to public education.

Having advocated the addition of the concept of design to the policy framework, we are mindful of the difficulties of achieving large-scale take up. How these were addressed in Victoria with Schools of the Future was described by Don Hayward in Chapter 3. Alignment is important in the sense we described in applying the Guthrie and Koppich (1993) model to explain the success of this reform. Absence of such alignment may impair the NAS effort. RAND was responsible for monitoring the design and implementation effort, drawing the conclusion that accomplishment to 1996 was impressive: 'the distinctive contribution of NAS has been to help capitalize, support and legitimise a new mechanism for the building of school-level capability for transformation: a design-based assistance organisation' (Bodilly, 1996, p. 321). Despite good progress in some important respects, school autonomy from districts proved 'elusive' unless it had been built in at the outset, prior to the design team's efforts. This has been recognized by David Kearns and John Anderson, respectively Chairman of the Board and President of New American Schools, who observed that 'school systems are frequently reluctant to change entrenched budgeting and allocation systems . . . Too often they view school-based designs as add-on programs . . . This way of supporting schools holds little promise for institutional improvement in education' (Kearns and Anderson, 1996, p. 21). Consequently, as scale-up gathered momentum, NAS included in teams some experts on school finance and budget restructuring. They would benefit from close examination of reforms in Britain, for the local management of schools, and in Victoria, for Schools of the Future.

Elements in a Policy Framework Based on the Concept of 'Design'

- That a range of new designs — core, comprehensive and systemic — should be created to extend the level of reform already attained.
- That for systems with a high level of local management or self-management, one systemic design should be the creation of autonomous schools within the public sector.
- That success in these new designs can only be achieved through strong alignment of policy-related forces, requiring above all an unrelenting commitment at the level of government or relevant central authority, even though design teams in systems of locally managed or self-managed schools have the authorities, responsibilities and accountabilities to proceed.
- That organizations and institutions in the corporate and foundations sectors should play a role in helping to energize school design, with tax incentives to encourage higher levels of involvement from these sectors and from other forms of private effort that increase the levels of resources for public schools.

Scenarios for the Future of the Public School

Let us return to the themes of Chapter 4. Our starting point was a set of reforms called Schools of the Future that Don Hayward had introduced in Victoria while serving as Minister for Education. We had noted the parallels in other nations and reviewed the evidence on processes and outcomes, especially on learning for students. We accounted for the success of the Victorian effort, described the shortcomings of single reform initiatives such as school-based management, and summarized progress in Schools of the Future in terms of its coherence as a multidimensional framework for school reform. In Chapter 5, we canvassed a range of issues on matters such as teachers and teaching, learners and learning, the relationship between education and the economy, the resourcing of schools and the role of government. We recognized that reforms such as Schools of the Future were necessary but not sufficient and that there were a number of pre-conditions to be satisfied if there was to be lasting reform for public schools.

Given this, there are basically three scenarios for proceeding. The first is to maintain current approaches and try to make them work better, preferably with a dramatic increase in resourcing from the public purse, trusting that things will be put right and that governments will allow schools to settle down and consolidate, rather than continue to cope with constant change. The comfortable times of the 1970s and 1980s will return. We reject this scenario because it does not recognize the way the world has changed in the last decade and that the societal transformation that marks the information age leaves no place for nostalgia.

A second scenario calls for major reform but within the current broad framework of policy and approaches to public schooling. This has been the approach in the USA where there has been a wave of reforms over more than a decade, but the momentum for even more change continues to build. In places like Britain and in Victoria, there is the sense that the agenda is incomplete and more remains to be done. Issues such as those we addressed in Chapter 5 just will not go away, so we reject this scenario. It may be necessary but it is not sufficient; it may be coherent, but it is not comprehensive.

The third scenario calls for the fundamental redesign of public education, starting with the concept itself. The issues we raised in Chapter 5 were fundamental and we must start with the fundamentals in seeking their redress. We set about this task in Chapter 6 by first expressing our commitment to the concept of public education and then offering a vision for schooling in the third millennium. We then selected four key concepts and developed a set of elements for each that would stand up in a coherent policy framework. These concepts were 'public', 'entitlement', 'contribution' and 'design'. This is our preferred scenario because it is coherent, comprehensive, conceptually based and connected to a vision for schooling.

The Preferred Scenario

Our preferred scenario is offered as a policy framework with fifteen elements, as listed below, these being drawn from the four sections of the chapter that dealt with the fundamental concepts. While many of our illustrations were drawn from Australia, especially Victoria, we intend the framework to be applied in comparable nations, although we acknowledge that some have been achieved already, such as the broader concept of 'public' that may be found in places like Britain, Canada Hong Kong, The Netherlands and New Zealand. We also acknowledge that the manner in which real policies are formulated in various settings may differ in the detail and the sequence. In some instances, governments may decline to proceed with some elements if the alignment of which we wrote in Chapter 4 cannot be secured. Nevertheless, it is important to have a blueprint and that is what is offered in the following.

1 That all schools that receive funds from the public purse should be designated 'public schools'.

2 That existing 'foundation arrangements' shall continue in respect to ownership of the school and its resources and the employment of its staff.

3 That schools whose communities and staff have the commitment and capacity should have the opportunity to change their 'foundation arrangements' from government owned and employed to privately owned and employed, with transition arrangements established to ensure such a change is a valid expression of intention and is feasible.

4 That to cover recurrent expenditure, all public schools should receive funds from the public purse on the same basis, payable as an entitlement that attaches to the student.

5 That the basis for funding schools in this manner be determined through an extension of current work on funding mechanisms for resourcing

     schools under conditions of decentralization, taking into account such matters as stage of schooling, special education needs of students and school location.

6   That where there are several levels of government, new funding agreements be established to facilitate the disbursement of grants that are currently managed separately.

7   That parents are entitled to expect an education for their children that is offered within a curriculum and standards framework and to receive information about how well their children are achieving against standards.

8   That existing arrangements in respect to entitlement to attend the nearest school shall be maintained.

9   That all public schools should be permitted to charge fees, determined by the school council or governing body, taking account of the kind of schooling to be offered and the capacity of parents to pay, but that such a fee for schools owned and operated by government shall not include a charge to cover the costs of tuition.

10   That fees for government owned and operated schools should take account of the policy of entitlement to attend the nearest school, with means-tested arrangements to accommodate parents whose incomes will not meet the level of fee.

11   That schools in some communities should be funded from the public purse at a higher rate than at present, especially in respect to capital and infrastructure, to take account of the overall high levels of resourcing needed for lasting school reform.

12   That a range of new designs — core, comprehensive and systemic — should be created to extend the level of reform already attained.

13   That for systems with a high level of local management or self-management, one systemic design should be the creation of autonomous schools within the public sector.

14   That success in these new designs can only be achieved through strong alignment of policy-related forces, requiring above all an unrelenting commitment at the level of government or relevant central authority, even though design teams in systems of locally managed or self-managed schools have the authorities, responsibilities and accountabilities to proceed.

15   That organizations and institutions in the corporate and foundations sectors should play a role in helping to energize school design, with tax incentives to encourage higher levels of involvement from these sectors and from other forms of private effort that increase the levels of resources for public schools.

If this is our preferred scenario, then how will it be achieved? In our view this calls for leadership of a high order, with some important changes in roles for individuals and organizations with an interest in public education. We deal with these issues in Chapter 7.

7   Leadership, Alignment and Will in the Transformation of Public Education

What we propose is a transformation of the system of public education, re-defining the concept itself, penetrating deep into the classroom and the processes of learning to ensure high levels of achievement for all students. To use the jargon, this is the re-engineering or re-invention of public school education. Such a transformation calls for extraordinary leadership.

Leadership is a process that involves setting a new direction or creating a new vision, and the building of commitment to moving in that direction or achieving that vision (based on a view of leadership offered by Kotter, 1992, p. 6). Don Hayward described in Chapters 2 and 3 how the vision for Schools of the Future was determined and we proposed in Chapter 6 a policy framework for achieving lasting school reform, with programs like Schools of the Future a necessary but not sufficient condition in accomplishing that purpose. The particular ways in which such a vision will be formed in each setting, be it a nation, system or school, will call for new acts of leadership.

In this chapter we focus on the notion of alignment, for this has emerged in various accounts as important to success in achieving large-scale change. It was the key element in the explanatory model of Guthrie and Koppich (1993) that proved helpful in Chapter 4 in explaining the success of Schools of the Future. Lack of alignment or lack of coherence between different elements of reform accounts for why there has been little discernible impact on outcomes for students in many instances, as illustrated by our review of research on school-based management in Chapter 4.

We believe it is important to achieve alignment among key organizations and institutions if there is to be large-scale change of a lasting nature to produce benefits for students. These include government, bureaucracies, organizations that wish to represent the interests of teachers and others who work in and support schools, and principals and others who lead at the school level. We address each of these in Chapter 7. We conclude by noting that the future is learning, not only in the primary sense that our focus should be on students, but in the sense that the future of school reform depends very much on what we have learned from recent efforts. We speculate on where the big breakthrough will occur. The ingredients are leadership, alignment and will.

Government

It is remarkable how quickly roles in government are changing around the world. It was only recently that Osborne and Gaebler (1993) startled many when they wrote of re-inventing government, articulating a principle that governments should be in the business of 'steering' rather than 'rowing', referring to a role that sees governments setting direction, providing standards, furnishing resources, and utilizing frameworks for accountability in the delivery of public services, but as far as it is effective and efficient to do so, vacating the arena of actually delivering the service. This principle has passed quickly into the currency of language and practice, although many issues remain to be resolved in some settings, including the extent to which governments should actually engage in the delivery of a service that meets a basic societal need such as school education.

The policies we have advocated see governments assuming this role in school education to a greater extent than at present, steering a system of public education and encouraging others to do the rowing, that is, actually delivering the services. Our proposal provides for more autonomy for schools, so that ownership and employment are in private hands rather than government, where it is desirable and feasible to do so, although many schools will continue to be government owned and employed. In the long term in some settings, this may settle at about 30 per cent so that, in the field of public education, 30 per cent are government owned and 70 per cent are privately owned, operating through councils, boards or trusts. Interestingly, this is about the balance that exists in The Netherlands, where equity in funding for publicly owned and privately owned is protected in the Constitution.

Adoption of this 'steering' role calls for a clear vision and strong leadership of a kind we hope was exemplified in Schools of the Future. Success depended on alignment and, in this case, it was alignment of a program of government with a problem in practice, about which there was general public agreement, with a window of opportunity created by a sweeping election victory and a 'political champion'. We acknowledge that some organizations were not aligned in this initiative, notably the teacher union, and we consider their role in another section. In general, we see it as the role of government and its ministers to help create this alignment, thus mobilizing public commitment to the reform effort.

Failure to secure alignment or maintain the will to reform will undermine the endeavour. The promise of the New American Schools program in the USA may not be fulfilled if some factors evident in a progress review are sustained (see Bodilly, 1996, p. 320). More significantly, the charter school movement in the USA may not achieve scale-up because of a lack of organized, well-financed support and the failure of some school districts to release the charter school from budget requirements that constrain district schools. Strong and sustained leadership, combined with political will, are essential if the pioneers are to succeed and more are to be encouraged to join the movement (see Bierlein and Bateman, 1996, pp. 164–8 for an account of forces that may limit the impact of charter schools). Bi-partisan support in Congress and greatly increased financial assistance in the budget proposed by President Clinton in 1997 are positive indicators.

An important ingredient of success in the organization of the future is trust, as eminent writer on management Charles Handy (1997) has made clear:

> Organizations which rely on trust as their principal means of control are more effective, more creative, more fun, and cheaper to operate. They are, however, very different from the organizations as we know them today, most of which are based on hierarchical control systems, with an unspoken undercurrent of fear. (Handy, 1997, p. 381)

Whilst the Kennett Government had secured alignment in the public arena, Don Hayward had to proceed with Schools of the Future at the same time as the Government had to deal with a major budget crisis and with a key organization, the teacher union, doing all it could to make things difficult. He attempted to build this trust by keeping the focus on students, as in the manner he applied the criterion 'does this add value to a student's learning?' to every decision that had to be made. This focus is crucial if governments are to build trust and secure alignment in leading the transformation of public school education.

Bureaucracies

An important aspect of 're-inventing government' has been the reform of the bureaucracy in many states and nations, for it is the bureaucracy that has a central role in the 'steering', assisting in setting directions, formulating standards, providing resources and utilizing frameworks for accountability. In that they are less involved in the 'rowing' means that they have been downsized rather dramatically, as was the case in Victoria. In a sense, Don Hayward's dictum 'does it add value to a student's learning?' also became the basis for determining need for a position in the bureaucracy.

It is paradoxical that Hammer and Champy's (1993) concept of 're-engineering' the public service entails a return to the original meaning of the practice, that is, serving the public by contributing to the design and implementation of the policies of the government of the day. In recent times it seems that the public service has become a major political force in its own right, apart from government, to the point where both Kenneth Baker and Don Hayward, in their accounts of ministerial experience, referred to the way bureaucrats had stymied reform in the past, and their determination to see a responsive public service in the large-scale reform to be undertaken, respectively, in the 1988 Education Reform Act and Schools of the Future.

Geoff Spring epitomizes the kind of senior bureaucrat needed under these conditions. Don Hayward described in Chapter 2 the manner of his appointment and his personal qualities, and his role in the implementation of Schools of the Future was critically important. Appointed initially as Director of School Education, he was elevated to the senior position of Secretary of Education in the second term of the Kennett Government.

Geoff Spring provided the commitment at the level of senior management that was required for a large-scale reform like Schools of the Future to succeed. His approach is consistent with the role of senior management in James Champy's illustration of why 'the larger the scale of a change program, the more likely it is to succeed':

> A change program aimed at incremental improvements creates too many fronts on which to fight battles. Sometimes the battles are quiet. You don't even know that they are going on. And sometimes, in fact, nothing is going on! People are just involved in continuing discussions or study — no action is being taken. The organization's antibodies are quietly killing the change effort. If the change program is large, however, and it has senior management's commitment, the organization must confront all that is required to manage the change. No hiding, no return to the current state. (Champy, 1997, p. 13)

The decision to scale-up the first intake of schools in Schools of the Future was a classic illustration of this, with an initial intention of fewer than 100 becoming more than 300, thus reducing the chances of the reform being undermined. Geoff Spring's strength and strategic sense were also evident in the simultaneous management, albeit at different rates, of the design and implementation of the four frameworks of Schools of the Future, a characteristic that distinguishes Schools of the Future from less coherent efforts at reform. These qualities are a requirement for senior executives in the further reform of school education.

A combination of strength in the Minister–Director team is important, as evidenced in the relationship between Don Hayward and Geoff Spring. It was also evident in Britain in the partnership leading up to and following the 1988 Education Reform Act, in this instance between Margaret Thatcher and Kenneth Baker. Similarly in New Zealand following implementation of *Tomorrow's Schools* with David Lange as both Prime Minister and Minister for Education, and Russell Ballard as Chief Executive Officer.

An illustration of apparent failure of commitment and will at the executive and governance levels is presented by recent experience in the Los Angeles Unified School District (LAUSD). A non-profit organization of business, education and political leaders was established in 1992 to help move the control of schools from central administration to the individual school. The initiative known as the Los Angeles Educational Alliance for Restructuring Now (LEARN) has had disappointing results, with only about a third of 660 schools agreeing to participate in the program that called for decentralization of budgets in return for changes in school governance to allow more involvement in decision-making by parents and teachers. Despite evidence of a slight increase in student achievement, there are a number of factors that are disincentives for schools to join, including delays in providing schools with essential and up-to-date information. Pyle compares the situation in 1997 with the apparent enthusiasm when LEARN began:

> But the LEARN landscape is different now than it was five years ago, with the chronic delays in transferring power and money to schools causing even some loyal LEARN teachers to join critics in questioning whether the district was ever really committed to reform and, more important, whether it is worth the effort. (Pyle, 1997, p. 6)

In an effort to revive the initiative, William G. Ouchi, an eminent writer and expert in modern management from UCLA's Graduate School of Management has been appointed to head up LEARN. Ouchi has signalled an intention to place greater pressure on state and federal authorities to reduce the mass of regulation that constrains the way resources are deployed in schools and for LEARN to become less involved in the detail of local transition arrangements. This strategy illustrates a key theme of the book concerning the importance of aligning key interests, including different levels of government. It will be interesting to observe the strength of this alignment and the will to sustain the reform by executive, governance and political interests, including Ouchi as Chair of LEARN, the Superintendent of LAUSD, and the Mayor of Los Angeles.

Teacher Unions and Professional Associations

Teacher unions in some places may need to be re-invented if they are to have a role in the future of schooling. Failure in this respect may serve to disempower teachers and place the profession if not public schooling in jeopardy. Unions must embrace and become leaders in the reform program. The roles of teachers will become so complex and, in many cases, so dispersed, that the professional will need the support of a top flight organization that is in the vanguard of change.

A Profession in Decline

From time immemorial, the teacher was viewed as a respected professional and looked up to by the local community. In recent years, the professional status and respect for teachers have declined. Why is this? It is possible to argue that, at least in part, it is due to the recent role of teacher unions. Because of their history, their nature and the fact that the continued relevance of their officials is dependent upon engendering 'industrial issues', teacher unions are now, in reality, inherently inconsistent with the concept of teacher professionalism, although we acknowledge that the best unions provide support for individuals in disputes in the workplace and have helped build and maintain a sense of professionalism.

At least three problems are evident in the role of the teacher union, or 'teacher trade union' as it may more accurately be described in respect to the matters we raise here. First, the focus of union officials must, of necessity, be on industrial representation. True it is that they have a focus on education industrial relations, but the issues that arise in education industrial relations are not necessarily the same issues as arise in the profession of teaching. Their essential interests are not necessarily the same as the professional interests of teachers.

A second inherent difficulty with the role of the union relates to the very rationale of unions, namely that of collective representation of members. The individual subjugates his or her individual interests to those of the group. In contrast, one of the delineating qualities of a teacher, and professional persons in general, is the individual's acceptance of (often onerous) personal responsibility or duty. In the case of a teacher, that personal responsibility or duty is owed variously to the student, parents, the school and colleagues.

A third aspect is a 'political' consideration. Teacher unions have allowed their role to become blurred. In some places, union magazines are a curious mix of industrial relations matters, professional issues, political comment, economic affairs and general consciousness-raising on issues ranging from sexism to overseas aid to the state of the world economy. It would be bizarre to find these themes in the professional literature of doctors, engineers or lawyers.

The power of teacher union officials derives from their ability to create a collective industrial dispute, usually concerning pay rates and working conditions, and then to use 'industrial action', such as a strike or the imposition of work bans, or the threat thereof, to attempt to force the employer to grant their demands. In Australia, the industrial relations system can be called in aid, and it will attempt to settle the 'dispute', usually by the making of concessions by the employer.

The politicization of the teacher unions, and the resort by officials of these trade unions to 'industrial action' has in our view undermined the concept of teaching as a profession in the minds of the general public and of teachers themselves. The general public tend to think of teachers in the same way as they think of other industrial employees who go on strike, although it may be that the general public regards teachers in a poorer light than other employees in this respect. It is an aspiration for many people that their son or daughter might attend college or university and become a teacher. It is a job which requires the use of intellectual power that is well paid by comparison with some other jobs. Teachers enjoy holidays far in excess of other employees. In that context, a strike by teachers can seem very luxurious to other working men and women, particularly when the people most adversely affected by the strike are powerless children.

The Future of the Professional Association

It is critical that, in the future, teaching regains its standing as a profession. Employers should treat teachers as professionals, recognizing that, if conditions of employment at the local level lose flexibility or fail to meet local needs, because they are determined by some central bureaucracy, the teacher will feel powerless. Thus, it is important that there be a minimization of central control in large bureaucracies. If the employer becomes too big or too remote, the employee will feel that he or she needs an ally who is equally powerful or big. Most desirably, responsibility should rest with the local school to develop a close, professional relationship with the individual teacher which will best promote good teaching at that school.

A resurgence of professionalism is likely to lead to teachers having their own individual service contract with their school or other provider of educational services. In these circumstances, teachers will need a professional association, as distinct from an industrial trade union. A fundamental aim of such a professional association would be the enhancement of the professional status of teaching and of the professionalism of its members. It would be a provider of professional development courses and other activities for teachers. It would provide advice for the teacher in negotiating his or her individual contract of service with the school or other provider of educational services, and could act as an advocate for the teacher in any dispute that may arise in connection therewith.

The challenge for the existing teacher unions is to transform themselves into such professional associations to serve teachers. In some countries, such as the United States, there are signs that some enlightened officials see that the future of their organization is in the provision of professional services, as distinct from the foment of industrial disputes. However, in other countries, including our own, their thinking on some matters is so entrenched in the past that the prospect of teacher unions re-inventing themselves appears at times to be quite remote. In these circumstances, they will continue to lose members, who will move to new professional associations that will emerge.

Can Such a Transformation Be Made?

Evidence that such a transformation can occur is starting to emerge in the United States, where leaders of both major teacher unions have an understanding of change in society and its implications for schools. The late respected long-serving President of the American Federation of Teachers, Alberta Shanker, re-positioned his organization as early as 1987, appreciating that the system had become bogged down in a mass of regulation due in part to the complexity of agreements secured through collective bargaining. He was a powerful supporter of national goals for schooling, school-based management, new approaches to incentives and rewards, and changes to the workplace. He became a key player in all decisions of note in the ongoing reform effort.

Shanker's counterparts in the larger National Education Association (NEA) came to the same view, with President Bob Chase making the following statement in early 1997 (Chase, 1997) which captures in remarkable fashion an appreciation of the need we have identified and the direction we have proposed. His view is so important that we quote at length.

> What are the sounds of a paradigm shifting? Listen closely. Linda Bacon
> is president of the local NEA affiliate in Florida that has made school
> quality a top issue at the bargaining table. At a recent union gathering, one

member rose to challenge her priorities: 'Your job isn't to look out for the children; your job is to look out for *me!*' Bacon respectfully disagreed: 'Our bedrock purpose as an association must be to improve student learning'.

These are the clashing voices of teachers working at the fault line of a remarkable paradigm shift. New schools are being created in our midst. And teachers like Linda Bacon are striving courageously to reorient — more accurately, to reinvent — their local union for a new era.

True, most educators are still stymied by the old industrial paradigm. Factory-style schools with as many as 4000 students are managed badly — by a top-heavy, top–down bureaucracy. Teachers are relegated to the role of production workers, with little say in decision-making.

But today, this old world is ending — not with a bang, but through countless acts of 'subversion'. For example, public charter schools, many of them founded and run by teachers, are proliferating rapidly. So are schools where principals and teachers collaborate in 'site-based' management.

In all of these new-style public schools, teachers and other employees are co-managing — and sometimes self-managing — the education enterprise. Talking with these professionals, you quickly realize that they are preoccupied with issues of school quality and renewal.

All of which confronts unions with a huge challenge. How do we advocate for these 'new paradigm' educators, while still meeting the needs of members in 'old paradigm' schools who insist that the union's job is to 'look out for me'. (Chase, 1997, p. 7)

The answer, for Chase, is a new view of 'looking after me', one that extends a union concern about working conditions (which alone is 'dangerously myopic') to 'pursuing an aggressive agenda of excellence and revitalisation in public education' (Chase, 1997, p. 7). Leaders like Chase and Shanker may in some respects be far ahead of their members, and of leaders in school districts in the United States, for progress is slow, as we reported in Chapter 4 in our review of the evidence of impact for school-based management. Certainly, where success was evident in the case of New American Schools, a prior condition was the freeing up of schools from many of the constraints that had accrued over decades of collective agreements and a mountain of state and district regulations (see Bodilly, 1996, pp. 308–10 for an account of these matters). On the other hand, both the NEA and the AFT have invested considerable sums to defeat public ballots on charter schools in order to head off, according to one view, the possibility of school vouchers (see Bierlein and Bateman, 1996, p. 165). In general, the unions in the USA face a daunting challenge to transform their roles. If successful, they will make a contribution to 'a revitalized system of public schooling in America' (Koppich, Kerchner and Weeres, 1997a, p. 43) (see also Koppich, Kerchner and Weeres, 1997b for their evocatively titled book *United Mind Workers*).

At times teacher unions appear to have done their best to thwart reforms of which we have written, sowing dissent on the fundamental direction of change even beyond the time when it had become clear to the wider community that the new approaches were a more effective and efficient way to operate the school. Hopefully, union leaders will align themselves and their members with the reform effort, in much the same way as leaders like Chase and Shanker have done in the USA. Such alignment within the profession will significantly empower teachers in the design and implementation of the next stage of reform.

Principals and other School Leaders

Principals of many public schools will have roles much like those of principals in the major private or independent schools now, with oversight of several campuses, a very large budget, the support of state-of-the-art technology, and the empowerment of many leaders in different parts of the school. One additional factor will be the existence of multiple providers, and many on the part-time payroll, in direct teaching, the support of teaching or the provision of other services. In some respects, elements of a 'virtual school' will be evident.

We focus on two aspects of the roles of principals and other school leaders in helping achieve the transformation of public education, and each is based on the notion of alignment. One is a capacity for strategic leadership in the sense described by Caldwell and Spinks (1992):

- keeping abreast of trends and issues, threats and opportunities in the school environment and in society at large, nationally and internationally; discerning the 'megatrends' and anticipating their impact on education generally and on the school in particular;
- sharing their knowledge with others in the school's community and encouraging other school leaders to do the same in their areas of interest;
- establishing structures and processes which enable the school to set priorities and formulate strategies which take account of likely and/or preferred futures; being a key source of expertise as these occur;
- ensuring that the attention of the school community is focused on matters of strategic importance; and
- monitoring the implementation of strategies as well as emerging strategic issues in the wider environment; facilitating an ongoing process of review. (Caldwell and Spinks, 1992, p. 92)

Given the scope of reforms like Schools of the Future, we believe that a starting point in the exercise of strategic leadership by principals and other leaders is a capacity to locate these reforms in the broader context of global change, generally within society as well as in school education. This is not easy, given the uncertain and contentious nature of many changes. However, we cannot feel confident that a school community can be aligned and committed to a sense of direction unless these people can take the lead in accomplishing the tasks in the list above.

The second aspect of the role is that of 'educational strategist'. The school leader must be more conversant than ever about strategies that will yield benefits for students, and that means knowledge based on research on school and classroom effectiveness and improvement that is now more extensive and sophisticated than ever before. Strategies will, of course, include those that utilize the new information technologies. Educational leadership in the past may have meant knowledge about a more-or-less static curriculum; being able to teach a class and teach it well, serving as a model or master teacher; being able to visit the classrooms of others and make constructive comments about what was observed; and articulating an educational vision to the community. These capacities will continue to be important but there will be more, much more, including the empowerment of other leaders in the school to do the same in their areas of responsibility. In some instances, especially in larger schools, the role will be broader, hence the concept of 'educational strategist'.

Associated with this aspect of the role will be a capacity to understand the resource implications of choices on alternative strategies in learning and teaching. Determining the cost effectiveness of these strategies will be critically important (see the work of Hanushek *et al.*, 1994, Burtless, 1996, and Thomas and Martin, 1996, for an up-to-date account of cost effectiveness in the context of advances in knowledge about school and classroom effectiveness).

These roles for principals and other leaders are very important if there is to be improvement in learning. The effects are indirect, because they impact the work of others who, in turn, will be at the front-line of efforts to secure that improvement. Other actions will also be indirect, but equally important, including leadership in professional development; providing incentives, rewards and recognition; and generally creating a purposeful and professionally satisfying climate for the workplace (see Gurr, 1996a, 1996b, 1996c for research on the role of the principal in Schools of the Future). Taken together these aspects of the leadership role are all part of the alignment we believe to be so important in securing commitment and capacity to achieve lasting school reform along the lines we propose.

The Future Is Learning

The title of this book is *The Future of Schools*, but its substance has really been about the future of learning, and it is on this theme that we conclude. We have two themes in mind. First, the future of learning for students and the role of teachers and those who support them. Second, the future as it is shaped by what we have learned about past efforts at reform, and this is what underlines the subtitle of the book *Lessons from the Reform of Public Education*.

A Future of Learning for Students

The *raison d'être* for reform is to achieve the highest quality of education that is possible for all students. In this sense, distinguished American teacher leader Stephanie Pace Marshall has it right when she observed that:

For well over a decade we have been barraged with reports and rhetoric about the crisis in public education. It is my belief, however, that the

espoused crisis in public education is predominantly a crisis about learning
... (Marshall, 1997, p. 178)

School education for the knowledge society as envisaged at the start of Chapter 6 is exciting, but challenging, given that learning can occur anywhere with the advent of new information technologies, and that the needs of society and the individual are continuing to change in remarkable fashion. But the whole must focus on the individual, so learning is and will continue to be an intensely personal experience that must be constructed for each student.

The need for outstanding teaching has never been more important. We have a picture in our minds, call it a vision, of teachers working in schools that are well constructed to the needs of learning for a knowledge society, supported by the best technology available; with a capacity to draw on state-of-the art knowledge about what works to ensure all students learn well; working in teams and in schools that have been empowered to set priorities, making decisions and allocating resources to address the unique mix of needs of students in their schools; enjoying salaries and other working conditions that are consistent with those of a top professional; being supported by a professional association whose first concern is that of students and quality schooling, but supporting the individual on matters related to individual work arrangements when that is necessary; all within a curriculum and standards framework that the community knows and understands, with accountability that is part and parcel of any professional effort, and freedom from oppressive bureaucratic control and industrial heavy handedness; and, above all, contributing to the well-being of the individual and society through the accomplishments of their students.

We can work through the elements of this vision and see some gains, but they present a daunting agenda. Reforms like Schools of the Future are taking up the challenge of technology, have provided a framework of curriculum and accountability, and have delivered, albeit in a still constrained fashion, a capacity for local management or school-based management. There is a sense where such reforms have been implemented that they are largely irreversible, but that much more needs to be done, and that is our view too.

A Future Shaped by Learning from Reform in the Past

We have learned from these recent efforts at reform in public education, from Schools of the Future and other initiatives of a kind described throughout the book. We have learned that reform must be comprehensive and coherent, and that single initiatives rarely deliver the range of benefits that are sought. Few have confidence that the ground has been laid for lasting school reform.

We have offered a policy framework that will remove some of the bottlenecks and provide some of the resources. This framework was built around the concepts of 'public', 'entitlement', 'contribution' and 'design'. These do not apply to all nations or all systems of education to the same extent. Most apply to Australia, where our primary interest lies, but each has its application somewhere.

We suggest that the concept of 'public' and our understanding of what is public education must become more embracing, so that Australia and other places where the analysis applies, can be freed of a divisive view about the role of government and approaches to the resourcing of schools. Similarly, with the concept of 'entitlement', for under the broader view of public education, all parents ought to expect a fair entitlement to resources according to the stage of schooling and the special education needs of their children. This fair entitlement is guaranteed in the Constitution of The Netherlands. We propose a scheme for attachment of resources to students because our vision of schooling places the needs of the individual at the centre. Standardized allocations to schools, even if they have a measure of sensitivity to the different needs of students, largely reflect an outdated view of schooling. The concept of 'contribution' calls for the most significant departure from what many see as a fundamental value in public schooling, namely, that it should be free in all respects. The reality is that it has not been free for many decades in most nations, especially our own, and given the limits to further resourcing from the public purse, we ought to now adopt policies that provide for a private contribution with due account of the circumstances of some parents who cannot afford to pay. The current approach is neither fair nor transparent, and cannot continue. The end result will be higher levels of resourcing for those schools that are presently underresourced, with the fabric and technology of what are now government schools more like those in the non-government sector, to use the distinction now applying in our own country. In many ways, the concept of 'design' is the most important, because it is here that schools ought to be supported, indeed empowered, to reinvent themselves in ways that are consistent with a vision for schooling and for learning and teaching such as that described above. We do not provide the detail, but we see enough of efforts in some places to know that it should now pervade the scene.

The astonishing thing is that we know how to do all of this. We have shown in Schools of the Future and in similar reforms in other places that a necessary but insufficient part of the agenda can be put in place if its design is coherent and comprehensive, but above all, if there is the will to do it, and alignment of interests can be secured. Removing unnecessary boundaries between schools to achieve a broader view of public education is straightforward, if there is the will to do it, for it has been achieved in other places that now enjoy a consensus about the role of government and approaches to resourcing the public school. Even attaching resources to students in ways that reflect the stage of schooling and special education needs can be achieved, for what was formerly discarded as an administrative nightmare can now be managed with the aid of new information technology, as is every-day practice in health care and financial transaction. Deploying new technology in challenging settings has been demonstrated and documented in this book, as in the case of the Koorie Open Door Education (KODE) school at the Woolum Bellum Campus of Kurnai College near Morwell, Victoria. Finally, the concept of 'design' is now starting to flourish in some settings; we need only to free the spirit and provide appropriate incentives and recognition to those who make the effort.

We have no doubt that the policy framework will be taken up in a new era of public education. It requires leadership, alignment and will. Where will the opportunity be taken first? Will it be in Australia in a new association between Commonwealth and States, perhaps extending the work of Schools of the Future? Will it be in the United States, where there is a continuing sense of crisis, a new alignment shaping up with professional associations in the vanguard, momentum in the charter school movement, and some exciting approaches to school design? Will it be in Britain, where there is now consensus that the major elements of reform were necessary but are not sufficient, and new ways to resource schooling and build a new alignment of interests are foremost on the agenda of the Labour Government? Will it be in Hong Kong that has already achieved high standards for its students but now seeks to provide quality schooling for all in a future that returns the territory to China?

The consequences of not responding will be catastrophic. We cannot afford to let the reform movement stall. We have learned much about school reform. We now know how to proceed. Let's do it, and claim the future in a new era of public education.

References

ARMITAGE, C. (1997) 'Shortage of teachers more dire than the 70s', *The Australian*, 27 January, p. 3.

BAIN, A. (1996) 'The school design model at Brewster Academy: Technology serving teaching and learning', *T.H.E. (Technological Horizons in Education) Journal*, **23**, 10, May.

BAKER, K. (1993) *The Turbulent Years*, London: Faber and Faber.

BARRINGTON, J.M. (1994) 'New Zealand: System of education', in HUSEN, T. and POSTLETHWAITE, N. (Eds) *International Encyclopedia of Education*, 2nd ed. London: Pergamon Press, **7**, pp. 4104–11.

BEARE, H. and BOYD, W.L. (Eds) (1993) *Restructuring Schools: An International Perspective on the Movement to Transform the Control and Performance of Schools*, London: Falmer Press.

BIERLEIN, L. and BATEMAN, M. (1996) 'Charter schools v. the status quo: Which will succeed?', *International Journal of Educational Reform*, **5**, 2, April, pp. 158–9.

BISHOP, P.W. and MULFORD, W.R. (1996) 'Empowerment in four Australian primary schools: They don't really care . . .', *International Journal of Educational Reform*, **5**, 2, April, pp. 193–204.

BLACKMORE, J., BIGUM, C., HODGENS, J. and LASKEY, L. (1996) 'Managed change and self-management in Schools of the Future', *Leading and Managing*, **2**, 3, pp. 195–220.

BODILLY, S. (1996) 'Lessons learned: RAND's Formative Assessment of NAS's Phase 2 Demonstration Effort', in STRINGFIELD, S., ROSS, S.M. and SMITH, L. (Eds) *Bold Plans for School Restructuring: The New American Schools Design*, Mahwah, NJ: Lawrence Erlbaum Associates Publishers, Chapter 11, pp. 289–324.

BROSNAN, M. (1996) 'Make it new: Brewster Academy reinvents itself', *Independent School*, Spring, pp. 12–16.

BROWN, D.J. (1990) *Decentralization and School-based Management*, London: Falmer Press.

BULLOCK, A. and THOMAS, H. (1994) *The Impact of Local Management in Schools: Final Report*, Birmingham, University of Birmingham and National Association of Head Teachers.

BURTLESS, G. (Ed) (1996) *Does Money Matter? The Effect of School Resources on Student Achievement and Adult Success*, Washington, DC: Brookings Institution Press.

CAIN, J. (1995) *John Cain's Years: Power, Parties and Politics*, Carlton: Melbourne University Press.

CALDWELL, B.J. (1994) 'School-based management', in HUSEN, T. and POSTLETHWAITE, N. (Eds) *International Encyclopedia of Education*, 2nd ed. London: Pergamon Press, **9**, pp. 5302–08.

CALDWELL, B.J. (1996) 'School reform for the Knowledge Society: An economic perspective', *Australian Economic Review*, **29**, 4, pp. 416–22.

CALDWELL, B.J. and SPINKS, J.M. (1988) *The Self-managing School*, London: Falmer Press.

CALDWELL, B.J. and SPINKS, J.M. (1992) *Leading the Self-managing School*, London: Falmer Press.

References

Caldwell, B.J. and Spinks, J.M. (1998) *Beyond the Self-managing School*, London: Falmer Press.

Caldwell, B.J., Gurr, D., Hill, P.W. and Rowe, K.J. (1997) 'The Schools of the Future Program in Victoria: The principal's perspective', Paper presented by Brian Caldwell and Peter Hill in a Symposium on School Reform and School Decentralization at the Annual Meeting of the American Educational Research Association, Chicago, 24–29 March.

Champy, J. (1997) 'Preparing for organizational change', in Hesselbein, F., Goldsmith, M. and Beckhard, R. (Eds) *The Organization of the Future*, San Francisco: Jossey-Bass Publishers, Chapter 1, pp. 9–16.

Chase, B. (1997) 'Paradigm lost: New schools challenge us to create new unions', *Education Week*, 22 January, p. 7.

Cheng, Y.C. (1996) *School Effectiveness and School-based Management: A Mechanism for Development*, London: Falmer Press.

Cheung, W.M. and Cheng, Y.C. (1996) 'A multi-level framework for self-management in school', *International Journal of Educational Management*, **10**, 1, pp. 17–29.

Cheung, W.M. and Cheng, Y.C. (1997) 'Multi-level self management in schools as related to school performance: A multi-level analysis', Paper presented at the International Congress of School Effectiveness and Improvement, Memphis, January 5–8.

Cooperative Research Project (1994) *Base-line Survey*, Report of the Cooperative Research Project on 'Leading Victoria's Schools of the Future', Directorate of School Education, Victorian Association of State Secondary Principals, Victorian Primary Principals Association, The University of Melbourne (Fay Thomas, Chair) [available from Department of Education].

Cooperative Research Project (1995a) *One Year Later*, Report of the Cooperative Research Project on 'Leading Victoria's Schools of the Future', Directorate of School Education, Victorian Association of State Secondary Principals, Victorian Primary Principals Association, The University of Melbourne (Fay Thomas, Chair) [available from Department of Education].

Cooperative Research Project (1995b) *Taking Stock*, Report of the Cooperative Research Project on 'Leading Victoria's Schools of the Future', Directorate of School Education, Victorian Association of State Secondary Principals, Victorian Primary Principals Association, The University of Melbourne (Fay Thomas, Chair) [available from Directorate of School Education].

Cooperative Research Project (1996) *Three Year Report Card*, Report of the Cooperative Research Project on 'Leading Victoria's Schools of the Future', Directorate of School Education, Victorian Association of State Secondary Principals, Victorian Primary Principals Association, The University of Melbourne (Fay Thomas, Chair) [available from Department of Education].

Cooperative Research Project (1997) *Still More Work to Be Done But . . . No Turning Back*, Report of the Cooperative Research Project on 'Leading Victoria's Schools of the Future', Department of School Education, Victorian Association of State Secondary Principals, Victorian Primary Principals Association, The University of Melbourne (Fay Thomas, Chair) [available from Department of Education].

D'Arcy, E. (1989) 'What is an Excellent School?', Remarks contained in a presentation to a breakfast seminar of leaders in education organized by the Centre for Education at the University of Tasmania and the Department of Education and the Arts, Hobart.

Dawson, R. (1997) 'Knowledge is power: Intellectual capital is emerging as the hottest company asset in modern management thinking', *The Bulletin*, 18 March, pp. 46–9.

DEAN, C. and RAFFERTY, F. (1997) 'Staff dissatisfaction peaks', *The Times Educational Supplement*, 1 January, p. 1.

DRUCKER, P. (1995) *Managing in a Time of Great Change*, Oxford: Butterworth Heinemann.

EDUCATION COMMISSION (Hong Kong) (1996) *Quality School Education*, Consultation Document for Education Commission Report No. 7, Hong Kong: Education Commission.

EDUCATION COMMITTEE (1994) *The School Global Budget in Victoria: Matching Resources to Student Learning Needs*, Report of the Education Committee (Brian Caldwell, Chair), Directorate of School Education.

EDUCATION COMMITTEE (1995) *The School Global Budget in Victoria: Matching Resources to Student Learning Needs*, Interim Report of the Education Committee (Brian Caldwell, Chair), Directorate of School Education.

EDUCATION COMMITTEE (1997) *The School Global Budget in Victoria: Matching Resources to Student Learning Needs*, Final Report of the Education Committee (Brian Caldwell, Chair), Department of Education.

EDUCATION WEEK (1997) 'The state of the states', *Education Week*, An Editorial in a Supplement on 'Quality Counts', 22 January, p. 3.

GOUGH, J. and TAYLOR, T. (1996) 'Crashing through: Don Hayward and change in the Victorian school system', *Unicorn*, **22**, 2, June, pp. 69–80.

GOVERNMENT OF NEW ZEALAND (1988) *Tomorrow's Schools: The Reform of Educational Administration in New Zealand*, White Paper, Wellington: Government Printer.

GOVERNMENT OF VICTORIA (1986) *The Government Decision on the Report of the Ministry Structures Project Team*, Ministry of Education, Melbourne: Government Printer.

GURR, D.M. (1996a) 'The leadership role of principals in selected "Schools of the Future": Principal and teacher perspectives', Unpublished doctoral thesis: The University of Melbourne.

GURR, D. (1996b) 'On conceptualising school leadership: Time to abandon transformational leadership?', *Leading and Managing*, **2**, 3, pp. 221–39.

GURR, D. (1996c) 'Reply to Gronn and Lakomski', *Leading and Managing*, **2**, 3, pp. 246–8.

GUTHRIE, J.W. and KOPPICH, J.E. (1993) 'Ready, A.I.M., reform: Building a model of education reform and "high politics"', in BEARE, H. and BOYD, W.L. (Eds) (1993) *Restructuring Schools: An International Perspective on the Movement to Transform the Control and Performance of Schools*, London: Falmer Press, Chapter 2, pp. 12–28.

HALLS, W.D. (1994) 'United Kingdom: System of Education', in HUSEN, T. and POSTLETHWAITE, N. (Eds) *International Encyclopedia of Education*, 2nd ed. London: Pergamon Press, **11**, pp. 6515–23.

HAMMER, M. and CHAMPY, J. (1993) *Reengineering the Corporation: A Manifesto for Business Revolution*, London: Nicholas Brealey Publishing.

HANDY, C. (1997) 'Unimagined futures', in HESSELBEIN, F., GOLDSMITH, M. and BECKHARD, R. (Eds) *The Organization of the Future*, San Francisco: Jossey-Bass Publishers, pp. 377–83.

HANUSHEK, E.A. (1996) 'Outcomes, costs, and incentives in schools', in HANUSHEK, E.A. and JORGENSON, D.W. (Eds) *Improving America's Schools: The Role of Incentives*, Washington, DC, Chapter 3, pp. 29–52.

HANUSHEK, E.A. *et al.* (1994) *Making Schools Work: Improving Performance and Controlling Costs*, Washington, DC: Brookings Institution Press.

HARRIS, J.F. (1997) 'Clinton urges tougher education standards', *Washington Post*, 23 January, p. A12.

HAYWARD, D. (1993) *Schools of the Future: Preliminary Paper*, Melbourne: Directorate of School Education.

HIND, I. (1996) 'School global budgeting in Victorian government schools', *Australian Economic Review*, **29**, 4, pp. 423–30.

JAMES, B. (1950) *The Advancement of Spencer Button*, Sydney: Angus and Robertson.

JÖRESKOG, K.G. and SÖRBOM, D. (1993) *LISREL 8: User's Reference Guide*, Chicago: Scientific Software, Inc.

JOUZAITIS, C. (1997) 'Charter schools sprout in search of a better way', *Chicago Tribune*, 23 January, p. 1.

KEARNS, D.T. and ANDERSON, J.L. (Eds) (1996) 'Sharing the vision: Creating new American schools', in STRINGFIELD, S., ROSS, S.M. and SMITH, L. (Eds) *Bold Plans for School Restructuring: The New American Schools Design*, Mahwah, NJ: Lawrence Erlbaum Associates Publishers, Chapter 1, pp. 9–23.

KOTTER, J.P. (1992) *A Force for Change: How Leadership Differs from Management*, New York: The Free Press.

KOPPICH, J.E., KERCHNER, C.T. and WEERES, J.G. (1997) 'The "New Teacher Unions": The stuff that fairy tales are made of', *Education Week*, 9 April, pp. 43 and 60.

KOPPICH, J.E., KERCHNER, C.T. and WEERES, J.G. (1997) *United Mind Workers: Unions and Teaching in the Knowledge Society*, San Francisco: Jossey-Bass.

LEVACIC, R. (1995) *Local Management of Schools: Analysis and Practice*, Buckingham: Open University Press.

LOUDEN, W. and WALLACE, J. (1994) 'Too soon to tell: School restructuring and the National Schools Project', Australian Council for Educational Administration Monograph No. 17, Hawthorn: ACEA.

MACPHERSON, R.J.S. (1993) 'The reconstruction of New Zealand Education: A Case of "High Politics" Reform?', in BEARE, H. and BOYD, W.L. (Eds) (1993) *Restructuring Schools: An International Perspective on the Movement to Transform the Control and Performance of Schools*, London: Falmer Press, Chapter 5, pp. 69–85.

MARSHALL, S.P. (1997) 'Creating sustainable learning communities for the Twenty-First Century', in HESSELBEIN, F., GOLDSMITH, M. and BECKHARD, R. (Eds) *The Organization of the Future*, San Francisco: Jossey-Bass Publishers, Chapter 18, pp. 177–88.

MISICH, T. (1996) *Options for Self Managing Schools in Western Australia: A Discussion Paper for WA School Leaders*, A report of experiences and recommendations of Australian and New Zealand principals as reported by Tony Misich, President of the Western Australia Primary Principals Association, as recipient of the Australian Primary Principals Association 1995–6 Telstra Research Award, Perth, WAPPA.

NEW SOUTH WALES (1990) *School-centred Education: Building a More Responsive State School System*, Management Review, New South Wales Education Portfolio (Brian Scott, Director), Milsons Point, NSW, The Review.

ODDEN, A. and ODDEN, E. (1996) *The Victoria, Australia Approach to School-site Management*, A Report of research sponsored by the Consortium for Policy Research in Education (CPRE) under a grant from the Carnegie Corporation and the Office of Educational Research and Improvement, US Department of Education, University of Wisconsin, Madison, CPRE, September.

OECD, DIRECTORATE OF EDUCATION, EMPLOYMENT, LABOR AND SOCIAL AFFAIRS, EDUCATION COMMITTEE (1994) *Effectiveness of Schooling and of Educational Resource Management: Synthesis of Country Studies*, Points 22 and 23, Paris, OECD.

OSBORNE, D. and GAEBLER, T. (1993) *Reinventing Government*, London: Macmillan.

PAPERT, S. (1993) *The Children's Machine: Rethinking School in the Age of the Computer*, New York: Basic Books.

PYKE, N. (1997) '£1m heals reading blight', *The Times Educational Supplement*, 31 January, p. 1.

PYLE, A. (1997) 'Riordan ally Ouchi is new LEARN chief', *Los Angeles Times*, 20 March, pp. B1, B6.

SLOAN, A.P. (1964) *My Years with General Motors*, New York: Doubleday.

SMITH, M.S., SCOLL, B.W. and LINK, J. (1996) 'Research-based school reform: The Clinton Administration's Agenda', in HANUSHEK, E.A. and JORGENSON, D.W. (Eds) *Improving America's Schools: The Role of Incentives*, Washington, DC, Chapter 2, pp. 9–27.

SMYTH, J. (1993) *A Socially Critical View of the Self-managing School*, London: Falmer Press.

SPENDER, D. (1995) *Nattering on the Net: Women, Power and Cyberspace*, North Melbourne: Spinifex.

ST. JOHN-BROOKS (1997) 'Blunkett pledges to clear the funding fog', *The Times Educational Supplement*, 16 May, p. 1.

STEHR, N. (1994) *Knowledge Societies*, London: Sage.

STRINGFIELD, S., ROSS, S.M. and SMITH, L. (1996) *Bold Plans for School Restructuring: The New American Schools Design*, Mahwah, NJ: Lawrence Erlbaum Associates.

SUMMERS, A.A. and JOHNSON, A.W. (1996) 'The effects of school-based management plans', in HANUSHEK, E.A. and JORGENSON, D.W. (Eds) *Improving America's Schools: The Role of Incentives*, Washington, DC, Chapter 5, pp. 75–96.

SWANSON, A.D. and KING, R.A. (1991) *School Finance: Its Economics and Politics*, New York: Longman.

TASK FORCE TO REVIEW EDUCATIONAL ADMINISTRATION (1988) *Administering for Excellence*, Report of the Task Force to Review Educational Administration, B. Picot (Chair), Wellington, New Zealand Government Printer.

THATCHER, M. (1993) *The Downing Street Years*, London: Harper Collins.

THOMAS, H. and MARTIN, J. (1996) *Managing Resources for School Improvement: Creating a Cost-effective School*, London: Routledge.

TOWNSEND, T. (1996) 'The self-managing school: Miracle or myth?', *Leading and Managing*, **2**, 3, pp. 171–94.

TOWNSEND, T. (1997) 'Teaching our children well', *The Age*, 14 January, p. A11.

VUYK, E.J. (1994) 'Netherlands: The system of education', in HUSEN, T. and POSTLETHWAITE, N. (Eds) *International Encyclopedia of Education*, 2nd ed. London: Pergamon Press, **7**, pp. 4067–77.

WALKER, A., BRADLEY, M. and DE KANTZOW, D. (1996) 'Restructuring for improved learning outcomes', *Education Journal*, **24**, 1, Summer, pp. 86–110.

WEST, E.G. (1996) *Education Vouchers in Practice and Principle: A World Survey*, Human Capital Development Working Paper No. 64 prepared for the World Bank, Washington, DC.

Index